Nina Otero-Warren
of Santa Fe

Nina Otero-Warren
of Santa Fe

by
Charlotte Whaley
With a New Foreword for this Edition by the Author

SOUTHWEST HERITAGE SERIES

SUNSTONE PRESS

SANTA FE

Sunstone books may be purchased for educational, business, or sales promotional use.
For information please write: Special Markets Department, Sunstone Press,
P.O. Box 2321, Santa Fe, New Mexico 87504-2321.

Library of Congress Cataloging-in-Publication Data

Whaley, Charlotte, 1925-
  Nina Otero-Warren of Santa Fe / by Charlotte Whaley ; with a new foreword for
this edition by the author.
    p. cm. -- (Southwest heritage series)
  Originally published: Albuquerque, N.M. : Univesity of New Mexico Press, 1994.
  Includes bibliographical references and index.
  ISBN 978-0-86534-635-2 (softcover : alk. paper)
  1. Otero-Warren, Nina, 1881-1965. 2. Hispanic Americans--New Mexico--Santa
Fe--Biography. 3. Santa Fe (N.M.)--Biography. 4. Los Lunas (N.M.)--Biography.
5. Hispanic American children--Education--New Mexico. I. Title.

F804.S29S759 2008
978.9'56004680092--dc22
[B]
                            2007041864

Published in
Santa Fe

WWW.SUNSTONEPRESS.COM
SUNSTONE PRESS / POST OFFICE BOX 2321 / SANTA FE, NM 87504-2321 /USA
(505) 988-4418 / ORDERS ONLY (800) 243-5644 / FAX (505) 988-1025

The Southwest Heritage Series is dedicated to Jody Ellis and Marcia Muth Miller, the founders of Sunstone Press, whose original purpose and vision continues to inspire and motivate our publications.

CONTENTS

THE SOUTHWEST HERITAGE SERIES / I

FOREWORD TO THIS EDITION / II

NINA OTERO-WARREN OF SANTA FE / III

I

THE SOUTHWEST HERITAGE SERIES

The history of the United States is written in hundreds of regional histories and literary works. Those letters, essays, memoirs, biographies and even collections of fiction are often first-hand accounts by people who wanted to memorialize an event, a person or simply record for posterity the concerns and issues of the times. Many of these accounts have been lost, destroyed or overlooked. Some are in private or public collections but deemed to be in too fragile condition to permit handling by contemporary readers and researchers.

However, now with the application of twenty-first century technology, nineteenth and twentieth century material can be reprinted and made accessible to the general public. These early writings are the DNA of our history and culture and are essential to understanding the present in terms of the past.

The Southwest Heritage Series is a form of literary preservation. Heritage by definition implies legacy and these early works are our legacy from those who have gone before us. To properly present and preserve that legacy, no changes in style or contents have been made. The material reprinted stands on its own as it first appeared. The point of view is that of the author and the era in which he or she lived. We would not expect photographs of people from the past to be re-imaged with modern clothes, hair styles and backgrounds. We should not, therefore, expect their ideas and personal philosophies to reflect our modern concepts.

Remember, reading their words and sharing their thoughts is a passport back into understanding how the past was shaped and how it influenced today's world.

Our hope is that new access to these older books will provide readers with a challenging and exciting experience.

II

FOREWORD TO THIS EDITION
by
Charlotte Whaley

NINA OTERO-WARREN would be delighted to know, at the time of this publication, that her life and accomplishments still generate interest more than forty years after her death, in 1965, and over thirteen years since this first biography was published. She would not, however, be happy to know that the name of one of the most distinguished members of her large family, Estella Leopold, Ph.D., had been omitted from the genealogy chart that prefaced the original 1994 edition of the book. Fortunately, Sunstone Press's edition in their Southwest Heritage Series provides an opportunity to correct such omissions and other errors.

The daughter of Aldo and Estella Leopold, Dr. Estella Bergere Leopold followed in her famous father's footsteps. Aldo Leopold is still considered one of this country's most influential conservationists, becoming a distinguished paleobotonist at Washington University.

In his close reading and good review of the first edition of *Nina*, New Mexico historian John P. Conron noted that the newlyweds, Alfred and Eloisa Bergere, probably traveled to Chicago in 1886 on the Atchison, Topeka and Santa Fe Railroad, not the Denver and Rio Grande Western railroad (page 29). Neither Los Lunas, the couple's starting point, nor Socorro were ever on the D&RGW's route. In addition to his helpful editing, John Conron closed his review with praise for the book: "a good, charming, detailed look at a fine lady that nephew Dr. Bergere Kenney described as 'very gracious, courtly'" (from *La Cronica de Nueva Mexico*, published by the Historical Society of New Mexico, April 1995).

For all her gracious courtliness, Nina also had a bravado and self-assurance that was unusual for Hispanic women of her generation. According to *The New York Times* in an article dated September 19, 1922, she was the "most picturesque" of the four women who "tossed their toques into the ring" as candidates for Congress that fall. Nina broke new ground when she won "a hot republican primary fight in New Mexico." Suffragists in New York were "elated over her victory." Nina "represented the old Spanish tradition in the Southwest. She is the new type of woman in politics, the daughter of a Spanish don, with a background of family wealth and culture, yet herself one of the vigorous younger generation who espoused the cause of the militant suffragists of the National Woman's Party and went for public office as soon as women won the vote.

"Mrs. Warren is reported to have defeated in the primary contest the present incumbent of the seat, also a Republican, and this fact was noted with great glee by Republican women politicians. . .as marking the passing of the time when women candidates were given complimentary nominations in districts where victory at the polls was highly improbable and where no male candidate was hungry for the post."

Nina lost that election to an Anglo male, but by a narrow margin. She continued to make important contributions in other ways. Thanks to her pioneering spirit, the land she homesteaded just outside of Santa Fe has appreciated in value and has become the meeting place of choice for large family reunions. In 2002, Nina's niece, Eloise Bergere Brown, organized a "Bergeriana Revelry." One hundred and ten relatives of all ages attended the festivities: a Friday night reception at Gerald Peters Gallery followed by dinner and dancing at La Fonda and group photographs at the Georgia O'Keeffe Center; a Saturday afternoon barbecue picnic with guitar playing, singing, and story telling at Las Dos; and a Sunday brunch at the Luna Mansion in Los Lunas. Four years later, in the summer of 2006, the reunion was repeated. This time, the genealogy chart was so long that it was wrapped around both homestead houses. Nina would have been pleased and proud to know that she had been the catalyst for it all.

III

NINA OTERO-WARREN OF SANTA FE

Nina Otero-Warren of Santa Fe

Charlotte Whaley

DESCENDANTS OF ELOISA LUNA OTERO BERGERE

Five Generations

Compiled by John J. Kenney, Jr. (1980)

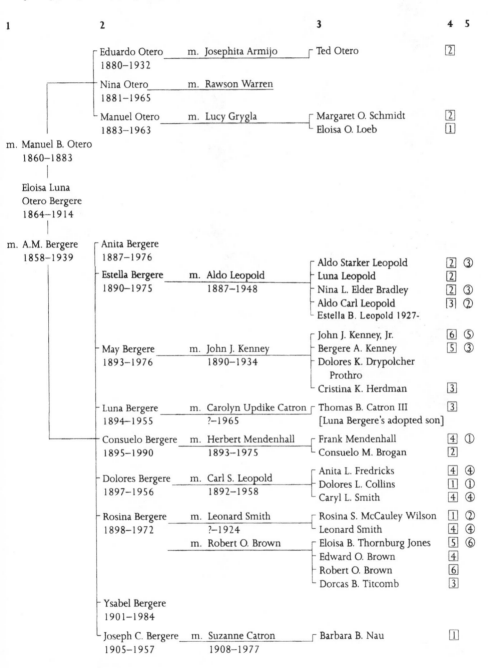

1	2	3	4	5
	Eduardo Otero 1880–1932 m. Josephita Armijo	Ted Otero	2	
	Nina Otero 1881–1965 m. Rawson Warren			
	Manuel Otero 1883–1963 m. Lucy Grygla	Margaret O. Schmidt	2	
		Eloisa O. Loeb	1	
m. Manuel B. Otero 1860–1883				
Eloisa Luna Otero Bergere 1864–1914				
m. A.M. Bergere 1858–1939	Anita Bergere 1887–1976			
	Estella Bergere 1890–1975 m. Aldo Leopold 1887–1948	Aldo Starker Leopold	2	③
		Luna Leopold	2	
		Nina L. Elder Bradley	2	③
		Aldo Carl Leopold	3	②
		Estella B. Leopold 1927-		
	May Bergere 1893–1976 m. John J. Kenney 1890–1934	John J. Kenney, Jr.	6	⑤
		Bergere A. Kenney	5	③
		Dolores K. Drypolcher Prothro		
		Cristina K. Herdman	3	
	Luna Bergere 1894–1955 m. Carolyn Updike Catron ?–1965	Thomas B. Catron III [Luna Bergere's adopted son]	3	
	Consuelo Bergere 1895–1990 m. Herbert Mendenhall 1893–1975	Frank Mendenhall	4	①
		Consuelo M. Brogan	2	
	Dolores Bergere 1897–1956 m. Carl S. Leopold 1892–1958	Anita L. Fredricks	4	④
		Dolores L. Collins	1	①
		Caryl L. Smith	4	④
	Rosina Bergere 1898–1972 m. Leonard Smith ?–1924 m. Robert O. Brown	Rosina S. McCauley Wilson	1	②
		Leonard Smith	4	④
		Eloisa B. Thornburg Jones	5	⑥
		Edward O. Brown	4	
		Robert O. Brown	6	
		Dorcas B. Titcomb	3	
	Ysabel Bergere 1901–1984			
	Joseph C. Bergere 1905–1957 m. Suzanne Catron 1908–1977	Barbara B. Nau	1	

Boxed figure is the number of children in the fourth generation.
Circled figure is the number of children in the fifth generation.

This
Edition
is
Dedicated
to
Eloisa Bergere Brown
and
in
Memory
of
Bergere,
Dode,
Jack,
and
Cristina

Contents

1   Introduction

CHAPTER ONE
7   The Years at Los Lunas

CHAPTER TWO
45   Santa Fe

CHAPTER THREE
77   A Keystone Falls

CHAPTER FOUR
101   The Educator

CHAPTER FIVE
131   Las Dos

CHAPTER SIX
167   The Matriarch

205   Epilogue

211   Chronology

213   Notes

241   Bibliography

247   Index

Introduction

N ina Otero-Warren, a descendant of Spanish conquistadores, was herself a pioneer. Suffragist, educator, politician, homesteader, writer, and business entrepreneur during the early decades of the twentieth century, she was on
the forefront of the first wave of feminism in the country her ancestors had explored and settled three hundred years earlier. In many
ways, her life paralleled the life of Santa Fe itself, in that both selected what they wanted from the changes introduced by the Anglo-
Americans who poured into New Mexico at the turn of the century,
while both retained the spirit and grace of their eighteenth-century
Spanish heritage.

Changes came rapidly to New Mexico after the arrival of the
railroads in 1881, the year Nina was born. With easier access to new
markets in Albuquerque and Santa Fe, American capitalists gradually
began appropriating the land and the livelihood of the early aristocratic *ricos*. The Spanish colonials who had been socially and politically prominent landowners during New Mexico's territorial days found
their influence diminishing and the customs and training of their

1

ancestors disappearing at an alarming rate. The Anglos—all those U.S. immigrants whose nationalities were other than Indian, Spanish, or Mexican—began taking over in the name of progress and prosperity.

María Adelina Isabel Emilia (Nina) Otero-Warren attempted to preserve the best of her native culture and at the same time find a place for herself in the emerging new order. She lived in Santa Fe from the time she was sixteen until her death at eighty-three, moving there in 1897 from Los Lunas, New Mexico, where she was born into a distinguished family that traced its origins back to eleventh-century Spain.

Conservative in many ways, but rarely a conformist, Nina Otero-Warren had an easy grace and intelligence that attracted others to her. While her marriage in 1908 to cavalry Lieutenant Rawson Warren failed, she maintained her strong sense of personal worth and, with her family's support, proceeded to build several stellar careers for herself. She had no children of her own, but after her mother's death she helped bring up her nine brothers and sisters and some of their offspring in the "Big House" at 135 Grant Avenue, now one of Santa Fe's historical landmarks.

Nina took advantage of the new era opening for women in 1914, when the demand for woman suffrage began earnestly in Santa Fe. As a leader in Alice Paul's Congressional Union, helping through her fluency in English and Spanish to persuade both Anglo and Hispanic women to join the fight for the franchise, she became one of the CU's most influential organizers.

From 1917 to 1929, Nina served as superintendent of public schools in Santa Fe County, first by appointment and then by winning election to the position that had previously been held by men. In 1922, she became the Republican party's nominee for the U.S. House of Representatives, the first woman to win a primary election in New Mexico. In the days of the Roosevelt presidency and the Work Projects Administration, she was made director of the state's literacy program for adult education, and in 1941 she represented New Mexico in Puerto Rico as director of the Work Conference for Adult Education.

Along with the artists and writers who had formed colonies in Santa Fe and Taos before World War II, Nina worked to restore and preserve the state's once-scorned adobe architecture and her people's ancient traditions. She feted and supported these creative men and women—Mary Austin, Alice Corbin Henderson, Witter Bynner, John Sloan, Will Shuster, and Gustave Baumann were her close friends— and they in turn enjoyed her wit and vitality. Although they were outsiders, as compared with her Hispanic friends, the Anglo painters and poets who made Santa Fe their home were also fiercely loyal citizens who respected the special qualities of their adopted city and state, an attitude she appreciated and encouraged.

In the twenties Nina met Mamie Meadors, who had come from Texas to New Mexico for her health, and together they homesteaded 1,257 acres of land fifteen miles outside Santa Fe, calling it Las Dos (The Two), which was also the name given to the real-estate business they began in 1947. Nina's farsighted decision to claim some of the few remaining tracts of New Mexico land available for homesteading reflected an enterprising spirit and an instinctive sense that the property she and Mamie lived on and improved would, in the later decades of the century, appreciate dramatically in value and become a welcome retreat for urban dwellers across the country. At Las Dos in 1936, in her small adobe house on a hill overlooking the Sangre de Cristo and Jemez mountain ranges, Nina finished her book, *Old Spain in Our Southwest,* fulfilling her promise to Mary Austin, who for years had urged her to write down her memories of the old days and ways on the family hacienda in Los Lunas.

Before her death in 1965, and for years afterward, Nina was honored again and again for her achievements, particularly for the improvements she made in New Mexico's methods of educating Hispanic children. Hers was a remarkably productive life, that of a woman successful in establishing an important place for herself in her time, in keeping with the contributions made in earlier days by her pioneering Spanish predecessors.

Writing Nina Otero-Warren's biography has been much like untangling a series of large hard knots, many of which will forever remain securely in place. She left no personal journals, only a few articles and her book, which provides some insight into her childhood experiences but which most modern-day critics consider a romanticized account of rural life in nineteenth-century New Mexico.

Files in the State Records Center and Archives in Santa Fe, the National Woman's Party Papers at Texas Woman's University in Denton, Texas, and interviews with Nina's family members and friends have been primary sources of information, although the four people who knew her best—her sister Connie Mendenhall, her nephews Jack and Bergere Kenney, and her niece Cristina Herdman—died during the four years this book was in progress. Consequently, Nina remains in many ways a charming enigma—clever, well-educated, facile, socially and politically successful, but a woman who revealed very little of her inner life.

For helping to straighten out some of the facts about the public and private Nina Otero-Warren, I am deeply indebted to Dolores (Dode) Kenney, Eloisa Bergere Brown, Josephine (Joey) Kenney, Luna and Carl Leopold, and Michael Berger. I also wish to thank Henry B. Meadors, nephew of Mamie Meadors, for providing some insight into the background and personality of his quiet, intelligent aunt. Thanks also to the friends of Nina and the Bergeres—Ruth Leakey, Amalia Sánchez, Roberta Brosseau, Anita Gonzales Thomas, Marguerite Claffey, Letta Wofford, Justine Thomas, Ford Ruthling, Samuel Arnold, and Dominguita Vigíl Ortíz—all of whom have made valuable contributions.

Virtually everything I have written about Nina's husband, Rawson Warren, can be attributed to the extraordinary research assistance of Lois Hudgins and Gerri Brannan in the Dallas Public Library, and the staff in the alumni office of Stanford University. Many thanks to them, and to Allen Schwartz at the Santa Fe Public Library, to the staff at the Santa Fe Archives (particularly Paul Saavedra), to Edwin Berry and Pat Graham in La Constancia, to Professor Charles DeBus for the splendid photographs he took of the original Las Dos homestead houses, and to those who generously read the first drafts of the manuscript—Margaret Lefranc Schoonover, Sandra Edelman, and Barbara Vigíl.

Working with Beth Hadas and Barbara Guth at the University of New Mexico Press has been a particular pleasure. And I am especially grateful to Gould Whaley, Jr., without whose encouragement and support this book could not have been written.

CHAPTER ONE

The
Years
at
Los
Lunas

L os Lunas—the land of the Lunas colonized by Spanish pioneers centuries before Nina Otero was born—encompassed
fertile fields along the Rio Grande some twenty miles south
of Albuquerque. It was a vast, unfenced region of sweeping
plains and lush valleys where the air was pure, crisp, cool, and dry,
with just enough rain to coax beans and grains and fruits from the
rich sandy loam.

The loosely defined Spanish land-grant boundary lines around
the village had been drawn on the north near the ruins of the San
Clemente Chapel, on the south along the northern line of the Chávez
family's grant, and stretched west from the Río Grande all the way to
the Río Puerco. One of the best irrigated regions of the southwest's
Rocky Mountain territory, the choice acreage was covered with gra-
ma and buffalo grasses that fed sheep and cattle introduced to the
New World by the Spaniards in the sixteenth century. For hundreds
of years since the explorations of Coronado and Oñate, *pastores* (shep-
herds) had roamed the ranges, tending their herds, camping at night
on isolated plateaus with only their dogs for company.

At the center of the Luna ranch lands was the patrón's hacienda, a self-contained community with kitchens, storerooms, and bedrooms, even salas for dancing, all constructed around a large central patio. There were lesser rooms and patios for servants, and walled enclosures for domestic animals and for the vaqueros, those indispensable ranch hands who had learned from their ancestors the art of building and repairing fences, of tanning hides and plaiting whips and weaving horsemane into cinches. Standing a few yards behind the Luna home was a small adobe chapel, built and maintained by the patrón, where the Catholic priest from Tomé came every two weeks for baptisms and confessions, weddings and funerals, and, always, the celebration of Holy Mass. The Lunas maintained the santuario and held the key.[1]

María Adelina Isabel Emilia (Nina) Otero, a descendant of the first Luna to seek his fortune in the New World (don Tristan de Luna y Arellano de Castillo), was born in La Constancia, just across the Río Grande from the Luna hacienda, on October 23, 1881—a time when her mother and father and a handful of other ricos controlled the land, culture, and politics of New Mexico's Río Abajo (lower river) region. The large ranches at that time were ruled by the aristocratic hacendados, land-rich Spanish ranchers who provided their peones with shelter, food, and security in return for their services and, when territorial elections were held, their votes.

From her earliest years Nina was told about the history and customs of her Spanish Roman Catholic people, learning from her parents and private tutors of those conquistadores who, in the name of God and the King of Spain, took the semiarid land from the Indians and shaped the territory according to their own traditions.

The Luna family name was acquired in Spain in A.D. 1091, when young Captain Bacalla led a successful charge against the Moors one night by the light of a quarter moon, winning for himself the title "de Luna" and a coat of arms. Bacalla was followed by Pedro de Luna, an Aragonese cardinal who became Pope Benedict XIII, an "antipope," one of three popes at the time of the great schism in the

Catholic Church (1378–1429). Refusing to abdicate after the general church council elected a new vicar, Pedro sequestered himself in the fortress of Peñiscola, Valencia, where he died in 1423, supposedly poisoned by a friar.[2]

Conde Álvaro de Luna (1388–1453) was one of the family's more colorful ancestors—a powerful politician, landowner, and nobleman, but also a thief and a scoundrel. Álvaro was the illegitimate son of one of the less affluent Luna families, but he went on to become high constable of Castile and command his own army of more than twenty thousand soldiers. He also had the ear and the trust of King Juan II, a gullible man who granted him enormous political power and made him the most influential, if corrupt, man in the country. Luna's notorious career was finally brought to an end by King Juan's Portuguese wife, Isabel, who accused him of witchcraft against the king and had him beheaded. Isabel also ordered his life-size articulated statue removed from the Toledo cathedral's Capilla de Santiago, claiming worshipers were distracted by the noisy antics of the mechanical man as it genuflected, sat, and stood at key points during the Mass.

In 1984, more than five centuries after Álvaro's death, one of his many descendants, Eloisa Bergere Brown, traveled to Spain to verify her family's ancestry. Horrified when she first discovered the facts about Álvaro, she later saw the humor of finding a skeleton in her family's closet:

> Bless you, Count Álvaro de Luna. You ornery reprobate. What a wonderful ancestor to claim kinship to: the most notorious legal thief in history. A man who designed his own portrait and then built it as a mechanized marionette to dance attendance at his own mass for the dead. He must have loved the fantasy of future generations worshiping at that lively shrine.
>
> I had been looking for a noble ancestor and found a scoundrel instead of a hero.
>
> I could hardly wait to tell The Family.[3]

Still, there were genuine heroes among the Luna ancestors, and at least one Luna accompanied each of the explorers Cortés, Coronado, Oñate, and Vargas on their expeditions to New Spain. Don Tristan de Luna y Arellano de Castillo was the first to come, arriving with his shipmate Hernán Cortés in 1530, just thirty-eight years after Columbus first made landfall in the Americas. On his third trip in 1540, Captain Arellano was second in command under Coronado and helped build the first bridge across the Pecos River—also the first in the United States. Because of his expertise in managing the livestock brought over by the Spaniards, he became the first sheepman in New Mexico, establishing his camp at Tiguex, the site of the land Spain later granted to the Luna family.[4]

Melchior de Luna was a colonist during Oñate's expedition to New Mexico in 1597–98; Captain Juan Gómez de Luna, a student of the American Indian languages, came in 1664 as an interpreter; Diego de Luna and his family were in New Mexico during the Pueblo Indian rebellion against the Spaniards in 1680 and twelve years later reentered the territory with Vargas, the reconqueror.

It was a woman, however, doña Ana de Sandoval y Manzanares, who was the catalyst in acquiring in the eighteenth century what eventually became the Luna land, traveling by burro some fifteen hundred miles to Mexico City and staying there almost two years in stubborn pursuit of the deed Governor Felix Martínez finally granted. For reasons undocumented, but perhaps because doña Ana was not "able, willing, and properly equipped" to work the land (a legal requirement for grant holders at the time), the Manzanares grant was changed to the San Clemente grant and the 110,000 acres later acquired by don Domingo de Luna, a cousin of the Duke of Alburquerque, thirty-fourth viceroy of Spain. The marriage of Domingo to the daughter of Ignacio Chaves added another 100,000 acres of rich Valencia farmland to the Luna estate.[5]

The Lunas were influential in persuading fifty families to settle the New Mexico colony, including the Oteros, the Chaveses, and the Bacas, all of whom became successful ranchers and farmers under both Spanish and Mexican rule and continued to prosper after the United States claimed all territorial rights in 1848. As the centuries progressed, the Luna, Otero, and Chaves families became to New Mexico what the Lowells, Cabots, and Lodges were to New England. But the first Luna came to the New World eighty years before the Bostonians.[6]

Colonizing the land and wresting it away from the Indians challenged the resourcefulness and patience of the pioneers and brought unsought hardships. Midway through the nineteenth century, the Navajo Indian tribes had been fairly well contained by the United States Cavalry and had resignedly gathered together on one large reservation, but the Apaches continued their war against the intruders until 1886. Nina's great-great-grandfather, Antonio de Luna, was killed by the Apaches on June 9, 1779. Along with his Los Lunas land, he left to his wife thirteen cornfields, two small houses, farm equipment, livestock, "useless blunderbusses," a pair of scarlet trousers, and a black jacket. His widow reported that she paid the trousers, jacket, and a horse for a total of thirty-six masses. She also exchanged an ox for a shroud and forty ewes for her dead husband's burial fee.[7]

Nina's grandfather, Antonio José Luna, fared better than his father, for he joined the prominent Baca family from Belén by marrying María Nestora Cristina Isabella Baca. He also increased the family's sheep and cattle business, attained civic and political importance, and became known around New Mexico as the "father of the community of Los Lunas."[8]

Although the Lunas owned large tracts of land, there was not much ready cash for exchange, and like all New Mexico colonists at the time they subsisted on a barter economy. That situation changed dramatically in the 1850s, when the *patrones* of the Luna and Otero haciendas followed trailblazers Richen Lacy (Uncle Dick) Wootton, Jesse B. Turley, and Benjamin Franklin Coons in defying the heat and barrenness of Death Valley to transport their herds of sheep (at one time some fifty thousand head) along five hundred miles of trails from Los Lunas through Apache territory to gold-rich California. Antonio José and his brother Rafael, along with Ambrosio Armijo and Miguel Antonio Otero (father of the future territorial governor, Miguel A. Otero), set out to test the California market in 1852 with twenty-five thousand head, eleven hundred of which were trampled to death while negotiating a stretch of deep sand west of Colorado.[9]

Still, most of the flock survived, and outside Los Angeles the *patrones* sold their sheep for $5.50 per head, truly a bonanza for the early pioneers. The local market value in New Mexico for one sheep at the time was fifty cents. After a sightseeing trip to San Francisco, the jubilant men returned home a year later with $70,000 in coin and gold dust. The Lunas and Oteros were suddenly very wealthy people, the "big ricos and the political leaders of the Río Abajo centered in Valencia County."[10]

Nina's aristocratic mother, Eloisa Luna, the youngest child of don Antonio José and Isabella Baca Luna, was given every advantage. She, her older sister, Luz, and her brothers, Jesús, Tranquilino, and Solomón, enjoyed the privileges of their upper-class status, one of which was an excellent grammar-school education under private tutors. In the early nineteenth century, a public school system had not yet been established in the territory, and while a few public-spirited citizens volunteered classroom space in homes or churches, finding qualified men and women to teach was difficult if not impossible. The only requirements for a teacher were that he or she be able to read and write.[11]

The Lunas, however, found the best of tutors for their children, and servants and retainers were always in attendance. As Nina would write later in her book, *Old Spain in Our Southwest* (1936), "the children of the hacienda, even when fourteen years of age, still had a nursemaid following after them, looking after their needs. If they went for a horseback ride, a man rode behind them at a respectful distance. . . . If they went for a walk, or to their siesta, a nurse was there to get their proper clothing ready."[12]

At the age of twelve, Nina's mother had crossed the Great Plains

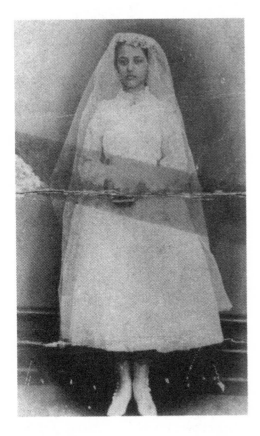

Eloisa Luna, age 12, dressed for her confirmation in the Catholic Church, Los Lunas, September 2, 1876. (Bergere Family Collection, photo no. 23232, New Mexico State Records Center and Archives, Santa Fe, New Mexico.)

with her parents—a two-week trip when the weather held—by horseback and stagecoach and steamboat to Kansas City, St. Louis, and finally New York, where she completed her high-school education in a private Catholic academy. Two years later, at age 14, she returned to Los Lunas and became involved in the social life of the Río Abajo region, Albuquerque, and Santa Fe. A onetime guest of the Lunas, Sister Blandina Segale, wrote in her memoirs that Eloisa was the most beautiful girl she had ever seen: "She carries the atmosphere of a convent education, and is entirely unspoiled by adulation."[13]

Bright, beautiful, articulate in English as well as Spanish (although she had some difficulty writing in English), with the refine-

Eloisa Luna, mother of Nina
Otero, ca. 1879 (Photograph
courtesy Eloisa Bergere Brown.)

ment and self-assurance that wealth and a good education bring,
Eloisa soon attracted the most eligible bachelor in New Mexico—
don Manuel Basilio Otero. Manuel was the son of Manuel Antonio
and Dolores Chaves Otero, wealthy landowners who claimed title to
over a million acres along the Río Grande, not far from Los Lunas.[14]

The Oteros who originally pioneered New Mexico—Pedro
Otero, his tubercular wife, and his son, Vicente—had come from
Spain to Santa Fe in 1786. A year later they acquired lush Río Grande
Valley land and named it La Valencia in honor of their Spanish home-
land. Pedro Otero's progenitors had distinguished themselves in Old
and New Mexico. Eloquent orator, legislator, and jurist don Mariano
Otero of Guadalajara was secretary of state in Mexico from 1842 to
1848; and don Antonio José Otero, Manuel B.'s great-uncle, was New
Mexico's first supreme court judge.[15]

Before the United States occupied New Mexico, Manuel Antonio Otero had purchased land from the Mexican government, paying

Manuel B. Otero, age 16, standing, with friends in Germany, ca. 1876. (*Bergere Family Collection*, photo no. 23231, New Mexico State Records Center and Archives, Santa Fe, New Mexico.)

500,000 pesos for half of the Bartolomé Baca grant that encompassed the Estancia Plains southeast of Albuquerque, in almost the exact center of New Mexico. His brother Miguel had bought the other half, bringing their total holdings to 1,232,000 acres.[16]

Manuel B. Otero had been educated at Georgetown University in Washington, D.C., and at Heidelberg University in Germany. He spoke four languages fluently. But while the Oteros were land rich, their liquid assets were modest. During his years at Heidelberg, Manuel's father wrote cautioning him about finances: "Try not to make too many costs. Remember that our household at La Constancia is scattered and this curtails our affairs in the future."[17]

Fair and handsome, courteous and brave, with the reddish blond hair and blue eyes of his ancestors from Valencia, Spain, Manuel seemed eminently suited for Eloisa. In 1879, less than a year after they met, the young people were married, uniting the Chaveses and Oteros of the Estancia Valley with the Bacas and Lunas of Valencia County. Between them, Manuel B. and Eloisa Otero owned more than 700,000 acres of land in and around Los Lunas, the Estancia Valley, and Antelope Springs. The Luna family alone owned 150,000 head of sheep.[18]

In late–nineteenth-century New Mexico, young couples of Spanish heritage could not be married without the consent of their parents, a rule that had been included in the Spanish law of 1766 to prevent marriages between people of unequal social status. Following protocol, the engagement formalities involved several exchanges of courtesies between the Oteros and the Lunas: Manuel's uncles and his father called on Eloisa's parents and presented a letter, which by custom was not read immediately, stating that the young man was favorably disposed toward their pleasing daughter. They respectfully hoped that the Lunas would pledge to them "the most precious jewel" of the Luna house.[19]

Once the Lunas expressed their pleasure and agreed to the union of their children—Eloisa was fifteen years old, and Manuel, nineteen—preparations for the engagement and wedding ceremonies proceeded with great industry and excitement. Since it was customary for the groom-to-be to furnish his future bride's complete trousseau, wagons began to arrive loaded with hand-carved marriage chests filled with fine linens, lingerie, dresses, and gowns for all occasions. Velvet boxes contained a string of perfectly matched pearls and the wedding ring.

The night the engagement was publicly announced, a dance was held at the hacienda, and Eloisa wore one of the heavily embroidered dresses from her trousseau. Guests were served enchiladas with frijoles (beans) and *posole* (hominy cooked with pork), New Mexico dishes that originated in Los Lunas.[20]

For her elaborate wedding, the bride was stunning in white satin, her luxuriant black hair carefully dressed, her pearls and orange blossoms accentuating the dark eyes and fair skin she had in-

The Luna Mansion as it appeared in 1992. The southern colonial, adobe-brick structure was built for the Luna family in 1881 by the Santa Fe Railroad in exchange for the right of way through their original homestead in Los Lunas. The portico and a solarium were constructed in the 1920s during the residency of Eduardo and Josefita Manderfield Otero. (Photograph by author.)

herited from her Castilian and Aragonese ancestors. Manuel had brought her a blue satin gown with Duchesse lace from Brussels, which she wore to the wedding feast he had arranged in the great hall. A barge draped with red velvet and flower garlands ferried bride and groom across the Río Grande for the festivities, since the river near Los Lunas at that time lacked a bridge.[21] Family and friends celebrated for two weeks after the newlyweds left in their carriage with outriders for their own hacienda at La Constancia, near Belén.[22]

In an interview just before her death at ninety-five, Consuelo (Connie) Bergere Mendenhall, Eloisa's eighth child (born August 28, 1895), recalled hearing about her mother's wedding, one of the most lavish and highly publicized social events in the history of New Mexico: "It was all very exciting. They went up and down the Río

Grande for a week in a gondola filled with flowers while Mexicans played guitars and sang love songs. I don't know how they were ever alone long enough to get together."[23]

But they managed, and their first child was a boy, Eduardo, born August 24, 1880, the strong healthy son they hoped would continue the family name. On October 23, 1881, Nina was born, and a year later Eloisa was again pregnant. These were prosperous and happy times for the young couple. The harvests had been plentiful, the warehouses filled with provisions, the wool from the flocks of sheep grazing their land abundant. Wet nurses were on hand around the clock to help the young mother with her infants.

Just down the road from their La Constancia home was the new Luna Mansion, built for Eloisa's father and mother by the Santa Fe Railroad in exchange for a right of way through their original homestead. Behind the mansion extensive vineyards flourished. The Muscat grapes grown there produced some of the country's finest wine and brandy, which, when returned from the presses near Algodones, were stored in the mansion's cavernous cellar. The Lunas had reportedly made a number of trips through the South and had been inspired by the grace and style of the architecture there. Their mansion was designed after the classic southern colonial homes but constructed with handmade adobe bricks.[24]

Unfortunately, Antonio José Luna did not live long in his elegant antebellum adobe home, for on December 20, 1881, he died, leaving the mansion to his eldest son, Tranquilino. A year later Manuel Antonio Otero died, and his only son, Manuel, took charge of the family estate (the Bartolomé Baca–Estancia land grant) and the thirty-five thousand sheep on its ranches.[25]

Less than a year after the deaths of the two patriarchs, Eloisa faced even greater personal tragedy when her young husband was fatally shot in the doorway of his family's Estancia ranch house at Antelope Springs in southeastern New Mexico. On a warm August day in 1883, Manuel left Los Lunas for Antelope Springs to challenge the claim of James and Joel Whitney to the Estancia ranch land, choice

Drawing showing the disputed Bartolomé Baca (Estancia) land grant, most of which was inherited by Manuel B. Otero in 1881. A portion of the grant was conveyed to Antonio Sandoval in 1845, who deeded it to Gervacio Nolan, who sold it in 1878 to Joel P. Whitney, a Boston capitalist. (SRC Misc. Collection, photo no.35519, New Mexico State Records Center and Archives, Santa Fe, New Mexico.)

acreage where natural springs fed a lake large enough to supply thousands of sheep and cattle with pure, cold water. Beautiful land of luxuriant grasses, shade trees, and flowering shrubs, the disputed property was truly an oasis in that part of the territory. Before the railroad intervened, Antelope Springs was a watering place for thousands of antelope and a mecca for hunters.[26]

The wealthy Whitneys of Massachusetts, owners of paper mills in Watertown and controlling partners in the Silver City, Deming, and Pacific Railroad enterprises, had challenged the ancient Spanish claims of those who had settled the Estancia land grant decades before. The Yankees had supposedly won a Territorial Supreme Court decision issued two weeks before the shootout. Although the case had been appealed and was pending in the district court of Valencia County, the impatient Whitneys went ahead with their plans to run the Otero ranch hands ("squatters," according to the Whitneys) off the valuable land, sending an armed posse to take possession.[27]

An Otero vaquero, Pablo Baca, his sick wife, and their three children were the only occupants of the ranch house on the day James Whitney and party arrived and ordered them to leave. Baca, suspicious of Whitney's story that he and Manuel Otero had "fixed matters up in Santa Fe a few days before," refused to go and became an eyewitness to the next day's tragedy. Whitney, his brother-in-law Alexander Fernández, and Arthur Bailhache made themselves comfortable in one room of the ranch house and spent most of the night drinking whiskey and playing poker.

Manuel Otero and his men—two vaqueros and his brothers-in-law, Dr. Edward C. Henríquez and Carlos Armijo—arrived around ten o'clock the morning of August 17. Despite Whitney's hostile attitude (he approached Otero with rifle in hand), young Manuel remained polite and cordial "and extended his hand to Whitney, who took it." Both parties entered the house to talk things over. The conversation became heated when Manuel confronted the Boston millionaire and demanded that he prove his claim to the property. It was then that Whitney pulled his pistol and fired point-blank at Otero, who was less than four feet away.

In the barrage of bullets that followed, Alexander Fernández was killed instantly; Whitney was shot in his side, hand, and lower jaw; and Dr. Henríquez was wounded in one arm. The bullet that struck Manuel splintered his collarbone and severed the carotid artery.[28]

Dr. Henríquez tried to stop the flow of blood from Otero's wound and summoned a justice of the peace to take statements from both men. Manuel found the strength to sign the document, but as his friends eased him back on a couch in the smoke-filled room, the blood clot in his neck ruptured and "he died in three minutes." Whitney, too weak to sign the paper, simply made his mark.[29] Riders raced ahead to notify Eloisa. The body of the young patrón was taken by wagon to Los Lunas, where it was met by his grief-stricken nineteen-year-old pregnant widow and her two small children.[30]

On the same day Fernández and Otero were killed, the severely injured Whitney was taken to Santa Fe's St. Vincent Sanatorium. Once his brother, Joel, heard the news, he arranged to have James secretly moved from the hospital, fearing retaliation by Manuel's friends. James was strapped to an improvised "contraption," lowered by ropes from his room to a waiting carriage, delivered to Joel Whitney's private Pullman car, and was on his way to safety in Las Vegas when Miguel Otero (a cousin of Manuel's and later territorial governor) and José Santos Esquibel, the county sheriff, intercepted the train. Showing due respect for Miguel Otero's "double action Colt pistol" and for an official order from the governor to proceed to Valencia County for a trial, the fugitives surrendered and the train headed south toward Los Lunas and a waiting lynch mob. When they arrived in Albuquerque, however, a Judge Bell boarded the train, held court in the Pullman car, released Whitney on a bail bond of $25,000, and permitted him to leave for California. Days later the judge in the Pullman-car case was roundly denounced by irate New Mexicans, who accused him of "assuming autocratic powers" in permitting Whitney to escape.[31]

Despite the outrage and demands for justice from Otero's family and friends, James Whitney was not tried for the murder until April 29, 1884, when he was acquitted on grounds that he shot in self-defense. According to Miguel Otero, Whitney had hired two prominent attorneys, had paid them well, and had bribed Judge Axtell, whose remarks to the jury were strongly prejudiced in Whitney's favor.[32]

The August 18, 1883, issue of the *Sunday Gazette* printed a telegram expressing the bitterness and sorrow of all who knew Manuel, "one of New Mexico's promising young men—cultured, kind, and noble. He died manfully contending for his rights, and his death is chargeable to the perpetrators and perpetuators of the system of land grant swindles that have for years crushed out the progressive industries of New Mexico and are now striking at the lives of her best and truest citizens."[33]

Once all rumors and testimony had been exhaustively sifted for the truth about what had occurred in the little ranch house at Ante-

The ranch house at Antelope Springs, site of the confrontation in 1883 between Manuel B. Otero and James P. Whitney. Otero, age 23, was shot and killed. (SRC Misc. Collection, photo no. 35520, New Mexico State Records Center and Archives, Santa Fe, New Mexico.)

lope Springs, Miguel A. Otero wrote his own account of the tragedy in his autobiography, *My Life on the Frontier* (1935). According to Otero, Manuel Otero and Charles Armijo had been at the ranch with the Whitney men the night before the tragedy on August 17. Both Otero and Whitney were in a friendly mood and had agreed to leave the matter of the land dispute "in the hands of the court." After an all-night poker party and considerable drinking, Manuel and Armijo rode off, leaving Whitney in full charge of the springs. On the way home, Manuel met Dr. Henríquez, who persuaded the young man to return to the ranch and demand that Whitney prove his claim by showing a court order. More drinks were passed around on the ride back. Whitney and his companions had also continued to drink in celebration of their easy victory. It seems that "all interested parties were in a very feverish state of mind" and very drunk on that fateful morning.[34]

At the time of her father's death, Nina was only twenty months old, too young to remember much about him, but she must have felt the grief of her mother and the servants in the hacienda at La Con-

Manuel B. Otero (1860-1883),
first husband of Eloisa Luna and
father of Nina Otero-Warren.
(Bergere Family Collection, photo
no. 21640, New Mexico State
Records Center and Archives,
Santa Fe, New Mexico.)

stancia the day the shocking news was delivered by a distraught
ranch hand. Her father's funeral, held in Belén with the Reverend Father Marra officiating, was the largest ever witnessed in that part of
the territory. Hundreds mourned the loss of the "brave, true-hearted
young man who died like a hero."[35]

Back at La Constancia, Eloisa went through the social rituals observed by Hispanic gentility in the late nineteenth century, politely
greeting the relatives and close friends who had gathered to offer
prayers and condolences, then quietly retiring to her rooms, resigned
to God's will. A few days later the widow and her two children
moved back to her parents' home, where her third child, Manuel B.
Otero, Jr., was born less than a month after his father was buried.

Eloisa began a period of mourning that by custom was to last
three years. Her privacy was respected, and only a few social calls

were permitted. The front door at the hacienda remained closed, the white lace curtains drawn at the windows. Black cloth draped both sides of the door and the lintels of the windows in front of the house. The harp in the living room was silenced, mirrors were covered with black veils. There was no laughter, no music, no joy in the household during the time the lovely widow mourned for her lost husband.[36]

A year after the death of her Manuelito, however, Eloisa's mother and brothers encouraged her to leave Los Lunas and go in search of an English-speaking companion-governess for her three children. With the large migration of Anglos into their region, the Lunas and Oteros saw the balance of political and social power shifting, and with it, the growing need to educate their children in American ways. Gone were the days when the Anglos found it advantageous to assimilate the customs and language of Spanish-Americans in order to maintain newly acquired land and gain access to positions of economic and political power. Having taken over much of the area in the 1880s, Anglos were now able "to impose their desire for and attitude toward land and business more effectively." Many of the wealthiest Hispanic families in New Mexico (only 5 percent of the territory's population) collaborated with the newcomers and reaped temporary benefits in the form of Anglo recognition and approval and, consequently, additional power and income. To succeed in the new economic order, the ricos believed that their children should receive "modern" education and training.[37]

To that end, Eloisa Luna Otero traveled during the summer of 1884 to Pittsburgh, Pennsylvania, where she met and hired Mary Elizabeth Doyle, an unmarried woman of twenty-four years who was working at the time in a convent. Eloisa "returned with a new ally," Connie Mendenhall said, "an indomitable Irish orphan called Teta." Teta and Eloisa were appalled at the condition of the Los Lunas hacienda when they returned from Pittsburgh. Among the general disarray and clutter, they found chickens eating off sterling silver plates in the patio. Taking over at once, Teta brought the sterling inside and

Mary Elizabeth Doyle, "Teta" (1860-1947), hired in 1884 by Eloisa Luna Otero as governess for her children, Eduardo, Nina, and Manuel. (Bergere Family Collection, photo no. 21754, New Mexico State Records Center and Archives, Santa Fe, New Mexico.)

hid it; she told Connie years later that "the chickens were never the same after that." Teta was charged with the care and instruction of Eduardo, Nina, and Manuel B., Jr., and developed a long, happy, and supportive relationship with them. For the next sixty-three years, until her death on April 1, 1947, Teta was with the family as nurturer and confidant, "surrogate grandmother, advisor, and friend."[38]

The year 1884 marked the beginning of a new and happier chapter in the lives of Eloisa and her three children. That winter, at the invitation of her brother Solomón, Alfred Maurice Bergere visited Los Lunas for a baptismal ceremony and there met his future wife. Eloisa was immediately attracted to Alfred, an intelligent, cultured man whose speech in both English and Spanish still retained the trace of a soft British accent. He made some effort to respect the widow's three-year mourning period, but Eloisa was only twenty

Alfred Maurice Bergere, ca. 1886,
second husband of Eloisa Luna
Otero. (Bergere Family Collection,
photo no. 23233, New Mexico
State Records Center and Archives,
Santa Fe, New Mexico.)

years old and much too beautiful, he felt, to be so strictly confined. He made it a point to see her again after that first meeting. Connie remembered stories of their "flowery courtship" carried on mostly through the mail: "Mama couldn't write English, so she and Teta would get down on the living room floor, and Teta would write the love letters."[39]

Because he was traveling at the time for the Spiegelbergs, five brothers who owned and managed a thriving general emporium operating out of Albuquerque and Santa Fe, Alfred Bergere found it convenient to schedule a visit to Los Lunas every two or three weeks to call on Eloisa. Obviously the rules for mourning were bent a bit, for in 1885 the young couple became engaged. Although, according to Alfred, a serious quarrel after one of his visits "ruptured" their relationship, a year later they met by accident in Socorro, made up, and in July of 1886 decided to renew their engagement.[40]

Alfred was nervous the Sunday he called on Eloisa's mother and her brothers Jesús and Tranquilino to ask for her hand in marriage. He and the family were well aware that the union would be a departure from the Lunas' centuries-old tradition of intermarrying with other old Spanish families.[41]

Alfred was an Anglo in the full sense of the word, born in Liverpool, England, on October 10, 1858, the second son of Italian parents whose forebears, by Alfred's account, came from the province of Peronne, France.[42] His grandfather, Francisco Luigi Berger, was born around 1760 in Trieste, which at the time belonged to Italy. His father, Joseph Charles Berger, owned the first line of steamships that sailed out of Liverpool. His mother, Nina Mandelick Berger, who died in 1865 when Alfred was seven years old, gave him his first lessons on the piano and encouraged his interest in music. His playing was impressive, and when only twelve years old he had performed in concert in Liverpool.

Educated there by tutors and in private schools, and later in London at Queens College, Alfred at sixteen left Britain for New York, where he lived with his aunt and uncle until he was twenty-one. One of the first calls he made on arriving in New York was to a Dr. Eberhardt at the city's famed Conservatory of Music. He told the distinguished musician of his longing to be a concert pianist and played two pages of the adagio from Beethoven's Fifth Symphony before the maestro abruptly interrupted him. It was already "too late" for Alfred, according to Eberhardt, who told him that he played very well "for a drawing room" but not well enough to go before the public. The crestfallen young man played nothing for a year and eventually resigned himself to pursuing a career in sales and marketing.[43]

Ambitious and resourceful even as a teenager, Alfred attended night school to learn the ways of his adopted America and worked days as an office boy for a weekly wage of $2.80. At the time he decided to leave New York for New Mexico in 1880, he was assistant cashier for Menier and Company of Paris, then the largest chocolate house in the world. After arriving in Albuquerque, he worked for the firm of Vose and Stein, representing his cousin's interest in the wholesale and retail merchandising business. The railroad had barely reached Albuquerque in 1881, and part of Alfred's trip from Las Vegas had to be made by stagecoach over primitive cart roads. A year later he went into business with H. B. Slaughter of Kansas City, Missouri, working from a tent store in Coolidge, New Mexico, supplying general stock to men working on the Atlantic and Pacific Railroad line.

For more than a year things went well with the commissary business—a second store had been opened at Belmont, Arizona, twelve miles south of Flagstaff—when Slaughter skipped town with all the money and goods, leaving Alfred stranded and in debt. Returning to Albuquerque, he joined Spiegelberg Brothers, first as a clerk and then as a traveling salesman covering the territory from the New Mexico–Colorado line to Chihuahua, Mexico. In the course of his travels he had made the acquaintance of Manuel B. Otero, but had not met his wife. News of Manuel's death came to Alfred in July, 1883, while he was in Fond du Lac, Wisconsin, recovering from an illness he described as "bilious fever." He was nursed back to health by a "young lady" to whom he was engaged to be married—but the following winter he met Eloisa, and two years later asked for her hand in marriage. [44]

Cross-cultural marriages between Anglo men and Hispanic women were not uncommon in New Mexico at the time, and such unions helped contribute to the Americanization of the Spanish Southwest. Many Hispanic women enhanced their opportunity for social and economic mobility through marriage to Anglo men, but this was not true in the case of Alfred Bergere and Eloisa Luna Otero. She was far more economically secure than he and already enjoyed the privileged status of New Mexico's elite class. For Alfred, who had been traveling the lonely roads of the Southwest for six years, marriage to Eloisa offered not only a full life with a kind and beautiful woman but also a connection with one of the most prestigious families in the territory.[45]

Alfred M. Bergere did not have the distinctive Spanish heritage of the Lunas, Oteros, Chaveses, and Bacas, but he was an honest and enterprising young man, well educated, and obviously in love with Eloisa. The Lunas not only accepted him, but treated him "royally." At first the couple planned a small wedding with only the immediate family in attendance, but when Eloisa asked that her dear friends the Hunings of Los Lunas be included, her brother Jesús insisted that since one outsider had been invited, all the relatives must come. Alfred then had to prepare for some three hundred guests.

Rising to the challenge, he arranged for an orchestra, doubled his order for flowers and refreshments, and, when the train transporting provisions and musicians to Los Lunas broke down, sent wagons to complete the delivery. After the wedding, Eloisa and Alfred left by train (the very latest form of transportation in 1886) for their honeymoon in Chicago, but when she became ill and the Pullman car broke down near Socorro, they were forced to remain there until the following night. Their confidence in the efficiency of the new trains shaken, they came to understand why the narrow-gauge Denver and Rio Grande Western Railroad (D&RGW) in time became known as "Dangerous and Rapidly Growing Worse."[46]

Despite their honeymoon's less than perfect beginning, the couple settled into a comfortable life at Los Lunas, Alfred assuming the care of Nina and her two brothers and taking over his wife's diverse interests, including the management of her land and several thousand head of sheep. Her property was to remain in his hands until her children came of age.[47]

Life for Nina and the other children in the hacienda was lived in accordance with the rules and expectations of their devout Catholic parents. All the little ones were instructed in the catechism and attended mass when the mission priest came through Los Lunas.

Whether the holy ceremony was held for a wedding or a funeral, Nina remembered that it was a time "to laugh, to love, and to pray. . . . Dons and Doñas came in high coaches, drawn by prancing bays. . . . The *peones* came in wagons, on burro-back or on foot. . . . It was always noticed if a neighbor did not come and he was considered a savage."[48]

When Nina reached seven, "the age of reason," she received her first Holy Communion, an occasion that featured elaborate breakfasts at neighboring houses and the lively music of fiesta to celebrate her new dignity as a first communicant.[49] Learning the more mundane subjects of reading, writing, and arithmetic came easily, as she was a bright and responsive student. She also had the advantage of having Irish Teta and British Bergere to help her with the English language. For several years she attended St. Vincent's Academy in Albuquerque, but by the time she was eleven it became clear to her parents that she was ready for a more formal education.

In the nineteenth century, daughters as well as sons of prosperous families attended boarding schools outside the territory. Since Eloisa and Alfred wanted and could afford the best education for their children, Nina was sent by train to St. Louis, Missouri, the nearest U.S. metropolis, to enter Maryville College of the Sacred Heart, an institution that forty-two years later (1936) would award her an honorary bachelor of literature degree for her achievements as author and educator.[50]

From 1892 to 1894, Nina studied under the Sisters of the Sacred Heart, and while no degrees were awarded in those days—Maryville being essentially a finishing school for young girls—she honed her skills in writing and speaking the English language. The college curriculum emphasized the importance of teaching careers for women, considered at the time the only respectable female occupation outside marriage and motherhood, and encouraged the girls to commit a portion of their lives to their community. This focus on social concerns laid the groundwork for the leadership roles she would assume twenty years later.

Nina Otero, Los Lunas, ca. 1894.
(Bergere Family Collection, Photo
no. 21696, New Mexico State
Records Center and Archives,
Santa Fe, New Mexico.)

Nina returned to Los Lunas from Maryville at the age of thirteen, two years short of the usual marrying age for girls at that time.
As the eldest daughter of her large family, she was expected to help
with the training and education of her siblings, a responsibility she
eagerly undertook. Friends and family members later said that even
as an adolescent "Nina wanted to be the boss. She took it upon herself to be in charge. She showed leadership qualities early on, and
she had the brains in the family."[51]

In predominantly Hispanic New Mexico during the last decade
of the nineteenth century, the rearing of daughters was not left solely
to the women. While doña Eloisa was the principal head of the
household and completely in charge of the servants and children, the
entire family, including Nina's uncles and older male cousins, helped
with her upbringing.[52] Once the wiry, energetic little girl had

learned to ride horseback, she would occasionally accompany her stepfather and her uncles Tranquilino and Solomón into the fields to watch the *peones* work the corn and alfalfa. Most farmers and ranchers found it advisable to carry a pistol or a shotgun when they were away from the safety of the hacienda, and when Nina was old enough to handle a gun, she badgered the men in the family to teach her how to shoot it. In later years she passed on her knowledge of firearms to her nephews, Jack and Bergere Kenney.[53]

Nina took pleasure in sharing all she had learned at Maryville with her brothers and sisters. She told Eduardo, Manuel, Anita, and even four-year-old Estella about their Spanish ancestors, information she would later put in her book for young adults, *Old Spain in Our Southwest.* The Spaniards, she proudly told them, were the people who brought to the New World all the domestic animals except the turkey and the dog; sheep, mules, burros, and horses were unknown to the Indians before the Spaniards introduced them. And of these the most important to *patrón* and *peón* alike was the burro, so special an animal that it was assigned a patron saint (San Antón) and its own feast day each year on the seventeenth of January.[54]

Nina's lessons were usually followed by a game of "rancho," where the older children imitated the handling of cattle and sheep and pretended to be stalwart vaqueros working the land. The younger ones would play with seeds, beans, and corn: pinto beans, including some brown ones, were the sheep; grains of corn were cattle, and pumpkin or melon seeds were horses. Baseball was a favorite sport for both girls and boys, and *taba*, a primitive dice game played with the ankle bone of a sheep, kept the youngsters occupied for hours.[55]

Nina discovered how difficult farming and ranching could be on the semiarid plains of New Mexico, where long cyclical spells of drought dried up crops even in the Río Grande Valley. She heard the ranch hands pray for rain and then protest the great flood brought on by the Child Jesus, complaining to the Virgin Mary about the damage her son had done after a deluge wreaked havoc on the land.

She remembered the flurry of activity early in the morning when everyone arose to begin the routine of the day, the field hands working from sunrise to sunset but breaking occasionally to gossip or take a siesta in the middle of the afternoon heat.[56]

Very little had to be purchased outside the hacienda. Men skilled as carpenters would build, carve, and finish essential furniture for the community—chairs, benches, cupboards, and tables, even the *santos* to be framed in wood or tin. Others repaired saddles and worked with leather. As the summer drew to a close, wood was hauled from the distant mountains to stock the house for winter and to provide fuel for the outdoor ovens where thin steaks from the butchered steers and lambs were partially cooked in preparation for storage.

The women would grind corn and chili, supervised by a regal Eloisa from her chair in the shade of the patio's *portal*. Bread was baked in outdoor ovens, removed on long-handled wooden shovels, and placed in earthen bowls to keep fresh. Harvest time each fall was a joyful event at Los Lunas. Nina, Eduardo, Manuel, and the children of Eloisa and Alfred Bergere, numbering five in 1895—Anita, Estella, May, Luna, and Connie—were taken each day to the great hall of the hacienda to watch the carding and spinning and weaving of wool, which was usually accompanied by violin and guitar music played by musicians brought in for the occasion. Corn was husked and ground, pumpkins cut and sliced. *Peones* served refreshments of sweet buns, cheese with honey, and a drink made of ground roasted peas.[57]

Nina would often visit the hacienda's dark, cool storehouse, where a six-month supply of food was preserved inside thick, adobe-insulated walls for the entire community. Meat, field corn, herbs, pumpkins in the winter months, and what vegetables the garden produced could be found in abundance.

For family celebrations and Catholic feast days, the housekeeper ordered the cooks to prepare a standard menu of clear soup, several meat dishes, including chicken and chili, and fresh or dried vegetables, depending on the season. Only dried vegetables were available in winter, since canned goods in late–nineteenth-century New Mexico were still not considered safe to eat. For dessert there were custards and *arroz con leche*, rice sweetened and cooked in milk, followed by coffee and chocolate.

On these special occasions the table in the family's large dining hall was covered with crisp linen cloths and featured an exquisite candelabra as the centerpiece. Gracing each place setting were heavy, hammered spoons and forks and plates glowing with the patina of old Spanish silver, all carefully arranged next to steel knives imported from the States. Food was served in large, patterned silver bowls.

After dinner Alfred Bergere would play the piano, entertaining family and guests with both popular and classical music. Then, as in later years, one of his greatest pleasures was performing the work of the masters and introducing Bach, Mozart, and Beethoven to the youth of New Mexico.[58]

The younger children were put to bed early, but Nina and her brothers would linger behind and beg for *cuentos* (stories) before they settled down for the night. They liked to hear their stepfather tell of his adventures in New Mexico before he married their mother. He was one of perhaps a dozen Anglos headquartered in Albuquerque during what he described as "the wild days" of 1881. Louis and Noa Ilfeld, Franz Huning, Edward Spitz, E. S. Stover, W. K. P. Wilson, R. C. Vose, and Albert Grunsfeld of Spiegelberg Brothers were among the few early Anglo businessmen seeking their fortunes in the Duke City.[59]

Alfred told his children of an encounter he once had with Mother Thatcher, a tough frontierswoman who carried a long knife in her boot and operated a hotel of sorts. The night he took a room in her shabby hostelry he overheard her conspire with her cohorts to rob him of what little money he had. Grabbing his coat, hat, and pistol, he managed to escape through a window before they moved in on him. He later learned that Mother Thatcher had been murdered by her son-in-law, Charlie Dyer.

The children of Eloisa Luna and Manuel B. Otero. Left to right: Eduardo, Nina, and Manuel, Los Lunas, ca. 1895. (Bergere Family Collection, photo no. 21644, New Mexico State Records Center and Archives, Santa Fe, New Mexico.)

Alfred mesmerized the children with his tales of robberies on the trails in the old days before the railroads stretched across New Mexico. On one occasion, when he was traveling alone on horseback from Belmont to Prescott, Arizona, two men forced him at gunpoint to turn over his pistols and relieved him of his signet ring, watch, and $92 in gold and silver. His new saddle was pulled from his horse and an old one substituted, but the thugs overlooked the $700 in bills he had sewed up in his black silk tie. Later that day, while he was having supper with some cowboys at a farm and cattle ranch in the Chino Valley, a wagon arrived with six men who had been severely injured while working on the new railroad line. An explosion had blown off one man's leg, another's arm, and the others were missing hands and had multiple and severe abrasions all over their bodies. The same thieves who had accosted Alfred had stopped the wagon and taken all the money the wounded men were carrying—something over $100.

Incensed by the brutality of the crime, Alfred and the cowboys went in search of the desperadoes, traveling night and day, changing horses at ranches along the way. Around midnight of their second night on the trail, they cornered one of the gang in a small sheepherder's shack. Walter Hill, one of the cowboys, decided to approach the hut and peer in the window, a serious mistake because in the bright moonlight he made an excellent target. The trapped man shot, wounding Hill in the forehead. Furious, Alfred and his friends threatened to set fire to the house if the villain did not come out in two minutes with his hands up. When he finally shuffled out the door he was met with a fusillade and fell with sixteen bullets in his body.

After helping with the renegade's burial, Alfred recovered his good saddle and $90 cash—the other thief had taken the rest—and on his arrival in Prescott went to the hospital and gave the injured workers the money that had been stolen from them.[60]

Life was not quite so violent on the ranches of Los Lunas, but there were many times when harsh weather and the great distances between communities tested the mettle of the sheepmen. Nina was eight years old when her stepfather and her uncle Solomón Luna lost twenty-one thousand head of sheep in an October snowstorm that stretched over an area five miles wide and one hundred miles long. The storm caught them as they were driving the herd back to pasture after a shearing in Grants, New Mexico. Alfred and Solomón lost all the sheep and their pelts, worth more than $80,000.

One winter the two patrones left Quemado before dawn in a blinding blizzard to buy provisions for their men and supplies for their herd at a store eleven miles away. Since they could not see the road to guide their horses, they had to give the animals free rein and as a result went full circle, ending their trip eleven hours later back at the ranch from which they started. Once the storm subsided, they managed to find the store but had to pay inflated prices for the staples they desperately needed—$50 for a sack of flour, $1 for a pound of coffee, $0.50 for a pound of sugar, and $1 a pound for salt pork. So scarce were these commodities at the time that the proprietor was reluctant to sell them even at those prices.[61]

In urgent need of cash, Alfred and Solomón agreed to sell some of their sheep to ranchers from Utah whom they arranged to meet at a specified place on the San Agustín Plains. With Solomón driving the buckboard, they headed off in what Alfred insisted was the wrong direction. Solomón wouldn't listen to his brother-in-law and kept on until the snow reached the hubs of the buckboard. After traveling all night in deep snow, with Alfred cursing most of the way and threatening to get out and walk, they finally came to a sawmill outside Magdalena, seventy miles north of their destination.

Once they arrived at the camp, two days late, they sold part of their herd to the Utah buyers for $3,850 and offered them two burros and two men to care for the sheep in the mountains. Alfred and Solomón tried to explain that it would be too risky to drive the herd any great distance in January, since the ewes were heavy with lamb. For a month or two the sheep needed a protected environment where they could be given food and water. Winter shelters for sheep were so important that, as Santa Fe writer Erna Fergusson wrote years later, the man-made lambing sheds sheepherders sometimes provided for their flocks were "only less comfortable than a hospital maternity ward."[62] Unconvinced and unwilling to wait for milder weather, the ranchers stubbornly insisted on driving the herd to Utah. Several years later Alfred heard that they had learned a costly lesson—all the sheep had died on the drive north.

Added to the constant threat of New Mexico's unpredictable weather was the fear of hostile Indians. Nina, Eduardo, and Manuel were told about the days when men and women throughout the territory kept shotguns and rifles at the ready to defend their homes and herds against possible attacks by Apaches. While there were many Indians who wanted work and were employed by the patrones, there were still those who violently resisted confinement to reservations and sought revenge for the confiscation of their land and destruction of their way of life.

One year when the Luna-Bergere flocks were being sheared by some Apaches near St. Johns, Arizona, an angry Indian drew a knife on Solomón Luna after the *patrón* fired him for badly cutting the sheep. Solomón, unarmed, ran for shelter in a nearby ranch house. The Indian was closing rapidly when he was stopped by a bullet through his eye, killed instantly by Mariano Chávez, the majordomo of the Luna herds, who had fired his rifle from the doorway. Chávez felt his act was one of justified vengeance, because Apaches had massacred his family and kidnapped him when he was a baby. He had been forced to live with the tribe for thirty years before he managed to escape and return to Los Lunas. After a brief investigation into the matter in the little town of St. Johns, Chávez was absolved of any crime.[63]

As the nineteenth century drew to a close, the danger and much of the adventure of living on the ranch lands began to fade. Travel became much easier. Nina, then a curious and bright adolescent, took every opportunity to venture away from the slow, predictable pace of the rural life she had known from infancy. She looked forward to trips north to Albuquerque and Santa Fe, towns that were steadily growing toward the status of cities as a result of their linkage by rail with the East Coast, for there she was exposed to new ideas, lifestyles, and lively young people who were quick to include her in their social gatherings. She made friends easily and was a popular choice for games, outings, and horseback riding contests when she accompanied her stepfather on his periodic trips to legislative sessions in Santa Fe.

Never much of a sheepman, Alfred's interests had turned to politics, particularly after he lost his legal battle for possession of the Baca-Estancia land grant. The ownership of the land was still being disputed after the murder of Manuel B. Otero when, in 1890, Alfred purchased from the heirs of Manuel Antonio Otero all their interest in the grant. This interest and that of Miguel A. Otero's heirs amounted to 1,282,000 acres. Alfred, on behalf of his wife, claimed four-fifths of the land, which the Miguel Oteros resented but, wanting to stay friends, decided not to contest.[64]

In their appeal to the U.S. Court of Private Land Claims in 1895, the Alfred Bergeres were awarded only forty-eight thousand acres of the contested property. Determined to fight the decision of the lower court, Alfred and Miguel A. Otero, who in 1897 was appointed New Mexico's territorial governor, appealed the case all the way to the United States Supreme Court in 1898.

Unhappily for the family, the Supreme Court decided against their claim on the grounds that there was "no proof that Governor Melgares had signed the approval of the grant as required by law," because the corner of the document containing the full approval and part of his signature was missing.[65] Because both the Otero and the Whitney claims to the land were denied, both grants were declared public domain and opened to settlement. Even the forty-eight thousand acres awarded to the Bergeres by the Court of Private Land Claims had to be forfeited.[66] "Now," Erna Fergusson wrote fifty years after the Supreme Court's 1898 decision, "the fine grassy stretches of the Estancia Valley are checkered with fences around forlorn little houses where perennially hopeful farmers are trying to prove that beans can be raised without water."[67]

Another factor contributed to Alfred's failure in the Supreme Court, according to Miguel Otero's account of the proceedings. A. M. Bergere, Otero said, had hired a "deadbeat" attorney, James W. Vroom, a "fine looking fellow from New Jersey, who excelled in drinking whisky and soda and in 'kiting checks'." In court, while Thomas B. Catron (Otero's attorney) was preparing to present their case in a dignified and reasoned manner, Vroom and his associate Harry S. Clancy burst into the room, "both full as ticks," and immediately began to take over the argument. Otero said that he never remembered "hearing a weaker and more rambling presentation. . . . Our case was hopelessly lost. . . . We all lost out."[68]

Unfortunately, such losses were all too common in New Mexico and its neighboring territories under the new Anglo legal system. From the Anglo's point of view, land used by Hispanics for grazing their flocks appeared to be wasted, vacant, and "not producing a profit." The U.S. Congress, therefore, recognized only the irrigated fields and home lots of the old land grants. The new law was interpreted rigidly, and land grants that had been held by Hispanics for more than a hundred years were rejected. Of the more than thirty-five million acres disputed in the 1890s in New Mexico, Arizona, and Colorado, only 2,051,526 acres were confirmed to Hispanics by the courts.[69]

Alfred and several of Miguel Otero's heirs managed to recover some of the land under the Small Holdings Claims Act of 1891, an acquisition that proved profitable later when they sold tracts to the Pennsylvania Development Company for the New Mexico Central Railroad's water tank.

Overall, Alfred M. Bergere was relatively comfortable financially, thanks to the support and influence of the Luna and Otero families.[70] But after trying his hand at sheep ranching for eleven years, with sometimes disastrous results, he concluded, and his relatives agreed, that his talents could be more productively used in the political arena. The late John J. Kenney, Jr., Alfred Bergere's grandson, admitted that while "AMB" was a charming and sensitive man who loved music and played the piano well, he was not a good businessman. "Grandfather mismanaged the sheep ranches," Jack said, "and so the family politicos got him a job in Santa Fe."[71]

Politics had always held a special fascination for Alfred, as it had for most of the male members of the family. On the recommendation of Solomón Luna, he had been appointed to various political positions in Valencia County from the time he married Eloisa Luna. He had traveled to the capitol in Santa Fe many times with Solomón to propose territorial legislation. When the Democrats at one time tried to divide Valencia County, "the greatest Republican County in the State," he paid key members in the House $400 to adjourn for

The Otero-Bergere family, Los Lunas, ca. 1895. Left to right, standing: Nina Otero, Alfred M.
Bergere, Eloisa Luna Otero Bergere; middle row: Eduardo Otero, May Bergere, Manuel Otero;
seated: Anita Bergere and Estella Bergere. (Photograph courtesy John J. Kenney.)

three days. This bit of bribery bought him enough time to line up
the necessary votes for the Republicans. Enraged by his high-handed
political maneuvers, two men from Gallup threatened to kill him on
sight, but he managed to avoid them even though they were all on
the same train out of Santa Fe.[72]

A. M. Bergere's commitment to the Republican party and his
ability to get the job done caught the attention of the territory's leaders, and in the last decade of the nineteenth century he, together
with Solomón and Tranquilino Luna, exercised strong influence in
Valencia County politics. In 1897, the election of President McKinley
swept Republicans into office, and Eloisa's cousin Miguel Antonio
Otero II was appointed governor. As a favor to Eloisa, "Gillie" Otero
recommended that Judge John R. McFie of the First New Mexico Ju-

dicial District appoint A. M. Bergere as his clerk. Despite the protestations of Solomón, who had serious doubts about Alfred's ability to handle such a job and who warned Governor Otero that he would "regret it" if he brought the Bergeres to Santa Fe, Otero held firm.[73]

Women in the late nineteenth century could not vote and were generally excluded from such matters, but even at the age of sixteen Nina was drawn to New Mexico politics. She would listen intently to the sometimes explosive discussions that began most evenings after dinner and lasted until the piñon logs in the corner fireplace were reduced to ashes. She commented later that for the Spanish-American male, the political arena offered the same drama and excitement as gambling or horse racing. "Just as at a horse race he bets on the pinto, so he bets on his political favorite. . . . He accepts defeat with a dramatic flourish—a shrug of the shoulder, a wave of the hand, and . . . 'It may be for the best.' "[74]

Nina must have been overjoyed at the prospect of moving to a larger city where she would have a better chance of finding a more interesting life. She had a certain bravado and self-assurance learned from her brothers, on whom she depended for companionship at home in Los Lunas, her half-sisters being so much younger. Eduardo and Manuel had the kind of freedom she would have wanted—freedom to come and go pretty much as they pleased, to take on responsibilities, to take charge, to choose a future in virtually any field of endeavor—but she must have realized at a very early age how limited her choices would be as a Catholic Hispanic woman living in a conventional paternalistic society.

The easy camaraderie she had with the young men in the family changed markedly as she reached adolescence. By the age of sixteen the male-female lines had been clearly drawn, and she had learned from her mother and aunts most of what she needed to know to prepare for marriage. As was customary and proper for young girls of her social class, her activities away from the hacienda—at fiestas and village dances—were carefully monitored and chaperoned.[75]

Nina undoubtedly resented the restrictions of being female in a male-dominated world, but she would go on to prove that she had the determination to work around them and find ways to fulfill her need for challenge, to take only what she thought useful from the prescribed roles for women of her time and place. She disdained learning how to sew or prepare meals, and such domestic skills were not demanded of her since the family could well afford servants. Developing social skills was another matter, for with them she could gain entry to the inner circles of power that held the best hope for achievement. Even in her teens she had a zest for reading and learning and for the intelligent exchange of ideas. Santa Fe would be a better place than Los Lunas to accomplish her goals, goals that in 1897 had yet to be clearly defined.

CHAPTER TWO

Santa
Fe

A lfred and Eloisa Luna Bergere, their eight children (ranging
from seventeen to not quite two years of age), and their
nanny, Teta, arrived in Santa Fe in 1897 in time for the
June 14 inauguration of Miguel Antonio Otero. The ancient city Pueblo Indians once called "the dancing ground of the
sun," the oldest capital in the United States, was still a drowsy little
town just before the turn of the century, but for the Bergere family,
coming from the quiet plains below Albuquerque, it was a metropolis of promise and opportunity. Here the girls would receive a better
education under the nuns at Loretto Academy on College Street, and
the boys could attend the new public high school and St. Michael's
College. The beautiful Cathedral of St. Francis, finished in 1869 under the direction of Archbishop Lamy, was within walking distance
of their first home on Lincoln Avenue, rented by Alfred Bergere from
the Thomas Catrons.[1]

Downtown Santa Fe, only a block away, was a motley assem-
blage of government buildings, shops, business offices, and private
homes, all facing wide, dirt paths around a fenced plaza where large

cottonwoods shaded benches and lanes. Narrow twisting trails that passed for residential streets branched out like spokes from the plaza and wound their way up toward the Sangre de Cristo Mountains, the soft, sensual foothills of the Rockies. Scattered about haphazardly were modest adobe houses, their fireplaces perfuming the air with smoke from piñon and juniper logs.

On the south side of the plaza, near Solomon Spiegelberg's grand building, bicycles and horse-drawn delivery wagons parked in front of Kaune's, the city's leading market. On the southeast corner, the Exchange Hotel (later renamed La Fonda), a one-story adobe structure with a portal supported by rough wooden posts and board sidewalks, offered comfortable rooms and generous family-style meals to the jubilant Republicans gathered to celebrate Otero's appointment. To entertain the more distinguished politicos, the Abraham Staabs opened their large Victorian mansion on East Palace Avenue, serving their guests fresh oysters and shad, aged liquor, and fine champagnes.[2]

In sharp contrast to the urban amenities, there were dilapidated corrals and stables a short walk away from the elegant Catron Block and the stylish Victorian homes in the city's center. Burros and horses stood tethered in Burro Alley, some loaded with bundles of firewood from the Sangre de Cristo forests.

The bright, festive inaugural day in June brought out merchants and shoppers, most of them on foot, some in carriages or wagons or on horseback. Thousands of men and women had assembled from across the territory to see and hear their newly appointed governor take the oath of office. "Enthusiasm for the inaugural was at fever heat," reported the Santa Fe New Mexican, when the governor-elect and his party circled the plaza in a rose- and flag-festooned carriage drawn by four spirited gray horses. "Cheer upon cheer" rocked the centuries-old Palace of the Governors, decorated for the occasion with bunting and American flags and freshly cut piñon tree branches tied to posts along the portal. Otero's inaugural speech was repeatedly interrupted with applause and bravos as he promised to "know no

Miguel A. Otero (1859-1944), Governor of the Territory of New Mexico, 1897-1906, second cousin of Nina Otero. (Courtesy Museum of New Mexico, negative no. 50608, Santa Fe, New Mexico.)

particular section; know no particular faction, swerve in no degree from the plain and clear duty of my administration." The loudest and most prolonged cheering came when Otero proudly said, "I stand before you as the first native-born governor of this fair territory."[3]

The Bergeres were among those who had the most to cheer about, for they were happily anticipating the years ahead with one of their own in high office. Miguel Otero and A. M. Bergere had been good friends for years and in 1895 had made a trip to New York together, hoping to trade the Estancia property for an estate at Pelham Manor outside New York City. Their dreams of acquiring prime real estate "with butlers, valets, masters of the hounds, gentlemen-in-waiting, and servants galore" were shattered when the deal fell through. But their friendship was cemented on that trip when Miguel became seriously ill after eating contaminated oysters at the Wellington Hotel in Chicago. For days Alfred took care of his ailing

The Bergere family, ca. 1906. Left to right, back row: Estella, Nina, Manuel, and Anita holding Joe; middle row: May, A. M. Bergere, Eloisa, and Luna; front row: Connie, Ysabel, Dolores and Rosina. Eduardo Otero was not present at the time the photograph was taken (Bergere Family Collection, photo no. 21648, New Mexico State Records Center and Archives, Santa Fe, New Mexico.)

friend "like a trained nurse." Once Miguel had recuperated and returned home, he and Alfred were again working together on money-making schemes when Otero received the good news that President McKinley had appointed him territorial governor.[4]

As New Mexico's chief executive, Miguel could now repay his friends for the kindnesses they had shown him, particularly his beautiful cousin Eloisa, who, he declared, was very excited about the prospects of living in Santa Fe during his administration. Eloisa and Miguel's Anglo wife, Caroline Otero, were also close friends, and both were happily looking forward to "a splendid time at the territorial capital."[5]

Eloisa did have a good time, even though she was pregnant with her ninth child when she arrived in Santa Fe and had four more children before Otero's three terms as governor expired in 1906. Two days after the inauguration she gave birth to María Eloisa Berenice Dolores. In 1898, María Rosina was born; in 1901, María Nestora Cristina Ysabel; and in 1905, her last child, Joseph Charles. Three children died in infancy. Her amused grandchildren offered one explanation for the astonishing number of Bergere children: "Eloisa would have a party, get pregnant, have her baby, turn it over to a wet nurse, have another party and get pregnant again."[6]

Much of the Bergeres' entertaining was done for political reasons, according to Eloisa Bergere Brown, who said her grandmother Eloisa was highly popular with the powerful people in state government and frequently invited them to luncheons and dinner parties in the warm, hospitable Bergere home. She also donated her time and money to small private charities, at times delivering baskets of food herself to poor families in and around Santa Fe. Since working outside the home was not socially acceptable for a woman at the time, Eloisa did a great deal of volunteer work through the St. Francis Cathedral altar society, and later as a member of New Mexico's Board of Education.[7]

Eloisa's first concern, however, was for her husband and children. The rented house on Lincoln Avenue became much too small for the burgeoning family, and given the political rivalry between their landlord, Thomas Catron, and Miguel Otero (Catron had vigorously opposed Otero's gubernatorial appointment, once accusing him of fraud and political chicanery),[8] Alfred and Eloisa believed it wise to move out. Two months after the birth of Ysabel, their seventh daughter, the family moved into a house on Grant Avenue. The residence was one of six once used as officers' quarters for the Fort Marcy Military Reservation, and it had at one time been the temporary quarters for former president Ulysses S. Grant and his family when they made a brief visit to Santa Fe in July 1880.[9]

La Casa Grande, or the "Big House," as it was soon christened by the family, was, and is still, located at 135 Grant Avenue. It was one of the many perquisites the Bergeres received through their close connection with the governor. After 1885, when there was no longer a pressing need for the fort, the residence had been offered rent free to politicians and prominent New Mexicans by the governor of the territory until he, as custodian of the property, could arrange for its disposal. Isabella Baca de Luna, Nina's maternal grandmother, had lived in the house for two years after the governor granted Solomón Luna permission to occupy it in 1899. But since Solomón had his own home in Los Lunas—the Luna Mansion—he encouraged the Bergeres to move in after his mother vacated the property.[10]

The family lived in the Grant Avenue house, which the local Anglos called the A. M. Bergere house, rent free until the Fort Marcy Abandoned Military Reservation Committee formally turned it over to the City of Santa Fe on January 5, 1904. A month later the property was transferred to the Santa Fe Board of Education, which in turn sold it to Eloisa Luna de Bergere on December 22, 1905, for $2,700. Ownership of the house remained in Eloisa's hands until her death in 1914 and afterward was taken over by her three Otero children— Eduardo, Nina, and Manuel. The Otero-Bergere family was to occupy the residence for more than seventy years.

The original structure was somewhat cramped for the large family because the cross-gabled, tin-pleated roof limited the bedroom space on the second floor, but over the years improvements were made. The original kitchen was converted to a master bedroom for Eloisa and Alfred, stables and a tennis court were constructed, and fruit trees planted. While the house was a departure from the flat-roofed, adobe-brick style characteristic of most New Mexico homes of the day, the exterior walls of the Big House were stuccoed, and there were wooden-planked floors in all the rooms.[11]

At the turn of the century the Bergeres, like many upper-class business and political leaders in New Mexico, were bent on joining the rest of the "modern" nation, hoping that their territory would soon be accepted as a state. To dispel decades of discrimination by those who looked upon the territory as the "final jumping off place for the American citizen" and not "fit to support a proper state government," there was a concerted effort in Santa Fe to put aside much of the city's Mexican and Spanish culture, including its Spanish-Pueblo architecture. Adobe homes and offices were regarded by prejudiced Anglo visitors as "a miserable collection of mud hovels," a "degenerate Spanish (Mexican) style of architecture."[12]

As a consequence, upper-class Hispanics and some Anglos living in New Mexico in the late nineteenth century began importing, from the East and Middle West, architecture that at the time was considered fashionable. In the early years of the twentieth century, more and more Victorian-style homes and buildings began to appear in Santa Fe—ornate, if banal, symbols of progress and prosperity. Brick began replacing adobe. The city's only newspaper, the New Mexican, had announced in 1889 that the Honorable Thomas B. Catron had ordered fifty thousand bricks for his new business block, and that more than six million bricks would be used in forthcoming city improvements. Decorative stone, bay windows, turrets, and stained glass windows became the choice for homeowners and merchants alike.

Along with adobe architecture, the Spanish language also became unpopular; the New Mexican was printed in English only. Given the Eastern political establishment's antagonism toward the Spanish-speaking populace, who wanted statehood but had not taken the trouble to learn English, the Anglo-owned newspaper claimed to be doing its part to remedy the "evil" of having children taught Spanish exclusively by public-school teachers who knew no English at all.

Despite negative perceptions of the territory in many areas of the United States, Anglos kept coming from across the country to Santa Fe, the largest town in New Mexico in 1900, touting a population of eight thousand enterprising people. An electric plant powering 320 lamps, including 30 street lights, had been operating since 1891; a "Hello!" telephone system had been installed three years before Otero's inauguration; and trains were arriving regularly on the spur from Lamy with the best of food, elegant furniture, statuary, pianos—all the things needed for comfortable, gracious living.[13]

Thanks to the money Eloisa had inherited from her parents and from the estate of Manuel B. Otero, the Bergeres maintained a high standard of living from the time they arrived in Santa Fe. Their home and the governor's mansion became centers for lively and at times lavish social affairs, attracting the territory's important political leaders, merchants, artists, and writers. Early in their occupancy of the Big House, the Bergeres gave a dinner party to honor their relative and chief benefactor, Miguel Otero, and included former Governor L. Bradford Prince and his wife, Captain and Mrs. Maximiliano Luna, and important attorneys from around the territory. Nina and her Otero brothers, then in their early twenties, also attended and were introduced to some of the most influential people in New Mexico.[14]

The younger children were carefully supervised by their ever-vigilant governess. "Teta," Connie recalled, "was more Irish than Pat's pig, and Catholic, oh my God! On a certain day, she'd put us all in a buggy and take us to have our throats blessed. The next day we'd all come down with tonsillitis." Life in the Big House had a certain rhythm, Connie said: "In the morning we'd all gather around the pot-bellied stove to dress. Then the girls stood in line while Teta brushed our hair. On Saturdays, we'd all take a bath and wash our hair ribbons in vinegar. We only had one bathroom: it had an overhead toilet chamber, so when you pulled the chain, you got sprinkled."[15]

Most of the children's clothing came from the East. Dresses for the girls—sensible plaid patterns for school, white for Sundays—were handmade by nuns in Columbus, Ohio. Nina and her sisters usually wore fringed black shawls to mass, a practice that caused some of the locals to call them "the Black Sisters" in their later years. As for shoes, Connie said, "Mama and Teta would put paper on the floor and trace our feet, then order brown shoes for school, and white for Sunday from Best & Co. in New York."[16]

Trips to the plaza were made virtually every day. There was usually a concert in progress on the bandstand, sometimes performed by African-American soldier-musicians from the U.S. Ninth Cavalry

Left to Right: Estella Bergere, Muriel O'Bryan, and Nina Otero, ca. 1900. (Bergere Family Collection, photo no. 23338, New Mexico State Records Center and Archives, Santa Fe, New Mexico.)

Band directed by Professor Charles Spiegel. The plaza was then, as it is today, central to the city's social life, the favorite place for Santa Feans to gather on pleasant afternoons and Sunday evenings to promenade and talk, the girls walking in one direction, the young men in the other, the older people chaperoning from benches on the square. There always seemed time for fiestas and siestas, music and dancing, debate and gossip. The plaza would come alive with music from guitars and violins and the spontaneous songs of young boys harmonizing through verse after verse of *cantilenas* from Mexico. "The same tunes played for dancing were played at mass," a custom that shocked the Anglo-Protestant newcomers, said Anita Gonzales Thomas, a native Santa Fean who grew up in the city at that time.[17]

Nina, like the other young people from privileged homes in Santa Fe, plunged into the social whirl generated largely by the family's ties with the governor. A product of one of the best Eastern finishing schools for women, she had learned something about the new assertive Anglo-American ways and anticipated the changes and growth in store for New Mexico. In the first decade of the twentieth century she metamorphosed from a skinny, nervous teenager into a graceful, intelligent young woman with an indomitable disposition. High-spirited and independent, she liked being the center of attention, and the quickness of her mind delighted her parents and friends. She hailed the day Miguel Otero fulfilled his "solemn promise" to her mother and recommended A. M. Bergere for Judge McFie's court, an appointment that brought her to Santa Fe and put her in touch with an interesting variety of people.

Beginning with the galas heralding Otero's inauguration and throughout the nine years he served the territory, Eloisa and Alfred Bergere, Nina, and her Otero brothers were included on most of the guest lists for parties and out-of-town excursions hosted by the governor. Trips with Gilly Otero's family were usually taken in private railway cars—to Denver, Chicago, Ohio, New York, wherever the trains rolled—with solicitous chefs and porters hovering in attendance, the Pullmans stocked with ice chests and larders filled with the choicest of foods and beverages.

On one trip to Cloudcroft and El Paso, Nina, Manuel, Eduardo, Nina's friend Julia Freeman, and the governor's family took a side trip by coach and four to Juarez, Mexico. Even though she was cautioned not to buy cigars in the Mexican shops, Nina tried to smuggle two boxes across the border, both of which were summarily confiscated and turned over to Pat Garrett, collector for the port of El Paso and the man who finally put an end to the rampages of Billy the Kid.[18]

While Nina appeared to be the little well-brought-up lady and dutiful daughter, like many Spanish women of the frontier days she had learned to drink alcohol and smoke at an early age (fifteen was the usual age for these rites of passage), which undoubtedly surprised some of her Anglo-Protestant friends. She considered smoking a feminine grace and herself sophisticated and glamorous when she held a cocktail and a lighted cigarette in a long holder, and she thoroughly enjoyed the banter, coarse jokes, and vigorous exchanges of the male politicians in her family.[19]

One of her favorite Southwestern historical personalities was the colorful gambling-hall proprietor, doña Tules (Gertrudis Barceló), a bold and independent woman of some social prominence who enjoyed drinking, smoking, and dealing cards at her *sala* on the corner of San Francisco Street and Burro Alley in the mid-1800s. Years later, at a party in the old Magoffin House, Nina would appear dressed as doña Tules, complete with cigarillo and monte deck.[20]

Nina and her family were delighted when Miguel Otero, after serving four years as governor, was reappointed by President McKinley in June, 1901. Otero was looking forward to another term working with his mentor, a man he respected and who had been strongly supportive of him, but three months later McKinley was gunned down at the Pan-American Exposition in Buffalo, New York, and died on September 14. Otero grieved deeply over the loss of his good friend, declaring in his public eulogy, "I shall not look upon his like again."

Not only did the assassin's bullet end McKinley's life, but it also left Otero in a precarious position under the new president, Theodore Roosevelt, who was immediately bombarded with petitions from ambitious Anglo politicians in the Thomas Catron faction—Eugene A. Fiske, William M. Berger, L. Bradford Prince, and General Lew Wallace—asking for Otero's removal. His enemies tried to convince Roosevelt that Otero was "an uneducated Mexican who favored Spain," and they urged the president to choose former Rough Rider Captain Frederick Muller as the next territorial governor. Fortunately for Otero, the unfounded accusations were ignored and he was reappointed, but his relationship with the new president, whose "enthusiasms came and went," was never the pleasant, easy one he had with McKinley.[21]

"We got along somehow," Otero wrote later in his autobiography, and when Roosevelt made a brief stop in Santa Fe on May 5, 1903, the governor and Santa Fe's socialites arranged for a proper celebration. During his address on the steps of the capitol, Roosevelt paid tribute to the New Mexico veterans of the Spanish-American War, acknowledging that more than half of his famous Rough Riders came from the territory and had served admirably. He also emphasized his commitment to preserving the forests in the Pecos wilderness—"I do not want the land skinned"—and promised that the government would help "somewhat" in the development of New Mexico.

After bidding the crowd good-bye, the president climbed into his carriage and paraded down Washington Avenue, passing the governor's mansion where thirteen-year-old Estella Bergere, dressed as the Goddess of Liberty, tossed him a wreath of roses. "Rising in the carriage he doffed his hat to the little lady amid a shower of roses," reported the *New Mexican*. At an informal reception that evening at the mansion, "several bottles of cold champagne were served to cool the parched throats of the party," and Nina was among the young women who helped the governor's wife introduce Roosevelt to some of the "citizens and ladies" of the city. That ladies were not voting citizens probably did not concern Nina at the time, but at twenty-one she was learning the way things worked in the capital and making social connections she would find useful in the years ahead when she led New Mexico's suffrage movement to make women full citizens.[22]

For the most part, Nina played the traditional role of gracious guest and hostess, appearing with the other young daughters of important families in receiving lines at gala receptions. On one occasion (February 12, 1902), described in the newspaper as the most brilliant social affair Governor and Mrs. Otero had given during their five years' residence in the capital, Nina came dressed in an exquisite cream-colored crepe de chine gown that highlighted her hazel eyes and orange red hair, and took her place in the receiving line. To honor the newly appointed territorial secretary, James Wallace Raynolds,

Nina Otero, ca. 1900. (Bergere
Family Collection, Photo no.
21698, New Mexico State
Records Center and Archives,
Santa Fe, New Mexico.)

"the executive mansion on Washington Street [now the site of the
First Interstate Bank building] was ablaze in the glory of electric
lights and from 9 o'clock in the evening until after midnight, a
steady and large stream of guests entered, representing the beauty,
the grace, the wit, and the gallantry of Santa Fe society." Guests
danced to the strains of the First Regimental Cavalry band in rooms
festooned with portieres of similax, masses of white carnations, pink
tapers, and bridesmaid roses. The governor's wife, "a vivacious and
charming hostess," wore white silk and carried American Beauty roses, her dress "a master creation of a skilled modiste." Nina and her
beautifully gowned girlfriends made "as handsome and bright a receiving party as ever gathered at a social function in Santa Fe."[23]

The elaborate affair closed Santa Fe's spring social season for
1902 in time for the beginning of Lent the following day. And a

would-be poet on the paper's staff closed the expansive report of the gala with a prophetic rhyme:

The lights, the beauty and blossoms
And from eyes in fair faces the gleam,
The music, the laughter and radiance,
They came and went like a dream.
A dream of the fragrance of roses,
A dream of a sweet low refrain,
A dream of love's softest whisperings,
But a dream that will not come again.[24]

Miguel Otero's nine years of pomp and power and competent leadership had indeed come and gone like a dream, ending in 1906 when Roosevelt appointed Herbert J. Hagerman to succeed him. Otero said at the time that he had no personal regrets about leaving office, as he doubted his "ability to satisfy Mr. Roosevelt," but he would have stayed on if he had been asked. The two men had clashed several times after the president reappointed Otero to the governorship in 1902, disagreeing over a New Mexico–Arizona joint statehood proposal (Otero was opposed) and some of Miguel's controversial political appointments. For his part, Miguel had found the chief executive an immature man of "uncertain temper . . . too egotistical and overbearing."

Otero went on to fulfill other dreams. He toured Europe, played key advisory roles in territorial politics, and wrote a three-volume autobiography before his death in Santa Fe in 1944 at the age of eighty-four. Although he was dubbed "the little governor" because he was a small man, he proved to be a powerful leader, and his tenure as governor was the longest in the history of New Mexico.[25]

Much of the good life Nina and the Bergeres had enjoyed with the Oteros also ended. Nina continued to socialize with the many friends she had met at the mansion, but not as often. What work she did was in keeping with the standards for women of that time—some tutoring and volunteer work for church and local charities.

While she was not particularly interested in housekeeping and children, she could hardly avoid domestic duties and was still expected to help tutor the younger Bergere children, numbering nine in 1905 with the birth of Joe. She helped her mother and Teta cope with the constant round of family parties for birthdays, christenings, weddings, and anniversaries and with the usual activities and confusions engendered by nine children, uncounted relatives, house guests, wagons, carriages, horses, and pets. When there were disciplinary problems, Nina felt no hesitation in freely offering solutions. "She liked to be in control," said Connie, who always resented what she considered her half-sister's "officious" nature.[26]

Nina was not unattractive, but neither did she have the dark voluptuous beauty of her mother. A small, slim woman, barely five feet tall, with thick red hair, hazel eyes, and freckles, she not only resembled her deceased father but she also had Manuel B.'s impulsive energy and decided temperament. Her lively mind and vibrant personal charm attracted men and women of all ages and ensured her a place at every party of importance in Santa Fe, even after her cousin Miguel left office.

Yet as the years slipped by and she saw her friends marry and start their own families, she became at twenty-six one of the very few single women of prominence left in the city.[27] Although she was courted by a number of eligible young men during her early twenties, she found none who particularly interested her until the spring of 1907, when, at a party in Albuquerque, she met First Lieutenant Rawson D. Warren, the commanding officer of the Fifth U.S. Cavalry stationed at Fort Wingate.

Born to Thomas and Fanny Fisk Warren in Oil City, Pennsylvania, on December 2, 1872, Rawson had spent most of his formative years in Pennsylvania, New York, and California. A well-educated man, he had graduated from Leland Stanford, Jr., University (class of 1894) and had been a postgraduate student for a year at Columbia University before completing his master's degree at New York University in 1896. Prior to joining the U.S. Army in 1899, he had stud-

Rawson Warren, back row, second from right, Stanford University Glee Club, 1894. (Photo #7910, Department of Special Collections, Stanford University Libraries, Stanford, California.)

ied at the Union and General Theological seminaries and had attended the University of Southern California.[28]

This intelligent older man—nine years her senior—who had served his country loyally for eight years appealed to Nina. Both Rawson Warren and her cousin Maximiliano Luna had fought in the Spanish-American War in the Philippines and Cuba, Max serving with Teddy Roosevelt's Rough Riders during the United States invasion of Cuba in 1898. Rawson had joined the army in September, 1899, two months before Max lost his life in the line of duty, drowning as he attempted to cross the swollen Agno River (Río Grande de la Pampango) in the Ecija Province of the Philippines.[29]

Max had been captain of the Rough Riders' Troop F during the Spanish-American War and had been in the forefront of the charge to secure Kettle Hill before the larger battle at San Juan Hill. Theodore Roosevelt himself had praised the young man for wanting to be a part of the U.S. volunteer cavalry: "The only man of pure Spanish blood who bore a commission in the Army . . . he demanded the privilege of proving that his people were precisely as loyal Americans as any others. I was glad when it was decided to take him."[30]

Luckier than his friend Max, Rawson Warren had returned from the Cuba confrontation unscathed and with singular military honors. Exuding the pride, glamour, and dignity of a triumphant cavalry officer who had been tested in battle, he was, according to Nina's sister May, "one of the handsomest men she had ever seen." Warren was indeed dark and handsome, though at five feet ten inches, not especially tall. With his carefully groomed dark brown hair, ruddy complexion, soft brown eyes, and engaging smile, he was as physically attractive as any man Nina had met.[31]

Their courtship began with the usual dances and dinners and pleasant trips outside Santa Fe, riding over the hills and mesas, picnicking in the canyons, visiting family and friends. Nina was an expert with horses, an accomplished and sometimes daring rider who refused to ride sidesaddle like most ladies of propriety at that time and who preferred to jump her horse over the corral gate at the Big House. This maverick, contrarian attitude would have appealed to a cavalryman looking for a wife to fit into his rugged life at Fort Wingate.[32]

Changing her name from Otero to Warren offered advantages for Nina because prejudices had developed throughout New Mexico toward people with Hispanic surnames, particularly after the bitter war with Mexico in 1836. According to historian David Weber, "Hispanophobia found its most strident and enduring rhetoric in Texas." For close to a century after "the bloodshed in Texas at the Alamo, Goliad, and San Jacinto . . . Hispanophobia, with its vitriolic anti-Mexican variant, also served as a convenient rationale to keep Mexicans 'in their place'." For many of the Texans who had moved to the Territory of New Mexico after the war, the term *Mexican* defined most Spanish-speaking people. Nina's pride and that of all Hispanos had suffered from the discrimination. Having Warren as a surname would be helpful in gaining wider acceptance within the ever-growing Anglo community where social and political power was increasing.[33]

At twenty-seven, Nina had few options available to her. Even though New Mexico was entering a new, progressive era, little had changed for women, and marriage still afforded them the best protection and economic security. An unmarried woman lost her "certification of ladyhood," her friend Mary Austin once observed, unless, of course, she entered the convent, and Nina had neither the temperament nor the inclination to be so confined.[34]

On the surface, Rawson seemed the perfect choice for a husband. He had distinguished himself in academe and in his army career, and he had the approval of Eloisa and Alfred Bergere, who encouraged the romance and invited him to their home when he was in Santa Fe on leave. Connie gleefully described the family's efforts to entertain him: "The children had to really perform. Poor Mr. Warren. Stella played 'Bells of St. Mary's,' Dolores and Rosina sang 'Two Little Sisters,' I played 'Hearts and Flowers' on the violin, and little Joe had to turn somersaults. Oh, it was awful. Imagine listening to all those kids!"[35]

It took only a few months after meeting Rawson for Nina to decide to marry him, and a year later, on June 25, 1908, their wedding took place in the sacristy of St. Francis Cathedral, the Right Reverend Vicar General Fourchegu officiating, assisted by a number of priests at a high nuptial mass. Following the service, the couple obtained a special dispensation from the church after Rawson signed an affidavit solemnly promising

> to leave [Nina] free to practice her Catholic Religion at all times. To my Dear Wife María Adelina Otero, now Mrs. Rawson Warren, I promise that I will not try by any suggestion or other ways to bring or lead her to abandon her religion. I promise that all

the children who may be born to us will be baptized and raised
according to the Catholic, Apostolic, Roman Church."[36]

A reporter from the Santa Fe New Mexican covered the "magnificent wedding . . . the most elegant and finest which ever occurred
in Santa Fe." Nina was described as "one of the best known young
society women in the capital, in Albuquerque and in Central New
Mexico . . . very popular, very bright, charming, finely educated and
attractive . . . endowed with many graces of heart, mind and
body . . . the descendant of one of the oldest and best families in
New Mexico."

The bride, carrying a rose and lily bouquet, was "a picture of
loveliness" in her "elegant ivory satin gown with point lace, princess
style." Solomón Luna's wife, Adelaida, was her matron of honor; her
half-sister Anita, wearing "pink point de mull with white lace," was
her bridesmaid; and Alfred Bergere gave his stepdaughter away. "Sol-
dierly and gallant" Rawson Warren, "an army officer of excellent
reputation, of splendid character and of many attainments," was in
full dress uniform and "looked very handsome and happy." He chose
his friend First Lieutenant Daniel D. Gregory as his best man.

In addition to the entire Bergere family, the marriage ceremony
and subsequent wedding breakfast at the Big House was attended by
ex-governor Miguel Otero and his wife, the Honorable and Mrs.
Thomas B. Catron, Governor George Curry, Mayor José D. Sena, Probate Clerk George W. Armijo, friends from Albuquerque, and uncounted members of the Otero, Luna, and Sena families living in
Santa Fe.

The New Mexican reporter summarized the idyllic Otero-Warren
courtship and honeymoon:

> The happily married people met about a year ago in Albu-
> querque, became acquainted, the acquaintance ripened rapidly
> into affection, the affection turned into love with the result of
> the happy marriage today. . . . After the wedding breakfast the
> happy couple departed overland in Territorial Secretary Nathan

Jaffa's automobile, gaily and properly decorated for the occasion, for the Field Cottage in the Pecos National Forest. The first nine miles were made in the auto and thereafter the bride and groom mounted and rode overland to the cottage where they will remain a few days enjoying their honeymoon, and will then proceed to Lt. Warren's station in Fort Wingate. . . . Hearty congratulations were extended to the groom on his very good fortune in securing a wife who possesses all the qualities and attractions to make him a happy and lovely home, and to be all that a wife should be."[37]

For thirteen-year-old Connie, it was a "wonderful wedding." The dining room chandelier in the Big House was replaced by a bell of fresh lilies of the valley, the table resplendent with roses, fine crystal, and a centuries-old silver breakfast service. "There was a little red satin slipper filled with rice in front of each place," Connie said, "and there were monogrammed boxes to carry home pieces of the cake." There were toasts all around, everyone wishing the newlyweds happiness and long life.[38]

The Warrens' "happy and lovely" home at Fort Wingate, near Gallup, New Mexico, was very much like the Bergere house in Santa Fe—there were even quarters upstairs for servants—but there the similarities ended. Life as an army officer's wife proved to be vastly different from the one she had just left in the city. Nina quickly learned that to be "all that a wife should be" to Rawson Warren meant absolute conformity to military rules and the subordination of her life to his career. As well educated as she was, only her husband's achievements and status were important in the closed society of the military base. She was expected to support him as a pleasant, well-dressed hostess and dutiful, uncomplaining companion in order to further his advancement in rank.[39]

As on all military bases, there was a clear line of demarcation between the enlisted men's quarters and those of the officers, sometimes so sharply drawn that one military wife once commented, "They might as well run barbed wire down the middle of the street."[40] Nina was told she could fraternize with officers' wives only, a rule that particularly irked her, for she had spent much of her life with interesting people of her own choice, regardless of their social status.

There was a stultifying sameness to the days spent at Fort Wingate, particularly when the men left the base on scouting assignments. Nina felt lonely and bored away from the loving closeness of her family and friends in Santa Fe. The boredom was broken occasionally by dances, card games, reading, and gossip, but when Warren was transferred to a fort in Utah, she was forced to leave behind the few friends she had made and what little identity she had developed at Wingate. Everything she said or did was carefully noted and discussed by the wives of senior officers at both bases. She was constantly on guard, because a derisive remark or a divergent opinion could jeopardize her husband's career.[41]

After several months of hardships and, for Nina, unconscionable restrictions, the more she was pressured to conform, the more rebellious she became. One evening at a party for all the soldiers stationed at the fort, she broke the rules and defiantly danced with a private. On another occasion she rode Warren's horse while he was away, even though he had expressly forbidden her to do so. During the wild ride the stallion reared, threw up his head, and broke her nose, giving her a "souvenir" she carried with her the rest of her life.[42]

Nina's willfulness, her dissatisfaction with army ways, and the shattering of her expectations for a more companionable marriage were undoubtedly the principal reasons for her decision to leave Rawson Warren after less than two years. But another probable cause surfaced months later when she confided to a few close friends that he had deceived her. Soon after they had settled in at Fort Wingate, he confessed to having had a common-law wife and two children in the Philippines at the time he married her. That amounted to bigamy in the eyes of the Catholic church, and certainly in hers, and was reason enough to separate. When news of the troubled marriage reached the Big House through Nina's despondent letters, Teta took a train to Utah and brought her home.[43]

Back in Santa Fe after her unhappy experience, Nina asked that Rawson Warren's name never be mentioned in her presence. From the time she left him until her death in 1965 she referred to herself as a widow, even though Warren did not die until 1942. A likely reason for her decision to opt for widowhood was that for many Spanish-Americans then, divorced women were considered eccentric—some were even looked upon as witches—and generated hostility from those who felt their conventional family values threatened. A widowed woman, on the other hand, had the freedom to manage her own affairs, engage in business, and even homestead land.[44]

As disillusioned as she was with Rawson Warren, however, Nina kept his surname throughout her life. Except for using "Adelina Otero" as her byline for an article in Survey Graphic in 1931, and "Nina Otero" when she authored her book, Old Spain in Our Southwest, in 1936, she signed letters and documents "Nina [or Adelina] Otero-Warren."

Once she had come to terms with her failed marriage, she began to look for ways to live a productive life without a husband, feeling fortunate that she had a large number of prosperous relatives nearby to help cushion the economic and emotional shock of her self-imposed widowhood. She was also thankful to be living in a tolerant city where she felt she could be useful and in some measure compensate for what she considered her greatest mistake.

She first decided to attach herself to one of the new women's clubs in Santa Fe that had been organized to address the community's social and educational needs. There she found a number of progressive, spirited women committed to broadening their horizons and overcoming political limitations imposed on them for centuries.

Since public policy making was off limits to women in 1910, Nina could only observe and try to influence in subtle ways her male relatives in the territorial legislature. Her uncle Solomón Luna was in a good position to help her, as he had been a political power broker in Valencia County for twenty-five years, serving at various times as probate clerk, sheriff, and treasurer of the county. For sixteen years he had been a member of the National Republican Committee. He was also an astute businessman, and because of his success in the sheep-ranching industry he was made president of Albuquerque's National Bank of Commerce. In 1910 he was territorial delegate to the constitutional convention in Washington, presenting well-reasoned and persuasive arguments to Congress on behalf of New Mexico in its bid for statehood.

Nina and other woman-suffrage advocates, most of them Anglo members of the New Mexico Federation of Women's Clubs, saw the state-constitution debate as an opportunity to change the political status of New Mexico's women. Fortunately, Solomón Luna was sympathetic to their cause and pushed for immediate partial suffrage for women in school district elections, and for women's right to hold public office. This resolution seemed reasonable inasmuch as several women had already been elected, by men, as superintendents of public schools, and the territorial governor had appointed a woman to the office of state librarian.

Limited woman-suffrage legislation had been introduced repeatedly to New Mexico congressmen in the decades before the constitutional convention—in 1893, 1895, and 1899—only to be ignored or defeated. "I do not believe in having women enter politics," said one male school superintendent in 1908; "they are more liable to be led into the deeper tricks of the trade than is a man, because of the lack of experience of women in business." Nevertheless, he grudgingly admitted that women might be an improvement over "some county superintendents now who are worse than dead men. . . . The question is still debatable, but I feel no difficulty will arise from this point if women are elected in several of our counties."[45]

Despite the gratuitous granting of a few public offices, New Mexico women were still denied the vote, and much as Solomón tried, nothing changed for them with the final drafting of the new state constitution of 1910. His resolution promoting partial suffrage for women was compromised by Article VII of that document, which restricted the right of women to vote for school officials if enough men objected—a compromise that gave women tenuous political rights at best and made it virtually impossible for them to petition for the franchise. Women who had been granted the franchise in several other western states had no such laws to overcome. Article VII did, however, protect the voting rights of Spanish-American men.[46]

Ten years would pass before New Mexico women finally won the right to vote in all local and general elections. While there was great joy in Santa Fe on January 12, 1912, when President Taft made New Mexico the forty-seventh state, Nina and other disillusioned and still disfranchised women felt cheated. Yet helping to rectify the injustice provided an outlet for her talents and energy and opened opportunities that would soon place her in the forefront of the country's first great feminist battle. Unfortunately, she had to carry on without the help of her Uncle Solomón.

Eight months after New Mexico's transition from territory to statehood, Solomón Luna died tragically at the relatively youthful age of fifty-four. Before dawn on the morning of August 30, 1912, he was found floating face down in a sheep-dipping vat on the ranch of Montague Stevens at Horse Springs in the Lueros Mountains. The *New Mexican* reporter wrote from Magdalena that "apparently Mr. Luna had gone to the vat early this morning to wash his hands or to get a drink of water. No one saw him fall. . . . It is believed he leaned over the vat to wash his hands at a faucet and either suffered a stroke of apoplexy, heart failure or fainted, falling into the vat which was filled with three and a half feet of sheep dip composed of lime, tobacco and water."[47] Edwin S. Spindler, the first of the ranch overseers to find the body, testified at a coroner's inquest that the dipping solution of cresylic acid and soap (Cooper's Fluid Dip) had so destroyed the outer tissue of the body that Solomón's silk underwear, scapular medal, and shoes with laces tucked inside were the only means of

Solomón Luna (1858-1912),
patrón and political leader in
New Mexico, uncle of Nina
Otero-Warren. (Bergere Family
Collection, photo no. 21653,
New Mexico State Records Center
and Archives, Santa Fe, New
Mexico.)

identification. While speculations of suicide or homicide spread, fu-
eled by rumors about the Lunas' supposed marital difficulties and the
questionable transfer of Solomón's herds to Eduardo Otero a day or
two before the tragedy, the jury ruled his death accidental.[48]

In her master's thesis on the life of Solomón Luna, written in
1941, Sister Lucretia Pittman mentions some of the rumors surrounding his death:

> Friction between Solomón and Adelaida was gradually deepen-
> ing. . . . "Every one knew" that their characters did not harmo-
> nize. The fear of public scandal [divorce] or of notoriety of any
> kind was unbearable to this gentle man. So, crushed with the
> thoughts of having a public scandal, . . . he ended his life by suf-
> focation in the poisonous liquid.
>
> It does seem that Solomón's property was not settled ac-
> cording to the only will available at the Los Lunas court house. . . .
> Eduardo took possession of the Los Lunas home, but the will

leaves it to Mrs. Luna. The will indicated that Eloisa is to be the recipient of several thousand sheep, but Miss Doyle [Teta] stated that Eloisa received nothing from Sol's estate and Mr. Spindler wrote, "Everything concerning that transfer [of the outfit to Ed Otero by Sol just before the beginning of the dipping] showed that it was a temporary settlement of Sol's property."

A third and more imaginative rumor was that

> Don Solomón was for many years after his supposed disaster, among the living. There is absolutely no authority for supposing that he had a sheep herder thrown into the vat. This man, unidentifiable after the disfigurement brought on by the strong dip, was taken for his employer who had slipped off to Washington and New York. Here he met his beloved, caught the first boat for Europe or unknown parts, and there lived happily ever after. The need of a continuous supply of funds from the ranch explains to adherents of this story why Eduardo was the recipient of such a generous share of Mr. Luna's fortune. He had to send to Sol in Europe, considerable sums periodically.
>
> In offices of attorney, or banker or politician, as well as at the fireside in family gatherings, Solomón's life and mysterious death are still sometimes the subject of discussion and speculation.[49]

Ridiculous as the stories were, they persisted over the years, and one of Nina's goals in later life would be to write a book refuting them all.

The premature death of this respected statesman was mourned throughout New Mexico. The shocking loss was particularly stressful for his family, since Solomón had managed so long and well the Luna ranch lands at Magdalena. Eduardo Otero, Eloisa's eldest son, succeeded his uncle, taking over the Luna Mansion and flocks and becoming in time one of the state's wealthiest and most influential politicians. Along with the family fortune, he inherited the position of political jefe of Valencia County. As his reputation grew, he personally handpicked candidates for county offices through clever maneuvers behind the scenes, and when his recommendations were presented to the Republican convention assembled at the courthouse, they were usually given a rubber-stamp approval.[50]

Eloisa Luna de Otero de Bergere inherited nothing from her deceased brother Solomón, but she had considerable holdings of her own. Her income from investments had been the chief source of revenue for the Bergere family; Eloisa and her children could not have lived so well on Alfred's salary alone.[51] After Miguel Otero left office, Alfred's position as clerk to Judge McFie also expired, and the father of twelve children earned only a small salary as manager of a local insurance company from 1907 until 1915. Eloisa's money was essential to the financial security of her husband and children, particularly her daughters, but after 1907 she and all married women in New Mexico lost the community property rights they had been given under Spanish and Mexican laws. Under the old rules, she could have kept her estate separate from her husband's and disposed of it as she wished.[52]

After researching the inequities toward women generated by the new American law, Nina resolved to do what she could to protect her mother's fortune. Since Eloisa no longer had the right to make a will or designate heirs, Nina convinced her, after she had been hospitalized at the Mayo Clinic in 1910 for a severe gallbladder attack, that she should establish a trust fund for her eight unmarried daughters—Nina, Anita, Estella, May, Connie, Dolores, Rosina, and Ysabel. The youngest, Ysabel, had been born mentally retarded and had the greatest need for financial security. As for her four sons—Eduardo, Manuel, Luna, and Joseph Charles—Eloisa felt they would have ample money-making opportunities and successful careers.[53]

Eloisa had been treated at one of the very best medical facilities in the United States in 1910, and the experienced staff at the Mayo Clinic had worked feverishly to save her life. Alfred wrote in his autobiography that "she was so ill that nothing could be done for ten days." After "Dr. Will Mayo removed one hundred forty-two gall stones . . . she rallied pretty well for the first five days and then had a

Eloisa Luna Otero Bergere (1864-1914). (Bergere Family Collection, photo no. 21637, New Mexico State Records Center and Archives, Santa Fe, New Mexico.)

hemorrhage of the wound—through carelessness—and almost died. She was near death for sixty hours, but pulled through."

Four years later, on September 3, 1914, Eloisa had another attack, and after four days of intense suffering, she died of heart failure. Her husband was stunned, "desolate and grief-stricken. Nothing in the whole world," he wrote, "could take her place either in my heart or my home. Of my life since then I have nothing to say except that I have probably been the most lonely man conceivable with a broken life and a broken heart."[54]

The death of beautiful, gracious Eloisa, only fifty years old and "in the full vigor of mature womanhood," shocked the Santa Fe and Los Lunas communities. She was praised for her "big mother heart," for her compassionate concerns for the poor and sick in Santa Fe, for her loyalty and love as wife and mother, for her unquestioning devo-

Monument marking the grave of
Eloisa Luna Otero Bergere, Rosario
Cemetery, Santa Fe, ca. 1914.
(Photograph courtesy of Dolores
K. Kenney.)

tion to the Catholic church, and for the training she had given her
children in "old-fashioned courtesies that are a joy to meet in this
day." Her comforting philosophy, which had helped Nina and others
through times of crisis, was quoted in her obituary: "We do not have
to always succeed in what we try to do, but we can offer up our efforts, that is our duty, and leave the issue with God."[55]

Hundreds attended Father Fourchegu's requiem mass and funeral services for Eloisa and followed the somber cortege to Rosario
Cemetery on the outskirts of Santa Fe, where the legendary doña of
the Río Abajo was laid to rest in the large, fenced family plot. A high
stone monument still marks her grave, and the east nave of the ceme-

Joseph Charles Bergere, youngest
child of Alfred and Eloisa Bergere,
ca. 1917. (Bergere Family Collection, photo no. 23247, New
Mexico State Records Center and
Archives, Santa Fe, New Mexico.)

tery's historic chapel contains a splendid stained-glass window de-
picting La Conquistadora (Our Lady of Victory), given as a memorial
tribute by Eloisa's husband and children.

Within two years the Luna and Bergere families had lost two
beloved members, and New Mexico, two of its most respected citizens. While Eloisa did not have her brother's powerful political status, she had worked hard for the schoolchildren of New Mexico and
at the time of her death was serving as chairman of the board of education in Santa Fe. A devoted Catholic wife and mother, she had
given life to twelve children, several of whom, particularly Nina,
would continue her crusade. At the time of her mother's illness, Nina
had been living in New York, keeping house for her half-brother
Luna, who was attending Columbia University. She was also working
part-time for Miss Anne Morgan's Vacation Committee, supervising

dancing, singing, and dramatic classics. Her stepfather called her home just before Eloisa died.[56]

Alfred also sent for Anita, who had entered a convent and was preparing to take her final vows, and he asked his two eldest daughters to stay with him and help care for the family of nine. Eduardo and Manuel, in their thirties when their mother died, had already left home: Eduardo had married Josefita Armijo and was managing the family's property in Los Lunas; Manuel and his wife, Lucy (Grygla), had moved to Albuquerque. But nine-year-old Joe and eight young women were still living in the Big House. Compliant Anita dutifully agreed to give up her religious vocation but later complained that in doing so she had "ruined her life."[57]

Most of the responsibility for running the house became Anita's, for although Nina lived at home and helped with family decisions, she was more interested in a professional career—for her own personal satisfaction and for financial independence. As chairman of the Child's Welfare Department in Santa Fe, she began working with the state legislature again, this time to promote bills to help delinquent and dependent girls.[58] But she still chafed at the bonds that prevented her and other women from fully participating in the political affairs of her country.

Nina had tried filling the approved roles of socialite, wife, tutor, and surrogate mother. She had succeeded at some and, by the standards of her time, had failed miserably at one. While she had great motivation, she still lacked direction. She had read enough history to know that others felt as she did about the grievous inequality of women in a country that prided itself on guaranteeing freedom and justice for all. Like her reform-minded friends, she wanted the same opportunities as men: to participate in political power, to influence social choices, to be economically secure. With new resolve she became involved once more in the pursuit of voting rights for women, along the way moving up as a leader in the national suffrage movement and beginning a twelve-year career as superintendent of public schools for Santa Fe County.

A
Keystone
Falls

The twentieth century's second decade was a turbulent time for women, with the push for voting rights, the emergence and sometimes brutal suppression of Margaret Sanger's birth-control movement, the passage of the essentially woman-sponsored prohibition amendment, and, in 1917, the mobilization of women across the country to help win World War I. By the end of that frenetic period, Nina Otero-Warren had become a respected leader and educator, and one of the most influential women in New Mexico.

In 1913, *Century* magazine ran an advertisement for the New York–based Women's Political Union:

Is marriage the highest destiny of women? Or is achievement? . . . The Keystone is falling: women are refusing—and must refuse—to accept the old ideals of the relations between men and women. . . . Humanity respects and reverences power, material and spiritual, and it holds weakness in hearty contempt.[1]

Here was a philosophy that would have appealed to Nina, thirty-two, single, and looking for a way to achieve something in life without benefit of husband, home, and children. Her unsuccessful challenge in 1910 to the disfranchisement of women by New Mexico's benevolent but indifferent patriarchal establishment had left her and her feminist friends convinced that only through a well-organized movement of suffrage supporters could the existing political walls be breached.

History had shown her the futility of bringing about significant change in society without careful organization and a great deal of struggle. From Abigail Adams's letter to her husband, John, in 1776, warning him that women would "foment a rebellion" if they had no voice in the law, to the fractious women's rights conventions of the mid-nineteenth century, it was clear that divided movements and the gentle prodding of men in power had not worked.

Once women united in 1890 as the National American Woman Suffrage Association (NAWSA) under the leadership of Carrie Chapman Catt and Anna Howard Shaw, some progress was made. By 1913, twelve states and territories (Wyoming first in 1869) had granted suffrage to women living within their borders. These successes encouraged Alice Paul, Lucy Burns, and other members of the more militant Congressional Union (CU) to use the voting power of the newly enfranchised women to force a suffrage resolution through the United States Congress.

For all the activism on the part of women's groups in western states before 1900, there was no organized support for the movement in New Mexico. Most women—Anglo, Hispanic, and Indian—remained uninvolved. In the 1890s only one woman in the territory, Mamie Marble, subscribed to NAWSA's Woman's Journal; in 1910 the organization had only two New Mexico women on its subscription list—one was dead, the other a patient in a Silver City sanatorium. In 1914, New Mexico was the only western state that denied women the vote.[2]

The general perception among suffragists in other parts of the country was that the prejudiced attitudes of Hispanic men were primarily responsible for the political ineffectiveness of New Mexico women. But more than that, responsibility lay with New Mexico's "reactionary," virtually unamendable constitution requiring a three-fourths vote of both houses and a two-thirds vote of each county to change the law. The state also lacked a strong, organized group committed to change. "Still," suffrage activist Katherine Patterson of the Women's Christian Temperance Union (WCTU) wrote in 1915, "the women are presenting their bills and arguments and serenely attending to their program and the steady pressure of this method is telling upon them and we expect to emerge from the clouds some fine day, even in New Mexico."[3]

But when Nina and other women throughout the state—most of them Anglo—who belonged to the influential National Association of Women's Clubs saw that the serene, steady pressures were not working, they finally took matters into their own hands, joined forces with the CU, and launched a new campaign. Nina's involvement with Alice Paul's group was to lay the foundation for the leadership roles she would take in the years ahead.

Her renewed activism came at a revolutionary time for women around the world, particularly in England and North America. British suffragists led by Emmeline Pankhurst were heckling political speakers and being thrown in jail for their efforts. Some of the more stubborn protesters were force-fed through tubes in their noses—twelve times in twelve months in 1913 before the Cat-and-Mouse-Act (Prisoners, Temporary Discharge for Health Act, 1913) ended that authorized torture. Under the British Parliament's "humane" act, rebellious women were released long enough to recover from their self-imposed fasting; once they regained their strength they were imprisoned again.

In the United States, Margaret Sanger was publishing *The Woman Rebel* and touring the country promoting birth control, and angry suffragettes (some twenty-five thousand at one time) wearing purple and gold "Let Mother Vote" buttons were marching in Washington and New York. Tables in suffrage meeting halls held felt pennants with "Miss Liberty" themes, bright posters proclaiming "Justice Demands the Vote!", and white satin ribbons emblazoned with "Women's Rights. Not Unscrupulous Men's Will" in bold purple capital letters. Periodicals such as The Suffragist, The Woman Voter, and The Woman Citizen circulated urgent appeals to hold the party in power responsible for the powerlessness of women and to "agitate" for an amendment to the federal Constitution.[4]

Things were more sedate in Santa Fe. Many Hispanic women had long been stereotyped in the role of suffering, deprived wife and mother (la mujer sufrida), resigned to a life of constant struggle (la vida es la lucha)—economically, socially, politically, and even within the realm of the male-oriented religious system.[5] Nina and other well-educated Hispanas recognized that the powerless-victim self-image helped to keep women "in their place" and reinforced the generally held notion that a woman had no interest in voting or governing.

Actually, as Sarah Deutsch has pointed out, Hispanic women were neither powerless nor especially submissive, but rather autonomous beings who helped sustain their communities physically and spiritually, who were usually consulted in important family decisions, and who managed their own property. In Hispanic villages throughout northern New Mexico, "relations between sexes were characterized by flexibility, cooperation, and a degree of autonomy," although women had traditionally avoided public roles.[6] For the suffragists, the immediate goal was to raise the political consciousness of these women, and to do that, Nina and her friends chose nonmilitant tactics of subtle but firm persuasion.

On May 1, 1914, the New Mexican ran an article announcing a mass meeting of the New Mexico Woman's Suffrage League. "The New Mexico women are going at the matter sensibly and wisely," the paper reported, "the suffragists in New Mexico are in no sense of the word 'suffragettes'."

The women of the state who want the ballot intend to convince the electorate logically and earnestly of the justice of their cause, without any fireworks. . . . That they have unanswerable arguments makes it the more unnecessary to employ any pyrotechnics in placing their case before the voters. That the women of New Mexico are as well able as those of any state in the union to use the ballot rightly and intelligently has already been amply demonstrated in school elections in the state; and that the organized women of the state are becoming a powerful influence no one will deny in view of the progress made in the woman's club movement throughout New Mexico in the past few years. . . . If you are a fair minded person it is well worth your while to go and hear the woman's side of the case.[7]

In 1915 the CU made its first campaign swing through New Mexico. While they were far more militant and sophisticated than their NAWSA sisters, CU leaders wisely restrained their pressure tactics in the conservative Republican state. Alice Paul sent four organizers to the Southwest between 1914 and 1920, and all but one—Lillian Kerr, the first to arrive in Santa Fe—worked well with Nina. In 1920, when she was chairman of the Women's Division of the Republican State Committee of New Mexico, Nina would write to Mabel Vernon that "Mrs. Kerr's actions . . . antagonized the very people we were depending on to help us straighten out the work of the anti-suffragists and democrats in trying to divide the Republican vote." Kerr, according to Nina, was "a Texas Democrat . . . who should have left her views in Texas." She had made threats and misstatements "which were uncalled for and were greatly detrimental to us at the time." Nina went on to say that she had to do a

> great deal of explaining to the men who had previously been for us but on account of her talk were beginning to take the stand that, if her expressions were the beliefs of the women of the state, they would work against ratification. . . . This is the first woman sent out by your organization who has not received my full support and endorsement.[8]

Even without Solomón Luna, Nina had male relatives with strong political pull to call on: Alfred Bergere and her brothers, Eduardo and Manuel, agreed to support her. Eduardo Otero was a staunch Republican national committeeman, and Manuel was moving up the political ladder to become in 1924 the Republican candidate for governor.

New Mexico's Senator Albert Fall (convicted and imprisoned in 1929 for bribery in the Teapot Dome scandal) also supported the movement, but Senator Thomas Catron, who at the age of seventy-one had finally fulfilled his desire for a seat in the U.S. Senate (1911–1916), was adamantly opposed. Catron, a Republican party boss for twenty years, was as much an irritant to Nina as he was to Miguel Otero, who once described the portly senator as a "brainy man, one of the ablest lawyers in the territory . . . but thoroughly selfish and a notorious kicker."[9] Rebuffed suffragists complained that the aging Catron scorned their cause. Disgruntled women left his office feeling that all they were good for was "to stay home, have children, have more children, cook and wash dishes."[10]

Catron's male chauvinism was shared by Nina's brother-in-law, John Joseph Kenney, who had married her half-sister May (María Bernadette Bergere) on June 13, 1917. Shortly after the wedding, Kenney wrote a long, impassioned dissertation entitled "Should Women Vote?", answering his own question with an emphatic "No! Woman's place is not in politics." She would be rendered "too callous, too mannish," he said. Her reliance on man would be forgotten, "her weakness, and chance of destruction, uncounted." A wife should love and respect her husband and vote his ticket, "not seek beyond his opinions for right, or wrong." According to Kenney a woman had all the privileges she needed and should stay above the fray. She was "more refined, more virtuous, more spiritual than man. . . . Woman's power is something better, deeper, nobler than man's. It is the power of love, of tenderness, of faith. . . . She points the way, he scales the perilous cliff."

For Kenney, a voting woman would resemble Eve in the Garden

of Eden—beautiful, loving, tender, but willing to trade her "good looks for a cheap fame," to lose her "youth and beauty, often happiness and peace, by her misdirected zeal." "What touches mud is stained," Kenney concluded, shuddering at the very thought of a "woman politician."[11]

John Kenney's opinion had little effect on Nina, who decided not only to scale the perilous cliff of political reform herself but also to point the way for other women. Having bilingual skills and Otero-Warren as a surname proved highly advantageous to her and to the CU, giving her entrée to the highest Anglo circles and also generating confidence and trust among other Hispanic women, most of whom were socially marginal, unwilling to go against the grain of the entrenched patriarchal system, and unconcerned about their lack of voting rights. Although she was timid at first when speaking before large groups and was severely criticized at times for leaving the "woman's sphere" to speak publicly, she soon overcame her shyness and began taking on all assignments given to her by Anne H. Martin, CU legislative chairman, and Mabel Vernon, the organization's national secretary.

Mabel Vernon first tried to organize New Mexico women in support of the Nineteenth Amendment early in 1914, working through the Women's Christian Temperance Movement, but had little success. The WCTU was largely supported by rural and radical Protestant church groups bent on closing the "dampness joints" around the country,[12] but the organization had little influence with Nina and other prominent women in northern New Mexico, particularly those from Catholic homes where social drinking was a part of everyday life. While the *New Mexican* had righteously reported in 1908 that "the best and most solid citizens favor absolute prohibition,"[13] Santa Fe's Anglo citizens and some Hispanics voted wet a year later. Nina and her friends, both Anglo and Spanish-American, liked to drink, and cocktail parties were almost daily rituals. Nina preferred scotch or bourbon, straight or with water, and on trips out of the state she would be sure to have a "drinking basket" with her on the train.[14]

Discouraged in their attempts to work through the WCTU, CU organizers Mabel Vernon and Ella St. Clair Thompson located the most influential Anglo women in Santa Fe. The new recruits soon established a state network of suffragists who planned mass meetings, parades, teas, and dinners and literally bombarded Senators Catron and Fall with demands for the vote. To encourage the participation of Hispanic women, six key Hispanas were chosen, including Aurora Lucero, daughter of the secretary of state of New Mexico, Anita Bergere, Estella Bergere Leopold, and Nina Otero-Warren.[15]

Nina's persuasive arguments urging women to participate in the fight for their voting rights galvanized suffrage groups and sent a steady stream of vocal, single-minded women to the offices of the state's representatives in Santa Fe and Washington. Yet despite the avalanche of sentiment for justice and change, crusty Thomas Catron remained unmoved and opposed, and even introduced an antisuffrage statement to Congress. The only New Mexico member of the U.S. House of Representatives, Benigno Cárdenas Hernández, voted with Catron.[16]

Fortunately for the movement, Catron was not renominated in 1916, defeated in his bid for a second Senate term by a prosuffrage Republican candidate, Frank Hubbell. And Congressman Hernández changed his mind when, at the national level, his Republican party's platform and candidate for president, Charles Evans Hughes, declared in favor of the women. Hernández wrote to Nina in September 1916 saying he was in "full accord" and would do everything in his power to further the suffrage amendment.[17]

That considerable arm-twisting on the part of Nina and others was having a positive effect on the New Mexico legislators in Washington was evident. She had brought to the battle her knowledge of the bureaucracy, learned at an early age from her stepfather and uncles. And A. M. Bergere unquestionably brought some of his own political skills to bear, since he was serving at the time as secretary to Congressman Hernández, a position he held from 1915, shortly after Eloisa's death, until 1920.[18]

Sentiment for a suffrage amendment was growing stronger across the country in 1916, and NAWSA organizers continued to send representatives west to bring reluctant states into the fold. Mrs. L. L. Walker made a tour through New Mexico, stopping in Albuquerque on May 19 and urging the state's women to support nonpartisan demonstrations at the fall conventions of both parties. A "monster parade" of fifty thousand women was planned for the Republicans in Chicago, and at the Democratic convention hall in St. Louis women were to

> mass about . . . everyone in uniform and all carrying yellow parasols. Every doorway to the hall will be guarded by the suffragists. Going in and coming out the Democratic delegates will see vast fields of yellow parasols, and the spectacle is counted upon to present the 'picture' that will impress the delegations with the importance and size of the suffrage question. While the demonstration at St. Louis will be 'walkless' and 'voiceless,' the work there will not be 'speechless.' There will be speeches at different places in St. Louis the night of 'demonstration day.'"[19]

In the general election that followed the noisy 1916 conventions, Democrats swept the Republicans out of Congress and reelected Woodrow Wilson president. In New Mexico, the women's movement for voting rights gained two champions at the federal level in Senator Andrieus Aristiens Jones of Socorro, who replaced Catron and became chairman of the Senate Committee on Woman Suffrage, and Senator William Walton, who agreed to consider passage after receiving urgent calls and letters from Otero-Warren.[20]

Nevertheless, victory at home still evaded the suffragists. On March 1, 1917, state legislators turned down the voting measure once again. The Albuquerque *Morning Journal* reported that it was a "sorry week and a glad week" for the women of New Mexico. The glad news was that Suffrage Bill 366 lost by only four votes, and the "cream of the legislature, the men who really count" stood by the women. "Next time," the newspaper reporter predicted, "those four votes and one more will be cast for instead of against suffrage."[21]

In debating the issue, eighty-year-old Judge J. H. Dills of Chaves County argued that it was "ridiculous to talk about elevating the womanhood of this country by sending them out to mix with a lot of dirty politicians. . . . There never has been a time when the women didn't do the voting, since Eve persuaded Adam to bite that apple." Yet the venerable old solon voted yes with the minority, one of whom (Mr. Pardue of Guadalupe County) asserted he was "man enough" to hold his own against a woman if he gave her an equal chance. Of the nay sayers, Mr. Ortíz of Río Arriba considered it "a duty not only to his family and the people generally, but a duty to his God, to vote against woman suffrage." With that, Mr. Sánchez of Valencia County moved to table the resolution, the motion passed, and the house adjourned.[22] More than three years would pass before enough male minds were changed.

Regardless of the defeat, women had been given wider recognition and could sense eventual victory ahead. Their pressure tactics were having some effect. So impressed were the CU's Washington leaders with Nina's work that Alice Paul wrote to her in September 1917 asking her to join the CU advisory council as vice president, and a few months later to head the state group:

> Since Mrs. [Joshua] Raynolds' resignation leaves you as our chief officer in New Mexico, we hope that you will be able to help in arranging the meetings which we have planned for Miss Martin and that you can assist her in re-organizing the New Mexico state committee and secure a new chairman. . . . Miss Martin . . . will be glad to speak . . . at lunches, mass meetings, dinners, teas or any kind of gathering which can be assembled to hear her.
>
> I am sure I need not tell you how earnestly we hope that we may have your help.[23]

Nina's response was prompt and her commitment strong: "I will keep out of local fuss," she wrote Alice Paul, "but will take a stand and a firm one whenever necessary for I am with you now and always!"[24]

Letters from Anne Martin toward the end of 1917 encouraged

Nina Otero-Warren, Superintendent of Public Schools, Santa Fe County, ca. 1918. (Courtesy Museum of New Mexico, negative no. 89756, Santa Fe, New Mexico.)

Nina to keep up her "intense and concentrated work" by sending delegations of women to lobby the New Mexico congressmen who had come home for the Christmas holidays. Urge them "not only to vote," she said, "but to work in every way possible for the passage of the Amendment."[25]

"Beginning as a timid woman unwilling to speak in public, Otero-Warren gradually became a political force," Joan Jensen wrote seventy years later in her carefully documented account of the suffrage movement in New Mexico.[26] Nina had discovered the joy and drama of revolutionary politics and of breaking down stereotypes, and in the process she had learned to trust her own strength and judgment.

In acknowledgment of her impressive leadership ability, the all-male Republican-directed New Mexico Board of Education appointed Nina in 1917 to the office of superintendent of public schools in Santa Fe County. In 1918 she ran for that elective position and won, defeating her male opponent handily and setting a precedent for other women. At age thirty-seven, she became the youngest superintendent in the state.

Winning by both appointment and election, Nina had proved to her friends in politics that she had the grit to campaign—through countless schoolhouse meetings, enchilada suppers, dances, and teas—and the popularity to win. But with winning came heavy schedules and more responsibilities. Along with her suffrage work, she at once began promoting ways to improve rural school conditions and elevate teaching standards. And just as she was beginning to make progress on both fronts, the United States declared war on Germany, joining its European allies in a war Woodrow Wilson believed would ensure for all time the safety of democracy around the world.

Despite the significant gains she had made as an educator and political lobbyist, Nina had some difficulty keeping the woman's voting issue in front of the legislators at a time when New Mexico and the rest of the country were preoccupied with World War I. Indeed, the picketing of the White House by militant suffragists during the war deepened the resentment of the opposition. From the beginning of the voting-rights movement, antisuffragists had taken every opportunity to ridicule the character and even the sexual orientation of women favoring the franchise. Newspaper editorials heaped abuse on marchers, and such derisive songs as the "Dark Town Suffragette Parade" (to the tune of "Dark Town Strutter's Ball") gave opponents considerable satisfaction.[27] Most women opted to postpone their suffrage activities, hoping to diffuse accusations that their behavior was unpatriotic. Instead, women came to Santa Fe from all over the state in May 1917 for the special legislative session called by Governor W. E. Lindsey to enlist their help with the war effort.

On May 6, 1917, less than a month after the United States entered World War I, New Mexico women formed the women's auxiliary of the State Council of Defense (later reorganized as the Woman's Committee of the National Council of Defense). The auxiliary was described by Alice Corbin Henderson—a Chicago poet and literary critic who had recently moved to Santa Fe—"as a vast clearing-house of women's activities . . . as a telephone or railway system in a country that had before been without one; as an artery . . . of ideas and inspiration. . . . New Mexico was thus one of the first states—if not the first—to mobilize its women for war service through an effective, state-wide organization."[28]

Nina had been appointed chairman of the auxiliary for New Mexico's First Judicial District and worked closely with her Albuquerque friend Erna Fergusson and with Alice Corbin Henderson in Santa Fe to encourage civilian cooperation in the war effort. Together they called on Santa Feans and went from farm to farm in rural areas, distributing Hoover Food Administration Pledge Cards (in Spanish and English), placing war posters and bulletins in libraries, and selling Liberty Loan Bonds. Liberty choruses going door to door "literally sang the Liberty Loan over the top," Alice Henderson reported. She also described the extraordinary difficulties involved in rolling up the returns on the Hoover food pledges in New Mexico:

> Little things like getting stuck in the middle of an arroyo during a cloud-burst and having to wait until the water subsided—if luckily one were not drowned by it. . . . Just what a house-to-house canvass in New Mexico means can only be understood by one who has "jitneyed" by narrow-gauge railway, stagecoach, bronco, or burro, over some of the rugged or sandy landscapes of New Mexico—where distances between houses are measured not by blocks but by arroyos, mountains, or mesas. Nor is there another state in the Union in which one half of the population cannot understand the other half without an interpreter.[29]

Despite obstacles, the people of New Mexico willingly tackled their problems, moved by their common impulse to win the war.

Most of the able-bodied men between the ages of eighteen and forty-five had left for Europe, and in New Mexico as in the rest of the country women were expected to take over their jobs at home. Erna Fergusson took charge of the Woman's Land Army, made up of patriotic female "harvest hands" who labored in the fields, picking, grading, and packing fruit for home and overseas. Indians helped them by growing and preserving fruits and vegetables.[30] Sugar-conservation demonstrations by women were set up outside private homes in Santa Fe. Even children were put to work making gun wipes.[31]

So much antipathy existed toward the enemy at home and abroad during World War I that the German language was taken out of New Mexico's public schools. German-Americans were accused of blowing up the country's factories, burning wheat, and poisoning food and water supplies. "The German is essentially a coward," the *New Mexican* reported on April 18, 1918. "What America most needs at home right now is a considerable number of Hun tombstones."[32]

While New Mexico legislators felt justified in putting the women's voting rights issue on hold throughout the war, the prohibition amendment received their full attention. To make sure the liquor traffic would not hamper the war effort, they adopted the Volstead Act forbidding the manufacture, sale, import, or export of intoxicating liquors. On October 1, 1918, all the state's saloons closed their doors, opening a fifteen-year period of unparalleled illegal drinking in the United States. While the *New Mexican* reported on November 17, 1917, that the dry victory would result in "happier and more contented and more prosperous people," the newspaper's editor, Bronson Cutting, reputedly "maintained perhaps the finest wine cellar in the Southwest," and alcoholic tea parties soon became fashionable in Santa Fe.

Scion of a wealthy New York family, Bronson Cutting had come to Santa Fe for his health and had acquired the *New Mexican* in 1912. He was a champion of Spanish-Americans, but he was also "ruthlessly competent in politics and intensely ambitious," according to Pulitzer-prize–winning author Oliver La Farge. Nina and the Bergeres were wary of Cutting, particularly after his paper challenged status quo politics and "set about walloping local Republicans."[33]

During the war Nina added to her work load as county school superintendent by taking on the chairmanship of the Red Cross membership committee for Santa Fe County. She was also serving as an officer with that organization's executive bureau and was preparing for overseas service with the Rocky Mountain Division of the Red Cross in Europe when the armistice was signed and her trip canceled.

Although relieved to have the war over, she was also disappointed that she was denied the adventure of a trip abroad. She had been looking forward to seeing her brother Luna and her stepfather. Alfred Bergere had been in Europe for several months at the height of the war serving as head secretary of the Knights of Columbus. While in France and Belgium, he had established three "huts"—one in a deserted convent—safe, temporary recreation centers for soldiers returning from battle. Luna Bergere, commanding officer of the 143d Machine Gun Battalion of the 40th Division, was also in France at the time. The stress of Alfred's overseas assignment took its toll on the sixty-year-old man, who was ill when he returned home in the spring of 1919 and remained in poor health for two years.[34]

With over ten million dead and twice that number wounded, the Great War came to an end in November 1918, only to be followed by an influenza epidemic that took the lives of twenty million more. The Bergere family was fortunate to be spared the casualties of war and fatal illness. But while there was victory for the Allies in Europe, the women's battle for the ballot in the United States had still to be won. The work Nina had done before and during the war and the success she was having in revitalizing county schools and curricula had given her the confidence she needed in the final push for voting rights legislation. Once the armistice was signed, the suffragists' campaign moved ahead with renewed vigor.

With Thomas Catron out of office and his successor, A. A. Jones, chairing the Senate suffrage committee, the Nineteenth

Amendment granting women the vote was finally passed by the U.S. Congress in June 1919.[35] It was now up to the states to ratify the amendment, and Nina would need all her persuasive powers to make that happen in New Mexico.

Her success by then in securing legislation to provide higher salaries and additional training for teachers, compulsory school attendance, and additional taxes to cover the new laws had received national attention. In August that year she was featured in *Holland* magazine, where she was said to "have mastered the best attributes" of the American and the Spanish woman. "No American woman could be more emancipated, more businesslike, more efficient, more wide-awake," and also possess "that peculiar Spanish charm, graciousness, modesty, and the poise and consideration of others found so often in the convent bred woman. Mrs. Otero-Warren shows how the daughter of a Spanish Don, but one generation removed from old world traditions in regard to the life of woman, can emancipate herself from what is useless in the old life, still retaining what is charming and really worth while."[36]

As a result of Nina's growing popularity and her tireless efforts to lobby Hispanic legislators, the suffrage amendment sailed through the New Mexico House of Representatives in the January 1919 session. Yet, to the astonishment of the majority of the voting public, it failed in the Senate, where it was shelved in favor of an unpopular and unpassable substitute referendum.

The lawmakers were roundly scored in newspapers around the country for their failure to pass the law. "Down there," the Portland *Oregonian* reported, "they prefer to marry the women when they find them and keep them out of politics." The *Christian Science Monitor* pointed out the prejudice involved in the decision: "Equal suffrage resolved itself into something of a racial question in New Mexico this week . . . three-fourths of those voting in the negative being Spanish speaking members." New Mexico's Governor A. O. Larrazolo fired off a scathing letter to both parties, denouncing their members who voted no and declaring that it was "neither fair nor honorable to betray the confidence" of the voters. He admonished his Republican colleagues to "discharge their duty" and fulfill their promises made at the general election: "redeem these pledges and thus save the future of our party; or . . . betray them and doom the party to defeat."[37]

Nina and her friends were crushed. They had hoped New Mexico would be among the first states to ratify. She did find some consolation, however, when two welfare bills providing for the protection of children and young women passed that year, thanks to her considerable personal efforts.[38]

The failed campaign in New Mexico and the need for fourteen additional states to join the twenty-two that had ratified brought a new sense of urgency. The opposition was becoming more of a threat, organizing in greater numbers to fight ratification. Some opponents went so far as to accuse suffragists of being aligned with Russian revolutionaries. The violent postwar overthrow of the Czarist government, led by Lenin and Trotsky, had created a "Red scare," and radical feminists with the CU, now calling itself the National Woman's Party, were suspect. To regain majority support for the suffragists, Carrie Chapman Catt, leader of the more temperate NAWSA, toured the country denouncing militancy and acting as mediator between the two organizations.[39]

On February 13, 1920, the New Mexican announced Catt's Chicago appearance with the headline "Republican and Democratic Ladies in Lively Spat at Suffrage Meeting," and quoted her as saying "No Earthly Power can do more than delay by a trifle final enfranchisement of the women of the United States."[40] Carrie Chapman Catt, who was to become the founding mother of the nonpartisan League of Women Voters, urged women to find their way to the centers of power once they received the franchise, for there, she said, "is the engine that moves the wheels of your party machinery."[41]

Inspired by Catt's rhetoric, Nina persisted in her efforts to take her message to the men in power. Night letters and telegrams jammed the lines between Washington and Santa Fe as she reported to Alice Paul and received her leader's instructions and encouragement. Alice Paul's confidence in Nina's ameliorative skills was under-scored in a telegram she sent Lillian Kerr, saying "People here [in Washington] say Mrs. Otero-Warren and [Holm] Bursom can do more than anyone else to save the situation,"[42] the situation being that the opposition was developing more strong-arm strategies and plotting another substitute referendum to prevent ratification. Three days later Otero-Warren reported her caucus plans to Paul with an upbeat telegram, announcing "situation in Senate favorable Fight on in House But we will win."[43] In the last days before the New Mexico legislature's final vote, she had gained admission to the Republican caucus, becoming the first woman in the state ever to participate in that previously all-male enclave.

The women finally won the right to vote on February 19, 1920, when the House followed the Senate and voted thirty-six to ten for ratification. New Mexico became the thirty-second state to approve the amendment proposed more than fifty years before by Susan B. Anthony and Elizabeth Cady Stanton. That same day, Nina received a cheerful telegram from Alice Paul: "Congratulations on New Mexi-co's victory All women in the country are indebted to you on your splendid leadership We have deepest admiration for your cam-paign."[44]

Nina clearly had shown that she had an instinctive understand-ing of ways to work with the New Mexico legislators. Her assertive campaign of persuasion and conciliation, without needless antago-nisms toward the men, had paid off. She emerged from the voting rights battle as something of a heroine in Santa Fe, an intelligent, re-sourceful woman with a strong sense of justice who had been re-markably successful in overcoming long-standing social and political obstacles. More than any other New Mexico woman of that time, she had become a role model for both Anglo and Hispanic women in the state.

And more fences fell in 1921, when a special election was held in New Mexico to pass an amendment to the state constitution per-mitting women to hold public office. Although many Hispanic men voted no on the ballot *para tener oficina las mujeres*, Anglos in the "Little Texas" counties of the southeastern part of the state approved, and the amendment passed.[45] A few months later, Nina became the overwhelming choice of Republican women in New Mexico to run for a seat in the U.S. House of Representatives.

The Republican party's male incumbent at the time was Néstor Montoya, a flamboyant congressman who had little respect from Santa Feans. He had been ridiculed in the *New Mexican* for his outlandish appearance, at one time "wearing a tile sombrero [with] 'soup-to-fish' make-up." The paper went on to report that "while Mrs. Warren hasn't made any announcement, friends say she is trimming her hat preparatory to tossing it into the ring."[46]

Feeling that she would have a better-than-average chance of winning the nomination, Nina announced her candidacy. Néstor Montoya was particularly annoyed at having the state's leading suffragist as his political foe because he had championed women's issues during his campaign in 1920, even threatening to challenge his Democratic opponent, Antonio Lucero, to a duel for making "pale pink remarks about the lady voters."

Montoya's friends began to spread propaganda about Nina in an effort to "nip in the bud any ambition she might cherish to spend the summer sweltering and the winter shivering in Washington." The *New Mexican*'s columnist sarcastically noted that Nina's friends felt she would be as qualified as amateur astrologer Montoya "when it comes to handing out the dope to eager constituents on the Transit of Venus, the kind of veils Venus is wearing this season," the origins of the "sun's spotted complexion," and whether "Mars wants to subscribe [to] the Congressional Record." Implying that Nina was not a candidate to be taken seriously, the columnist alleged that "Mrs. Warren is attracted by the bright social lights; not to monkey with the tariff, the transit of Venus, or that statesmanly stuff." But, Montoya should understand that he would have Mrs. Otero-Warren to beat if he expected to return to Washington, D. C., and "trips on the presidential yacht Mayflower, by invitation."[47]

Nina Otero-Warren, boarding
an electric automobile to take
the campaign trail in her bid for
election to the U. S. House of
Representatives, 1922. Seated in
the car, from left: May Bergere,
May Van Hunter (behind the
wheel), and Anita Bergere.
(Bergere Family Collection, photo
no. 21252, New Mexico State
Records Center and Archives,
Santa Fe, New Mexico.)

Backed by the supportive networks she had formed over the
preceding seven years as suffrage leader and lobbyist, Nina took the
primary trail against Montoya and began the arduous task of canvass-
ing the state for votes. She was at the same time serving as Santa Fe
County school superintendent, chairman of the state board of public
welfare, chairman of the department of public welfare of the State
Federation of Women's Clubs, and executive committee member of
the New Mexico Teacher's Association. Her days were full.

In the months following her announcement, the diminutive
"woman politician" made the rounds of New Mexico towns and villages, smiling, shaking hands, making campaign speeches, and
courting votes, her voice becoming hoarse from trying to project her
words without the benefit of a microphone. "Her voice was naturally

high-pitched," her niece, Eloisa Bergere Brown, said, "and when she tried to lower it, her speech seemed strained. She would always clear her throat just before she spoke, and when in small groups made a conscious effort to soften her voice."[48] Still, she articulated her views with a grace and poise that earned accolades for her aristocratic bearing and clear, intelligent presentations.

She accepted all invitations to speak, typically appearing at public forums dressed in long full skirts and sensible medium-heeled shoes, her red hair drawn back in a bun, soft waves framing her oval face. She usually wore a wide-brimmed hat decorated with a fashionable ribbon or flower to match her gown. Her bright hazel eyes behind steel-rimmed glasses took in everything and everyone around her.

If nominated, she promised the mostly female and Hispanic groups she addressed, she would run on a platform for better education, solutions to labor problems, a protective tariff and reclamation, and (though reluctantly) "for strict enforcement of the Volstead law."[49] When the votes were counted, Nina won by a wide margin, 446½ votes to Montoya's 99½, carrying all but one of the state's predominantly Hispanic counties and becoming the first woman in New Mexico to be nominated for high federal office.[50] Her victory set such a precedent that it was even announced in the New York Times: "NAME WOMAN FOR CONGRESS. New Mexico Republicans Make Mrs. Otero-Warren Their Candidate."[51]

The real battle, however, lay ahead. Néstor Montoya was a relatively easy target, lacking the respect of the voters and the commitment of his constituents. Her Democratic rival was another matter. John R. Morrow commanded a large Anglo following. Nina toured the state calling on organized women's groups for their help, urging the women she had worked so hard for to work for her. She reminded Hispanics that "the Democratic Party was the White Man's [Anglo] Party; the Republican Party is the only political party that is distinctly American." Her candidacy made the Republican ticket an "honest American and Woman Suffrage ticket."[52] Republican party campaign leaflets emphasized her "illustrious ascendancy" and touted her skills as

> a ready and resourceful debater . . . well read and thoroughly familiar with the science of political economy and also with all the public questions which (at the present time) are agitating the entire nation. No person in New Mexico knows better than Mrs. Warren the condition and the wants of our State and the needs of its people. . . . If elected, she will make her mark in the national halls of Congress and that success will crown her efforts. VOTE FOR HER."[53]

While more than forty-nine thousand people did vote for Nina, Morrow defeated her by ten thousand votes, winning the House seat by less than 9 percent. That she lost was understandable: she was the first woman to challenge an all-male political system, and that year the Democrats elected a governor, James Hinkle, and most of the state officials. After the votes were counted, Nina was pleasantly surprised to find that she had carried all but one of the state's five Hispanic counties. A majority of the votes in all the Little Texas Anglo counties went to Morrow. She was grateful that her people were willing to have her represent them in Congress, even though they had opposed a woman's right to hold office just a year before. Their change of heart was a tribute to her party's organizing skills and her own persuasive powers. Despite the lack of female political role models before Nina's campaign, and with no tradition of participation in structured party politics, Hispanic women had quickly become active voters, and most had voted for her.[54]

Two women were elected to state offices in 1922, a Hispanic Democrat—Mrs. Soledad Chávez Chacón—as secretary of state and an Anglo Democrat [her name is undocumented] as state superintendent of public instruction. But not until 1946 did a New Mexico woman, Georgia Lusk, win a seat in the U.S. Congress. At the national level, Rebecca Latimer Felton, a Democrat from Georgia, served less than a month in the Senate after she was appointed in 1922. While both the Democratic and Republican parties encouraged women to vote for men and to develop and support the programs of male candidates, "women never had more than token power," even though in 1920 they had been promised fifty-fifty representation in party councils.[55]

The percentage of women in state and federal offices has grown somewhat in the seventy years since enfranchisement, but so slowly that at the current rate, according to *National Voter* columnist Marsha Whicker, not until the year 2582 will equal representation be reached.[56] Despite those projections, Vivian Gornick wrote in 1990 that women had been "released from a collective lifetime of silence" in 1920. Those with brains and visionary ideas were no longer considered eccentric, and many had discovered a sustaining "inner clarity" and strength.[57]

In her short-lived fling with politics, Nina had lost the election but had found that inner clarity. She could now chart her future course with confidence. She accepted her loss graciously, in the spirit of a true Hispanic politician who enjoyed the intrigue and excitement of the process—win or lose—and proceeded a year later to help her brother Manuel campaign for governor. Manuel also lost to an Anglo Democrat, Arthur T. Hannett, but by only 199 votes, the narrow margin causing much speculation about possible illegal ballot-box stuffing.[58] The Otero-Hannett race alerted the public to the outdated, inefficient 1924 election methods and prompted a *New Mexican* editorial that year to demand "sweeping reform in election laws." Voters' faith in the integrity of the antiquated system had been considerably shaken after years of persistent rumors of poll tampering.[59]

Reform did come eventually, but not in time for the Republicans, who saw their party decline in the late twenties when the political practices of the old *patrón* system broke down and the first hard years of the Great Depression began to cripple the country.[60] Nina temporarily withdrew from politics and directed most of her efforts to addressing the urgent educational needs of her community and to cultivating the close friendships she had made during her years of political activism. Just as she had helped expand the narrow limits of women's lives, she now worked to release children and adults from the bonds of illiteracy.

CHAPTER FOUR

The
Educator

Nina Otero-Warren had been defeated in her bid for the U.S. House of Representatives in 1922, but her general success in politics had given her personal life richness and meaning. It also set her apart from her sisters, all but two of whom—Anita and Ysabel—had married and left La Casa Grande. When it became difficult to manage the erratic behavior of mentally handicapped Ysabel, the teenager was placed in the care of a nurse in St. Louis.[1]

Anita, with Teta's help, had been dedicating her life to the family's welfare during the six years since her mother's death and had carried most of the burden of managing the household. The most fervent of Catholics and the only sister who had a genuine vocation, Anita's final vows had to be secular: the Church granted her permission to devote her life to her father and siblings as well as to God. In addition to supervising the shopping, cooking, heavy cleaning, and transporting of the younger children, she also helped Nina, whose days and evenings were crowded with business and social commitments.

Seventeen-year-old Joe, the youngest Bergere child, still lived at home with his older sisters and his father, who at sixty-five continued to be involved in Republican party politics. Alfred Bergere's eldest son, Luna, had married Carolyn Updike Catron and was beginning his career as an attorney. May had married John Joseph Kenney in 1917, and by 1922 had given birth to three children—John Joseph III, Bergere Alfred, and Dolores.

A distinguished new member was added to the family when Estella married Aldo Leopold, noted writer and conservationist, a founder of the Wilderness Society, and author of the environmental classic *A Sand County Almanac* (1949). Aldo's brother Carl married Dolores Bergere. Rosina divorced her first husband, Leonard Smith, who died in 1924. She and her two children, little Rosina and Leonard, moved back to the security of the Big House for a year, until 1925, when she married Dr. Robert Osgood Brown; in the following thirteen years four more children were added to the family.

On the return of Rosina and her children to the Big House, Nina ordered extensive renovations. A second story was added because the ceilings of the original dormer rooms upstairs were so low the children would bump their heads going in and out.[2] Five large bedrooms were thus created, and with the new flat roof and squared-off second story, the house conformed more closely to the Spanish-Pueblo style of architecture that was becoming popular again in the twenties. The renovation also included another bathroom, a sun room (the center of most family gatherings), and a single-car garage.[3]

The Bergeres had acquired an automobile in the early twenties, but the average citizen did without until the Model Ts of Henry Ford became available. Dr. H. P. Mera, who headed the city's lucrative hospital for tuberculosis, Sunmount Sanatorium, also owned one, but for most Santa Feans, horses, burros, wagon taxis, and buggies were the chief modes of transportation.[4]

People walked a lot and life was simpler in those earlier days, said Alice Henderson Rossin in a 1987 interview with Sarah Nestor.

The Big House restored. The A. M. Bergere House after a second story was added, n.d. (Bergere Family Collection, photo no. 23421, New Mexico State Records Center and Archives, Santa Fe, New Mexico.)

"Everybody helped each other.... There weren't so many people and there weren't all the cars and there wasn't all the noise.... If you didn't know who people were by nightfall, it was just as well if they left—they'd be gone by night if they hadn't identified themselves. Unless they'd adapted themselves to the community, they weren't acceptable."[5]

Entertainment was simple, too, said Anita Gonzales Thomas, a lifelong resident of Santa Fe. Almost everybody had a phonograph, some had player pianos, and "people would get together just to sing." On summer evenings, she and her cousins would sit on the porch of a friend or relative and "do a little bit of singing and pray the rosary, and then we'd just walk down the street to our house and go to bed."[6]

Life in La Casa Grande was not so relaxed, according to Connie Mendenhall: "My Lord, they were strict," she said of Nina, Anita, and her father. "We never swore, smoked or drank, and we couldn't move without a chaperone until after we got married." Nina, of course, had been smoking and drinking moderately for years. Most family celebrations for birthdays, anniversaries, and marriages began and ended with alcoholic toasts. Indeed, as time went by and parental restrictions eased, there was a rite of passage for children in the family who had reached the age of fifteen, when they were invited into the sun room and offered their first drink and cigarette.[7]

Connie grew up under the watchful eye of her Victorian-minded father, and she remembered Alfred Bergere's reaction one evening before she and her sisters left for a party:

> Wearing short sleeves and low necklines, we went to say good-night to Papa. "You're all naked, a disgrace to the family. You can't go," he stormed. We ran to Teta, our governess. She proceeded to open up the cedar chest and drape us with Venetian lace. Papa approved; now we looked like ladies. On the way to the party, we stopped at my sister's house and took off the lace.[8]

Connie admitted that she was more headstrong than most of her sisters. When, at Nina's urging, A. M. Bergere declared that she could see her boyfriend, Herbert Mendenhall, only once a week, the sixteen-year-old packed a bag and headed for the train depot, determined to leave the repressive regime forever. But reason prevailed. Connie was intercepted by one of her cousins before she boarded the train and was persuaded to go home. When the adults saw the genuine love and commitment the teenagers shared, they became reconciled to the relationship that culminated in marriage seven years later (1917).[9]

Despite Nina's initial objections to their courtship and marriage, Connie and Herbert Mendenhall spent fifty-seven years together. Yet even in her nineties Consuelo Mendenhall would weep in anger and frustration when her half-sister's name was mentioned. Nina obviously felt that she had to be the strong parent in the absence of her mother and was resolutely committed to overseeing the morals, manners, discipline, and behavior of the family. Appearances were very important to her. Familial well-being and propriety were maintained no matter what underlying tensions were generated at home, and there were many. The climate in La Casa Grande grew heated at times, with shouting, tears, and accusations from those who felt their individual rights usurped. Yet Nina, the leader, the teacher, the one who made most of the decisions, remained intractable.

When her niece Eloisa at eighteen wanted to marry a cowboy, Nina ordered her mother, Rosina, to "lock her up in her room! She must not marry a cowboy," Nina stormed. "People of our class don't live in trailers." She also disapproved of Eloisa's pigtails: "One only puts one's hair in pigtails when ready for bed." The more independent-minded of her younger sisters submitted to her demands but were resentful and remained so for most of their lives. By and large, all members of the family—male and female—treated her cautiously.[10]

Catholic influences in Nina's early years at Los Lunas and later at Maryville remained with her throughout much of her life, although as she grew older and began associating with the artists and writers who flooded into Santa Fe in the twenties, she became more openminded. Right conduct—piety, devotion to duty, and deportment—and the "proper" roles for women in church and community had been instilled at an early age, and she tried to conform. Now in her forties and living in a city that was becoming known around the country and abroad for its creative citizens and tolerant attitudes, she became more aware of the rigidity and demands of her religion.

On the surface Nina professed to be a good practicing Catholic, regularly attending mass on Sundays and special feast days and making sure her sisters and the children joined her. She once participated in a Penitente ceremony, the only woman in a group of chanting *hermanos* (brothers) as they moved in procession after dark over a rough, sandy path to the Cross of Calvary to celebrate the feast of Our Lady of Sorrows. Yet her cousin Amalia Sánchez observed that Nina was not particularly religious. Instead, she was "politically minded, and she "had the brains in the family."[11]

Nina was also proud and prejudiced: proud of her "pure" Spanish blood, prejudiced toward Herbert Mendenhall for being a "flashy ne'er-do-well" from a lower-class family and toward the Bergeres for being Jewish. Herbert Mendenhall supposedly "broke the code" about the Bergeres' ancestry by revealing Nina's stepfather's Jewish-Italian roots. That her mother's family, the Lunas, were also of Jewish descent she never acknowledged, if indeed she knew. The noble de Lunas of the Spanish Middle Ages "had Hebrew strains," according to historian William T. Walsh, although they were probably faithful *conversos* (new Christians) during the Inquisition and were protected from unjust suspicion and persecution. Such prejudices unquestionably reflected the bigotry of the times and Nina's early indoctrination by the Roman Catholic church.[12]

Nina was one of the Lunas and Oteros who had always had good connections and who identified with the aristocratic way of life. She did not have to work but did so because idleness bored her and because she wanted to take advantage of the knowledge, confidence, and stature she had gained as a political activist. She had cleverly avoided the opprobrium attached to being divorced and childless by declaring herself a widow and had found a way to support herself in a socially acceptable manner. She liked the idea of financial and professional independence combined with meaningful work and pleasant companionship. She found that and more in her capacity as Santa Fe County school superintendent and, in 1923, as inspector for Indian schools.

Nina and all New Mexico educators were faced with an enormous task in trying to improve school standards in their state. Education had made very little progress since 1832, when only six public schools were registered in the entire territory. Before United States annexation, the instruction of Indians and Spanish-Americans had been left primarily to the Church. There were no public high schools or colleges until 1889.[13] At the turn of the century the *New Mexican* reported that school-age children were reading dime novels and wild, woolly west stories. . . . A boy who has good literature, Cooper's and Scott's novels, Robinson Crusoe, a good juvenile magazine and his local daily paper to read at home will not go out and filch money to buy himself a blood and thunder story.

A girl who has access to the standard novels of the day, to several volumes of fairly [sic] tales, to a good woman's journal and the daily paper will not pine for the *Saturday Evening Gazette* or the *Family Story Paper* with their perverse and silly love stories.[14]

Nina was sympathetic toward poor families living in widely scattered rural villages who needed their children in the fields to help harvest crops during the first months of the school term. In nineteenth-century hacienda days "a child's practical education came from the soil itself," she wrote in *Old Spain in Our Southwest*: "all of his work included a poetry of motion that is too often lost today, and that seems to us, looking back upon it, as a song of the past."[15]

Nevertheless, by the 1920s the young people of New Mexico whose families could not afford private educations for them in Catholic academies or Protestant mission schools had to attend public schools, which in the early decades of the twentieth century were still plagued by inadequate funding, underqualified teachers, and short school terms—three months or less in some areas of northern New Mexico. Hispanic villagers were convinced that their children "just didn't learn, the teachers did not know how to teach, they were not educated." And many Anglo teachers were reluctant to teach Hispanic children, considering them "sadly lacking" in ambition, courage, determination, and respect for education—an attitude that inhibited the Spanish-Americans and eroded their self-esteem.[16]

While she was leading the woman suffrage movement in the state and at the same time beginning her twelve-year tenure as school superintendent, Nina began a search for better teachers and encouraged more public involvement and cooperation for the schools. She pushed for salary increases for teachers—in 1916, just a

"In the fourth grade with Helen Harrison," Santa Fe, ca. 1920. A typical classroom during Nina Otero-Warren's tenure as superintendent of public schools for Santa Fe county. (Adela Collier Collection, photo no. 32140, New Mexico State Records Center and Archives, Santa Fe, New Mexico.)

year before she took office, a teacher was paid an average annual salary of $546.03. She also lobbied for the renovation of dilapidated school buildings and for government funds to pay off school debts. She proposed that the school year be increased to nine months—an addition of two to six months, depending on the region—and she restored school credit in the county by insisting on prompt payment of warrants.[17]

The industrial age demanded a better educational system, and Nina was expected to see that state rules and regulations were enforced in all the schools in Santa Fe County regardless of her opposition to some of their requirements. She would have liked to see the rural school curriculum in mostly Spanish-speaking New Mexico include the traditional arts of wool dyeing, tin working, blanket weaving, and wood carving—all of which, if taught by experts in the community, would bring something of "lasting educational value" to her people. Instead, credits were given for reading, writing, and arithmetic only, and children were not permitted to speak Spanish in the classroom or on the playground. As a result, few Hispanic students from rural areas accumulated enough credits for graduation to high school. While she saw the difficulties and injustices of this Anglo approach to education, she appealed to the teachers and children in schools she visited to "acquiesce in the new order," for "it is to our best interests that we become educated according to the standards of the nation. It has, for us, its distinct advantages, its definite protection."[18]

Nina made calls regularly to her districts, near and remote, to learn firsthand the needs of teachers and pupils. In 1917, just after she had been appointed school superintendent, she had to pay her own traveling expenses, so she was pleased when the state legislators—probably in an effort to appease women for shelving the suffrage amendment—agreed to allocate money for travel (a considerable item given the vast distances between school districts). The solons also ordered a compulsory annual "clean-up" day in the villages and set penalties for exposing meat to dust and flies.

Nina, with a school nurse or a friend, would drive by automobile as far as the paved roads would take her from Santa Fe—to Nambe, Tesuque, Santa Cruz de la Cañada, Glorieta, La Cueva, Cañoncito, La Joya, and Chimayo. The "wood roads," rutted dirt roads over high passes to the mountain villages of Cundiyo, Chupadero, and Río en Medio, required a horse and wagon and a trustworthy driver. Finding skilled teachers intrepid enough to live and work in such places was one of her major concerns.

Anita Gonzales Thomas, who spent twenty-four years teaching in New Mexico's public schools, was one of the many capable women Nina hired. Starting at nineteen, with a year of college attained through a scholarship from Loretto Academy, Anita taught for two years in a little schoolhouse at Cañoncito, a tiny village off the Las Vegas highway. The first year, her mother and father drove her from their home in Santa Fe to Cañoncito on Monday mornings and picked her up on Friday afternoons. During the week she lived in a boarding house and taught children ranging in age from six to fourteen, all assembled in one room. Some had to furnish their own desks and tablets. When bus transportation became available, Anita commuted every weekday, but she never considered those years a time of hardship. She liked teaching the gentle, uncomplicated children and was grateful to have a job.[19]

The Spanish-American people in the scattered hamlets of Santa Fe County recognized "La Nina" as a superintendent who cared for them, and they showed their gratitude in subtle ways. On one occasion as Nina and her Indian driver left Cundiyo late in the evening, the school director, Teofilo, mounted his horse and quietly followed her wagon through the rugged mountains and dark canyons, telling her he too was going to Santa Fe, thirty miles away. Once she arrived at her car, which she had left parked on the main road, Teofilo doffed his hat, smiled, handed her a letter to mail for him in the city, and headed back to the village. Astonished, Nina realized that he had followed her for ten miles to see that she made it through safely. "These are my people, my friends," she wrote later in a moving account of her experiences for the editors of *Survey Graphic*.[20]

One of her young pupils, Dominguita Vigíl, lived on a farm in Santa Cruz de la Cañada in 1922 and looked forward to the superintendent's visits during Christmas week, when Nina and her friend Mamie Meadors would bring boxes of food and candy to the Vigíl family. Nina and Mamie would work with the children all afternoon, decorating the tree with candles and the house with piñon and juniper branches, then drive home in the dark. Nina was fond of Dominguita's grandfather, a fair, brown-eyed Spanish American who claimed aristocratic connections in the old country. Toribio Vigíl was one of the few people she told about her ex-husband's infidelity, and the Vigíls were among the few village families invited to the Big House. Dominguita was proud of her grammar school diploma, earned despite her long absences from school during the weeks she stayed on the farm to help with the planting and harvesting of corn, pumpkins, and beans. She regretted not going on to high school, but at that time there were no school buses from Cañada to Santa Fe, and her family was too poor to own an automobile.[21]

Nina relished her work and loved her people. She liked the idea of doing good and believed that education meant liberation for northern New Mexico's children, who were largely from the poorest of homes in distant mountain communities. Yet they were vigorous, sensitive people with "high ideals, loving the solitude of the wilderness and fearing no danger." They had found peace and contentment in the canyons and mountains. As an educator, Nina saw the advantages of a gradual merging of Hispanic and Anglo cultures, but not at the expense of losing the customs and traditions, the arts and crafts of the Spanish Southwest. "I am wondering," she wrote in 1931, after her last term as county school superintendent had ended, "if this progressive and advanced republic has still time and patience for charm? . . . I do not believe there is an Anglo who does not feel that unless he takes this country and the people to his heart—loving it, scars and all—that he is very happy among us. The moment he begins to resent any aspect of his life, we still remain foreign to him."[22]

For all her defense of the easy, charming ways of the Hispanic families in her school district, Nina also insisted on regularity and efficiency, order and discipline. She took her mission to improve the education of children as seriously as she took her responsibilities at the Big House. By 1920 her efforts were paying off and the *New Mexican* reported that Mrs. Otero-Warren had "lifted the Santa Fe county school system from its demoralized condition and made it one of the best in the state." There were

> no better rural schools than those in Santa Fe County. . . . School buildings are modern and in repair. County high schools are flourishing. An all-year school nurse is kept busy. Only first grade [the best] teachers are employed. They are adequately paid. There is a budget balance of $27,000 and the people of every district display interest and pride in their schools.[23]

Nina realized early on that she would need help in the office and on her routine trips outside Santa Fe. Bookkeeping was a tedious necessity, and she had neither the time nor the patience to pore over ledgers. In casting about for an assistant, she considered a number of well-educated, hard-working women who had helped in her campaign for Congress, two of whom had become her close friends—Alice Corbin Henderson and Mamie Meadors (pronounced Mea-DOORS).[24]

Like so many people suffering from respiratory ailments during the early twentieth century, both Alice and Mamie had come to the high, dry climate of Santa Fe for their health—Alice in 1916, Mamie two years later. Both had tuberculosis, both found a cure at Sunmount Sanatorium on Camino del Monte Sol. Sunmount had been offering hope and salvation for "lungers" from the time it began as a "tent city" in 1903.[25]

Alice Corbin Henderson, author and cofounder, with Harriet Monroe, of *Poetry: A Magazine of Verse*, came from Chicago with her husband, William "Whippy" Penhallow Henderson, and her fifteen-year-old daughter, "Little Alice" (Alice Henderson Rossin). Once she was discharged from Sunmount, she resumed her writing career and plunged into civic affairs, concerned primarily with the plight of the Indians in New Mexico. Nina admired Alice's agile mind and cheerful tolerance and had been impressed with her Red Cross work and her campaign for Liberty Bond sales during World War I. Alice was as fervent a suffragist as Nina, but she was first a writer, editor, and creative critic. Like Nina, she was, in Haniel Long's words, "a group person . . . at home in that civic world, and often a leader in it," but also a person who paid others "an attention full of perceptiveness of them as individuals."[26]

Alice eagerly sought firsthand information about the state's political policies from authorities in Santa Fe, including Nina, and took innovative action to find remedies when needed. She also continued the recognition and support of poets and writers she had begun in Chicago while editing *Poetry*, insisting always that "a perfectly fearless

high standard" be observed by the many gifted people who submitted their work for her critical judgment.[27]

Through Alice and Whippy Henderson, Nina was to meet and
socialize with the leading artists and writers who came to the city in
the twenties, including Mary Austin, Ruth Laughlin, Witter Bynner
and Spud Johnson, Frank Applegate, Mabel Dodge and Tony Luján,
John Gaw Meem, Randall Davey, Haniel Long, and the Cinco Pintores
(Will Shuster, Josef Bakoz, Willard Nash, Fremont Ellis, and Walter
Mruck).

Mamie Meadors, unlike Alice, was a quiet, timid woman with a
small, thin figure that appeared even more fragile after her bout with
tuberculosis. She had been told by Dr. Mera on her arrival at Sunmount that she could expect to live no more than six months at best.
Instead, she outlived him by twenty-five years, dying in 1951 at the
age of sixty-four.[28]

Born in Berne, Arkansas, in 1887, Mamie came to Santa Fe
from Wichita Falls, Texas, armed with a degree from the University
of Arkansas and practical clerical experience. After she regained her
strength, she found a position as secretary to Levi Hughes, Sr., president of the First National Bank of Santa Fe. Once established, she
wrote her cousin, Salome E. Anthony, encouraging her to come to
Santa Fe and share a house with her on Delgado Street. Salome and
Mamie had grown up together in Wichita Falls and were compatible,
independent women. Salome accepted Mamie's invitation, and on
her arrival took a job at the city's public library on Washington
Street, a facility made possible primarily through the efforts of far-
sighted women who in 1903 pressed the territorial legislature to al-
lot land and a building to provide free access to books. Salome had
been trained at Columbia Library School in New York and would advance to the position of head librarian in the thirty-three years she
lived in Santa Fe. During that time she was largely responsible for the
development and growth of the city's library.[29]

Nina's friendship with Alice and Mamie became long lasting,
warm, and intimate. With both she shared a lifelong intellectual rap-

port, but it was Mamie who soon occupied the privileged place in her life as hard-working disciple, confidant, and devoted friend. Alice had her husband and child and a privileged position of her own within the clique of Santa Fe writers and artists. Nina enjoyed a long and easy friendship with those creative people, but her relationship with Mamie was a symbiotic and essential one. They were united by their common interest in ideas and a need for closeness and support. They could talk to and argue with each other on the same intellectual level, and they were both diligent workers. But it was a friendship of opposites—Nina outer directed, Mamie quiet and introspective; Nina outspoken, personable, happy to take full charge of her life, Mamie more dependent, retiring, inept at casual conversation, uncomfortable in large social gatherings. Yet the strongest bond of friendship was forged, and the two women enhanced each other's lives for more than thirty years.[30]

Mamie had helped behind the scenes with the clerical work during the suffrage campaign and Nina's run for congressional office. After that they saw each other on a fairly regular basis. When Mamie moved from her job with Levi Hughes to become a secretary in Judge E. H. Wright's office, she met A. M. Bergere, who in 1921, at the age of seventy-six, had been appointed by President Harding to the position of register of the U.S. Land Office in New Mexico.[31] Mamie knew the workings of the capital city well, was efficient and capable, and could be counted on to maintain a discreet silence when political disputes arose. Mamie, Nina learned early on, was trustworthy and dependable and usually available when there was work to be done and deadlines to meet.

Nina needed someone like Mamie, particularly in 1923 when controversy over Indian land and cultural rights was high and Otero-Warren was appointed inspector of Indian schools in Santa Fe County, the first woman in New Mexico to hold that position. She took over the job at one of the darker times for the American Indian, when the federal government's 1922 policies had become alarmingly aggressive and were creating almost insurmountable problems for the Native Americans. New Mexico Senator Albert B. Fall, who at that time was Harding's secretary of the interior, had introduced the infamous Bursom Bill in Congress, legislation aimed at taking even more land and water rights from the Indians (the Anglos had already looted most of their rich landholdings) and destroying their languages and religious practices.

While the bill slipped through the Senate, it was killed in the House after vigorous opposition from friends of the Indians. Leading the lobby were Stella M. Atwood, chairman of the Indian welfare department of the National Federation of Women's Clubs; John Collier, research agent for the federation; the Santa Fe art colony "yearners"; and the Indians themselves, whose well-organized Pueblo Council took their case directly to Washington.[32] Nina, Mamie, Alice, and other prominent Santa Fe leaders sympathetic to the Indian cause joined in the general outcry against unjust government practices.

The one bright spot in the dim picture was the launching in the fall of 1922 of Indian Market, then known as the Southwest Indian Fair and Industrial Arts and Crafts Exhibition. Organized by Kenneth Chapman and Edgar Lee Hewett, the fair was meant to encourage American Indians to revive their native arts and crafts and to establish markets for their products. The event was extraordinarily successful, the largest fair of its kind then as it is today. The 1922 exhibition combined arts and crafts in four simple categories—Navajo rugs and silverwork, Pueblo pottery, beadwork, and children's government-school classroom art—which increased over the years to seven major categories broken down into hundreds of classifications and divisions and generating more than three hundred awards. Today more than one thousand American Indians from across the United States set up booths at the annual Indian Market in Santa Fe. Attendance has increased from several thousand prospective buyers in 1922 to close to eighty-five thousand in the 1990s.[33]

Once the market was over, however, the Navajos and Pueblos had to return to their reservations and to government schools whose bureaucratic overseers were apathetic or hostile, or both. "Children were taken at six years of age and kept in boarding schools," Indian-rights activist John Collier wrote. Like serfs, they were "indentured out . . . to white families during vacation periods, until the end of adolescence. Child labor, in school time as in vacation time, was standard. The children's day would often begin at six in the morning and end at eight at night."[34]

On their first trips to inspect the Indian schools in and around Santa Fe, Nina and Mamie found the facilities in scandalous condition—overcrowded, fly-infested, disease-ridden government boarding schools where children were beaten for speaking their native tongues and "often roped like cattle" if they attempted to run away. Children forced from their pueblo homes to be indoctrinated in the Anglo way of life were malnourished, some even starving, on the Indian bureau's allotted seven to eleven cents a day for food.[35]

On September 7, 1923, Nina received a desperate letter from Benjamin Naranjo, who lived with his wife and two children at Santa Clara Pueblo and who had accepted employment for himself and his wife at the Santa Fe Indian School in order to be near his farming interests at the pueblo. "We were not given any courtesy on our arrival here," he wrote. "My two children had to sleep two nights on the floor. The Superintendent was always too busy to see us or to give us instructions about our work."

> We find the boys' building in such a condition that we do not see how it can be cleaned up with the small amount of help Mrs. Naranjo has. The building is old and dirty and generally out of order. . . . The mattresses we are expected to put Indian boys to sleep on are not fit for human beings to try to sleep on. . . . No boy can any more rest on these beds than he could on a rock pile. . . . A big fire is the only thing which will do these beds any good. . . . We are told to eat in the Indian dining room. It is so full of flies that today I took my two children and my wife out of it and we are all four boarding at the employees club as it is too dangerous for my children to eat the fly-filthy food. . . . I cannot

afford to pay board for four. . . . You have seen us in our home in Santa Clara and know how we live there. We feel like animals here crowded into two little rooms without official friends in the place except you. We will stay until you call to see us. Please come soon.

Very Sincerely yours,

Benj. Naranjo.[36]

Nina quickly arranged a meeting with the Indian school's superintendent, John D. DeHuff, and made a thorough inspection of the buildings. A few days later she filed a detailed report in a letter to Charles H. Burke, commissioner of Indian affairs in Washington, "a small politician with an abysmal outlook," according to Oliver La Farge. In the spring of 1923, Burke had issued a letter "To All Indians," demanding that they discontinue their "pagan" ceremonial dances, which he described as "useless and harmful performances." By September, he was feeling the pressure of public outrage over his and the Bureau of Indian Affairs' appalling treatment of Native Americans.[37]

During her inspection Nina had found the dormitories and the dining room much too congested for the 450 children attending school—"30 children are now sleeping two in a bed." While the girls' dormitories were in "splendid condition, clean, plenty of air, fairly good beds and clean linen," the boys' quarters were in a shocking state of disrepair. Most of the mattresses were "old, frightfully dirty, lumpy and scarcely covered." They had never been cleaned or washed.[38]

Eighty-six children between the ages of twelve and fourteen used one wash room with six faucets and seven toilets. Towels were thrown into a large uncovered box where the children could "easily reach in and take a soiled towel of perhaps a child who has Trachoma or skin disease, thereby spreading it. . . . Tooth brushes are exposed to dirt and there is no way of keeping a child from taking some one else's brush—again a way to communicate disease." On visiting the Indian school hospital, Nina was told that 46 percent of the children had trachoma (contagious conjunctivitis), which can cause scarring and blindness.

In the dining room she found "tables of all lengths and heights with torn and badly worn oil cloth," children so crowded on benches that their backs touched, no space between tables, no one to serve the meals, screens off the windows and flies on the food—what there was of it: one slice of bread per child and no variation in the diet of beans for supper and rice with meat gravy (mostly gravy) at noon. The baker, Richard Tafoya, told Nina that his allowance for flour had been cut, even though student enrollment had increased substantially.

"The kitchen was full of flies and the boiler leaking," she reported. The bakery in the basement of the dining room was "simply a hole in the ground, dark, full of flies and cockroaches, no screens in the windows, panes of glass broken and rags stuffed in to keep out either the air or flies, or perhaps both." The storeroom for the bread had only one small light bulb, and there were cockroaches "even in the locked pantry where the fresh bread is placed to let dry out for two or three days before it is served." To balance her generally negative report, Nina wrote that "the baker himself seemed nice and clean and anxious to call attention to the difficulties under which he worked . . . and the oven is in good condition."[39]

At Nina's insistence, the school's superintendent made as many improvements as possible given his meager budget. She then urged the Honorable Charles Burke in Washington to make a thorough investigation himself into the deplorable conditions of one of the largest Indian schools in the country.

"The vigorous use of flyswatters" by a special detail of one hundred or more boys and girls was Superintendent De Huff's first simplistic solution to the fly "nuisance." But he later implemented all of Nina's recommendations, screening the bakery and dining room, providing sanitary towel disposal boxes with slots, training pupils as

Nina Otero-Warren, ca. 1929.
(Bergere Family Collection, photo
no. 21703, New Mexico State
Records Center and Archives,
Santa Fe, New Mexico.)

waiters and monitors, and burning contaminated mattresses and substituting army cots.[40]

Nina soon gained respect in Santa Fe and around the country as an authority on American Indian affairs, speaking frequently on the subject at home and in neighboring states. In the 1920s the Bureau of Indian Affairs and patronizing Anglos perceived American Indians as "stereotypes—savages, children, wards—inferior to civilized peoples," with no knowledge of what was good for them and "utterly devoid of the wisdom or ability to plan and manage their own affairs."[41] Nina's first-hand contacts in the schools and pueblos had proven to her that Native Americans were, instead, competent, intelligent human beings who could and should run their own lives.

She offered some basic solutions to what was generally referred to as "Indian problems." To "save the Red Race," she emphasized the importance of educating the mothers and creating better conditions in the pueblo homes. "Few Indian mothers have any idea of modern methods of hygiene or know any of the scientific ways of caring for their babies. We must teach them what we have learned."[42] One result of her crusade for better hygiene in the pueblos was the creation in 1923 of a "Best Baby" category at the Indian Fair. Not just a cute Indian baby contest, it was an attempt to generate more interest in health care throughout the Indian communities and give doctors an opportunity to examine the youngest children for possibly fatal diseases.[43]

Nina also pointed out the defects in the federal system of educating the Indian, a system that "alienates him from his home ties and creates a breach between the older and younger generations":

The Indian child trained in modern schools has little in common with his parents when he finishes. He must be taught to appreciate the history and traditions of his own race and thus inspired to continue the native arts of his own people as well as acquire a new type of learning. When he finishes school he should feel closer to his own people and desire to help them. Leaders and teachers should be developed from their own race.

Another need is to create markets for the products of the Indian—for his baskets, pottery, rugs and ornaments. . . . And finally we must teach the Indian to become self-supporting and ready and anxious to assume the responsibilities of citizenship as soon as he can.[44]

Nina's criticism of the then-current boarding-house educational system for Indians undoubtedly irritated Commissioner Burke. She found it necessary to defend the Indian Bureau in a diplomatic speech reported in the Los Angeles Daily News on June 6, 1924, when "she stressed the importance of withholding criticism of the bureau of investigation until each phase of the situation [the bureau's policies] is understood." The reporter went on to say that "Mrs. Warren is enthusiastically interested in her work, and one feels that the government has placed a dynamic force behind its Indian affairs in the west."[45]

Nevertheless, just as pro-Indian activist Stella Atwood had been driven out of office because of the bureau's objection to her vigorous denunciation of its educational programs, so was Nina. Her job as inspector was terminated after two years. During that brief time, however, she had helped considerably in the battle for reform that gained momentum in the late twenties, when Burke resigned from office and both Democratic and Republican parties pledged to correct government abuses.[46]

Torn between her commitment to the goals of the Indian bureau as one its five inspectors and her own doubts about the wisdom of its policies, Nina was relieved to be out of a political position that was causing so much controversy. But she remained a champion of the Indian. Beginning in the early twenties and throughout the rest of her life she associated with, influenced, and was influenced by people who fiercely defended the lifestyles of the Indians and fought to defeat congressional bills that would have further depleted their landholdings, destroyed their religious ceremonies, and educated them by force. She passed along to her literary friends her somewhat biased beliefs about early Spain's legacy to the Indians—full rights of citizenship, land grants, autonomy, and religious freedom. She, like her friend Charles Lummis, believed that "Spain's was the most comprehensive, humane, and effective 'Indian policy' ever framed."[47]

Lummis's *The Land of Poco Tiempo,* a book that, when it first appeared in 1884, not only defended Spanish rule in the New World but captured the beauty and drama of the Southwest, did much to attract the first tourists to New Mexico. The once-popular perception of Spaniards as innately cruel and depraved people (the "Black Legend") was dismissed as a myth. According to former secretary of the interior Stewart L. Udall, such negative perceptions can be credited to the Protestant Reformation, which evoked hatred toward all Roman Catholic Spanish people, and to Richard Hakluyt, an early seventeenth-century British geographer—"a resourceful propagandist—

who glorified English accomplishments and virtually ignored Spain's great epoch of discovery.[48]

Historian David Weber has pointed out that since the time of Spain's earliest explorations in the New World, there have been many contradictory viewpoints and historical reconstructions—"all of them valid, even if not of equal merit." Accounts range from the Hispanophobic writings of the late eighteenth and early nineteenth centuries to the pro-Spanish, often sentimentalized histories of the late nineteenth through much of the twentieth century. "Like all historical terrain," Weber writes, "the Spanish frontier seems destined to remain contested ground, transformed repeatedly in the historical imaginations of succeeding generations."[49]

The rich history and traditions of the Spanish-Americans and Southwestern Indians were ardently admired by Santa Fe's artists and writers, who, by 1925, had come in large numbers from all over the country. Most had settled in Santa Fe as either permanent or part-time residents, much to Nina's delight, for their presence not only enriched her life but the city's as well. Carlos Vierra, one of the art colony's early founders and the man principally responsible for the revival of the Santa Fe style of architecture still popular today, came in 1904 seeking a cure for his tuberculosis. He was followed three years later by Kenneth Chapman, whose articles in national art magazines and the Museum of New Mexico's *El Palacio* popularized Santa Fe as an artistic haven.[50]

For creative people with modest incomes, Santa Fe was a quiet, soul-enriching place where one could be productive and live comfortably for ten dollars a month in a two- or three-room adobe house.[51] For independently wealthy Witter Bynner, a Harvard-educated Phi Beta Kappa, Santa Fe was a city of warm, caring people who were tolerant of his homosexuality and appreciative of his literary talent and—more importantly—his gifts of loyal friendship and social leadership. For all, Santa Fe was their newly discovered aesthetic center, the heart of the seductive, inspirational beauty of northern

New Mexico, a unique city they felt had to be protected from materialistic urban-industrial blight.

Forty years after he arrived in Santa Fe, Witter Bynner wrote that Nina and her sisters and the William Penhallow Hendersons were his "first Santa Fe families," Nina being his "special tie" to the Bergeres in the Big House where he was invited weekly for tea, cocktails, dinners, and pleasant evenings of animated conversation and bridge.[52]

Beginning in 1925, Alice Corbin Henderson and her husband opened their home on Camino del Monte Sol to writers looking for a receptive peer group with whom they could discuss their works in progress and obtain unbiased criticism and much-needed encouragement. Alice's literary evenings, soon called the Poets' Roundup, became the primary social event of the week, featuring such accomplished writers as Haniel Long, Oliver La Farge, Willa Cather, John Gould Fletcher, and Mary Austin. Most went on to establish themselves nationally by promoting the Southwest through literature that would in time become classic. The intimate congregations of "mud-hut nuts," as Witter Bynner called them, typically came together for

> tea, coffee, cigarettes, white mule, and talk, talk, talk. . . . What a sudden warmth we whipped together—Lorenzo and Frieda, Mabel and Tony Luján, Alice Corbin, Willy Henderson and Little Alice, Spud and I. Mabel and Tony left early; but the rest of us talked by the fireplace into the snuggest of the small hours, all of us bobbing at Alice as children bob at apples on Hallowe'en. [53]

While the Henderson's gatherings could be boisterous, uninhibited affairs that lasted long into the night, the art colonists did not live the reckless bohemian life. They were, in fact, solid citizens with generally stable families, dedicated to the preservation and betterment of their beloved Santa Fe.[54] This commitment to community was reinforced when Mary Austin appeared on the scene in 1924 and began, at the age of fifty-six, to direct her considerable energies

Nina Otero-Warren in the front
yard of La Casa Grande dressed for
the Santa Fe fiesta, ca. 1924.
(Bergere Family Collection, photo
no. 21718, New Mexico State
Records Center and Archives,
Santa Fe, New Mexico.)

toward saving the city and the enchanting land surrounding it from
modern-age mayhem. Nina moved easily among the newly arrived
literati, entertaining them in the Big House or in rented halls on special occasions. Her celebrations of birthdays and Santa Fe Fiesta Eves
became legendary.

The involvement of Nina and her gifted friends in the 1924 Fiesta de Santa Fe set high standards for future celebrations and attracted national attention. The three days of "magnificent" merrymaking
began on September 1 and were heralded in El Palacio as "an unusual,
if not unprecedented piece of community work" under the expert
direction of Dr. Edgar L. Hewett. An annual event that traced its formal beginnings back to 1712, twenty years after Diego de Vargas's
reconquest of Santa Fe, the fiesta celebrated the history, life, and cul-

ture of the Southwest under Indian, Spanish, Mexican, and American rule.[55]

Nina was on El Pasatiempo (amusement) Committee—one of the "Pasatiempolice"—along with Witter Bynner, Dolly (Mrs. John) Sloan, José Sena, Willard Johnson, and Florence (Mrs. Randall) Davey, all of whom worked long hours to stage colorful, irreverent tableaus and burlesques—a "hysterical parade" that poked fun at local dignitaries and relieved the seriousness of the other events.[56] El Pasatiempo pageant appealed most to resident Santa Feans, but the extraordinary number of visitors to the city that year (three new hotels were full and fiesta guests were housed in private homes and St. Michael's College dormitories) preferred the Indian ceremonies and crafts. Indeed, the 1924 fiesta marked a turning point for the Indians, as the Indian Fair that year attracted a record number of tourists. María Martínez of San Ildefonso Pueblo, whose work today is found in the most prestigious museums and private collections, won a $5 first-place award for her splendid pottery, and more than $2,000 worth of baskets, rugs, and jewelry was sold.[57]

Nina enjoyed the parties and parades and stimulating exchanges with her newfound friends, but she was by nature more pragmatic than artistic, and the practical, civic-minded attitude of the group especially appealed to her. As Arell Morgan Gibson wrote sixty years after the art colony peaked in the mid-1920s, the creative community "demonstrated to a desensitized society the worth of this scorned land and, by developing an ever broadening public interest, even infatuation with it. They were, in part, responsible for the Southwest's maturation and eventual acceptance as a coequal region of the nation."[58]

Toward the end of the decade, with the advocacy and promotion of this special group of citizens, Santa Fe matured and prospered. The city's population swelled to twelve thousand people, a vital, cooperative mixture of artists, bankers, writers, ranchers, poets, and tradespeople. Even the city's fire department was made up of lawyers, insurance brokers, electricians, merchants and mechanics, an engineer and a doctor, some of them graduates of Yale and Harvard—an unpaid team that responded to emergencies simply because they saw the need and wanted to help.[59]

For the creative people, it was a time of enormous productivity and "mutual stimulation."[60] Alice Corbin Henderson had added to her list of published books The New Poetry anthology (1917), which she coedited with Harriet Monroe; Red Earth (1920), her own poetry collection; and The Turquoise Trail (1928), an anthology of the work of Southwestern poets. Brothers of Light: The Penitentes of the Southwest, her first prose piece, was in process. Her husband had produced critically acclaimed paintings and murals and had established his Pueblo-Spanish Building Company (1926), where he employed local craftsmen to build the beautiful furniture he himself designed. William Penhallow Henderson had also remodeled and restored public buildings all over town, including the Santa Fe Railroad Ticket Office, the White sisters' El Delirio (now the School of American Research), and Sena Plaza, which under his direction acquired a second story. The Hendersons, along with Gustave Baumann, Martha White, and Margaret McKittrick, founded the New Mexico Association on Indian Affairs, providing a much needed forum for American Indian artists, the best of whom were rewarded with cash prizes for their work.[61]

Like the Hendersons, Witter Bynner espoused worthy causes and helped turn Alice's weekly Poets' Roundup into an annual fundraising event for the New Mexico Association on Indian Affairs. His close friendship with Nina and her family heightened his awareness of Hispanic art and culture, which he began to promote vigorously. Poetry being his first priority as a writer, he supported struggling Southwestern poets by offering an annual prize of $150 for their best efforts.

Bynner had received recognition nationally as a poet and lecturer (advancing the Spectric verse theory over Imagism) before he came to Santa Fe to stay in 1921, but he was best known for The Jade Mountain, his brilliant translation of Chinese poetry. In 1922 his home became the overnight quarters for Frieda and D. H. Lawrence, who

Witter Bynner, self-portrait, 1945. Poet and community leader in Santa Fe, Bynner was a longtime friend of the Bergere family. (Farrar Collection, Photo no. 36633, New Mexico State Records Center and Archives, Santa Fe, New Mexico.)

had arrived with Mabel Dodge and Tony Luján, all on their way to Mabel's ranch in Taos. A year later Bynner accompanied the Lawrences to Mexico, the memorable trip recorded in *Journey with Genius* (1951). In the late twenties the versatile author worked with artist-actor Frank Applegate and the city's theater group to produce his own *Cake: An Indulgence*, a satirical verse play that had been banned in New York for its explicit dialogue.[62] Bynner produced a total of twenty books before and after his arrival in Santa Fe, some under the pen name of Emanuel Morgan.

For all his literary accomplishments, Witter Bynner was best known as the "premier host of Santa Fe," whose "vitality, strong personality, personal charm and natural leadership provided the social cement that held the Santa Fe colony, in all its disparate elements, together and converted it into a functioning community for promoting creative activity and the quality of life."[63] Witter Bynner and Alice Corbin Henderson shared the social leadership role in the colony. Her literary evenings and his afternoon "teas," Prohibition-era cocktail parties, topped everyone's list of priority social affairs.

The city's artists and writers could "put a party together between morning and evening," said Alice Henderson Rossin, and her mother and father were the main organizers. Visiting poets came repeatedly to the Henderson home—"this was a place where people wanted to be," she said. Vachel Lindsay would come up the *camino* joyfully shouting "This is so wonderful—this is so beautiful!" Carl Sandburg "sang his poetry," and Robert Frost delighted everyone with his sense of humor. At that time, Witter Bynner recalled, "Manuel Chávez was here, but not yet called Fray Angélico. Mabel Sterne was in Taos but not yet known for her memoirs. Erna Fergusson was in Albuquerque but was conducting tourists to the Indian country, not yet a courier in print. Ruth Laughlin's pen was not yet notably busy."[64]

Nina took in as many of the parties as she could, given her busy schedule, and she usually arrived alone. Quiet Mamie had never learned the art of small talk and tried to avoid loud crowds as much as possible. Nina fit well into the group. She had little trouble initiating conversations with almost anyone she encountered. She had an instinctive sense that drew her toward those who were her intellectual equals, and she made sure they noticed and remembered her.

As she listened to the writers rhapsodize about the splendors of the land that had been home to her for more than forty years, Nina saw northern New Mexico in a new light—through creative prose and poetry that reinforced her own appreciation of the region's rare beauty. That her gifted friends had found a rewarding environment and way of life was evident in the words that poured forth in their work. Witter Bynner's close friend Paul Horgan had written: "Every day at Santa Fe seems like a beginning, so fresh the strike of breath in that air, so clear the endowment of sight in that light."[65]

Peggy Pond Church wrote of the surrounding mountains: "a

silent beauty / Of wine-dark shadows shed on purple hills," and of Santa Fe: "in no other city could we find / Fruit trees by almost every blue-silled door; / Nor any other place where stars may shine / Serene undimmed above the lighted streets."[66] Haniel Long followed with "But a garden which is always in bloom / lies about the towns and between them, / a garden of cloud and mountain. / From the horizon, petaled with color, / the colossal flowers rise."

For Mary Austin, it was the "form and color and infinite variety of the landscape," together with the enriching social and cultural milieu, that brought her to Santa Fe to stay for the remaining ten years of her life. From her rented Casa Querida on Camino del Monte Sol, she held court and worked for the betterment of the ancient city. Mary Austin, like Nina, was a strong, opinionated woman living in an age when women were not supposed to have opinions. But even Nina was taken aback at times by Mary's air of infallibility and her arrogant, self-absorbed nature. She had developed a reputation as a woman who knew it all and who rarely listened to anyone, but on the several trips she took with Nina to the Río Abajo region, she obviously listened to Otero-Warren's account of her Spanish ancestors and her childhood memories of life on the hacienda at Los Lunas. In one of her classic books about the Southwest, The Land of Journey's Ending (1924), Mary Austin described the grand wedding linking the Lunas and Oteros,

> rich and powerful families with estates divided by the Río Grande about where the present towns of Los Lunas and Tomé now stand. You hear of the beauty of the bride of fifteen, of the trousseau made in Philadelphia and freighted across the plains, of the wagon-loads of provisions for the wedding festival . . . how wandering players drifted up the Río Grande [singling] out the handsomest woman . . . for their carefully prepared compliments . . . of Eloisa Luna Otero, who was, and remained, not only the most beautiful of the señoras y señoritas of the player's song, but, until her death, the most powerful lady of New Mexico.[67]

Both Mary Austin and Nina were feminist-activists during the woman suffrage campaign, both worked for the improvement of the educational system in New Mexico, promoting courses in the Spanish language in public schools, and both were devotëd to Indian welfare and to the restoration of Indian arts and culture. Nina, Gerald and Ina Sizer Cassidy, the Hendersons, Witter Bynner, and others followed Mary's lead in forming the Spanish Colonial Arts Society to advance the renaissance of Hispanic culture in northern New Mexico. In 1930, Mary Austin announced that "the Spanish-speaking group here is emerging after a long foggy period of Americanization with something of the force and freshness which we discover in Mexico since the Revolution."[68]

Nina must record her memories of her early life in a book, Mary Austin insisted. The Americanization of New Mexico must not bury the precious heritage of the Spanish colonials. When and where she would write it was up to Nina. Find a quiet place, better that it be away from town, take a sabbatical from her busy schedule and begin—that was Mary's advice. And Nina took it.

CHAPTER FIVE

Las
Dos

Mary Austin and Nina worked together for ten years until Mary's death on August 13, 1934, both gathering material for articles and books about the Southwest. While Mary wrote eight books during that period, Nina had yet to start hers, since half of that time was taken up with her county school duties. But as 1929 drew to a close, the Great Depression and a devastating drought throughout the Southwest dealt severe blows to the national and regional economies. Like hundreds of thousands of men and women across the country, Nina found herself without a job, but only because she chose not to run again for public office.

She missed her close contacts with teachers and students, and the income, modest as it was. Still, after twelve years as superintendent she was ready for a change, and as a shrewd politician she sensed that change was in the wind for the Republicans. Winning election to the school post would become increasingly difficult.[1] Rather than campaigning for a thirteenth term and risking defeat, she and the family's male politicos encouraged Anita Bergere to take over, which she did most reluctantly, running in the 1930 election and winning over her Democratic opponent by more than fifteen hundred votes.[2]

A year later, however, with Democratic Governor Arthur Seligman in power and "progressive" Republican Senator Bronson Cutting throwing his support to liberal Democrats in Washington, Anita's conservative, old-guard Republican base of support eroded. That year Franklin Delano Roosevelt led the Democrats to victory, and one of them, Manuel Luján, Sr., defeated Anita.[3] Losing the election was no great disappointment for her, since she was never comfortable in the public role she had been pushed into by her family. She simply wanted to please Nina and felt duty-bound to try to help the Republicans cling to some vestige of power in Santa Fe.[4]

Although Nina's role as an elected educator ended as the thirties began, she left behind a solid platform on which those who followed her could build a better system for public schools across the entire state of New Mexico. She, Mary Austin, and Witter Bynner had worked fiercely for innovative public school curricula, focusing on ways to improve the instruction of the Spanish language in the state's schools. The colorful linguistics and literature of the Spanish-speaking people were being smothered by the Anglo-dominated school system, Mary Austin contended. "Once Spanish speaking New Mexico produced interesting and vital literature of its own," she said. "Public speaking was an art and the common people composed songs and poems of genuine literary merit. But in the struggle to acquire an English vocabulary, this literary expressiveness has been completely lost," not only in English but in Spanish as well.[5]

Encouraged by Mary Austin, Nina wrote a proposal shortly after she left office, outlining the needs of Spanish-American schoolchildren and recommending programs that would enhance their education. Hoping to receive a grant from either the Laura Spellman Rockefeller Foundation or the General Educational Fund, Nina wrote to a Dr. Hermon M. Bumpus in Duxbury, Massachusetts, asking for his "criticism" and for his recommendations as to the "proper group for presentation." Mamie typed the long cover letter and the carefully detailed course of study Nina had tested in Santa Fe County schools. In the proposal she pointed out that older groups of Hispanics, those "with latent knowledge of the cultural background of the native arts and industries," should be interviewed and their knowledge recorded and incorporated into the general American educational system.

"These hidden resources are rapidly being lost," she warned: "the standardized methods adopted from the English-speaking schools to a large extent have discouraged and subordinated every semblance of Spanish culture in the educational life of the Spanish-speaking native people."[6] Her efforts apparently met with success, because she wrote five years later that her "comprehensive study of the life of the people, their needs, their mental attitudes," was adopted by the state superintendent of public instruction for general use in New Mexico schools.

Thanks to the trust fund her mother had established before her death in 1914, the income from the Otero's N-Bar Ranch southwest of Albuquerque, and the salary earned by her stepfather (Alfred M. Bergere was still serving as register of the U.S. Land Office), there was enough money without Nina's income for the permanent residents in the Big House—only four in 1930—to live comfortably. Young Joe had left after his marriage to Sue Catron, and only Alfred, Nina, Anita, and Teta remained.

The uniting of the Bergere and Catron families is interesting considering the animosity that existed at the turn of the century between Miguel Otero and Tom Catron, arch rivals for high political office. For Catron, Otero was an incompetent governor, "extravagant, impure, oppressive, and tyrannical"; for Otero, Catron was a bully, "very greedy for office and power."[7] Obviously, enough time had elapsed to heal the Otero-Catron feud. Joseph Charles and Suzanne Catron Bergere were married for twenty-seven years before Joe's death in 1957.

Even though most of Alfred Bergere's children had married and left home, La Casa Grande on Grant Avenue continued to be one of Santa Fe's main party centers. Nina had discovered early in her political life the importance of social contacts—"networking" in today's terms—especially in Santa Fe where dinners, lunches, and Prohibition "tea" parties were the small city's principal forms of entertainment. Her Fiesta Eve celebration in 1930 brought everyone together—relatives, local politicians, writers, and assorted friends—before the ritual burning of Zozobra (Old Man Gloom). Four years earlier, her good friend Will Shuster had created Zozobra, a comic-grotesque papier-mâché effigy of all the year's sadness and misfortunes, which was torched after dark to the cheers of happy and usually very drunk spectators.

The afternoon before her party, a regal "doña Nina" dressed in a nineteenth-century Spanish costume was smiling and waving from a flower-decked float featuring Las Bellas Fiestas de Santa Fe Antigua. That evening she hosted a gala at the "Hacienda Bergere," serving her guests margaritas and an authentic Spanish buffet dinner of tortillas and posole, tacos, guacamole, and carne adovado. She had sent out the invitations in Spanish: "Que siga la Fiesta! Vengan con alegría y coman con tortilla" (On with the Fiesta! Come with happiness and eat tortillas). All came joyfully and left reluctantly, some in the wee hours.[8]

Still, the life of a socialite did not long satisfy Otero-Warren. She needed to be occupied and challenged, but with the depression deepening and unemployment rising, she had time on her hands for the first time in twenty-five years. This slowdown in her once full and hectic schedule gave her an opportunity to collect her thoughts and seriously consider writing a book. She began to look around for a quiet, affordable place away from the city.

The best bargain in New Mexico at the time was land. In and around Santa Fe it was cheap and, in the case of homestead land, virtually free if one had the pioneering stamina to live on it for three to five years and make certain government-mandated improvements. Before the depression, Santa Fe land and property had been steadily appreciating in value because of the influx of tourists, many of whom decided to stay on permanently. Nina believed that the trend would continue once the economy stabilized and that an investment

in real estate would one day benefit her family just as the landholdings of her ancestors had sustained many generations of Lunas and
Oteros.

Her friends Will and Helen Shuster and Jozef and Teresa Bakoz
had already filed for homestead land, each couple choosing a 160-
acre tract off what is now Tano Road. John and Dolly Sloan also
joined the homestead movement, acquiring property adjacent to the
Bakozes and the Shusters and calling it Sin Agua—Without Water.[9]

Nina had been reading Will Shuster's columns in the *New Mexican*
describing his experiences at "Crazy Bear Ranch." During the depression he kept Santa Feans well informed of the joys and hardships of
family living in the piñon wilderness. He boasted once of making do
with one canteen full of water: "I have . . . made a cup of coffee,
brushed my teeth, shaved, bathed and washed out socks in the bath
water. I might have watered the geraniums if I had them. If you ever
try this, be careful you don't reverse the order. It would be tough on
the coffee."[10]

In addition to his breezy columns, Shuster's parties at Crazy
Bear attracted most of his art-colony friends at one time or another,
guided there by an all-purpose printed invitation which included a
rough map, drawn in typical Shusteresque style with comic sketches
of coyotes and cactus fields, Tesuque Indians and "unemployed
artists." The wrap-around message read:

> THE SHUSTERS at the Crazy Bear Ranch in New Mexico—where
> they raise dogs—jack rabbits—Cacti—piñons—geraniums—
> juniper berries—coyotes—wild kittys—somebodys horses sheep
> and cows—genuine hand painted pictures—etchings and a
> goodly measure of hell—send you from this menage—best
> wishes—and a lusty hope that when this new year hatches out
> that y'all will find it one of the healthiest and happiest you have
> ever experienced—Will— Helen and Don. Also Happy Easter
> and a Jolly Fourth of July.[11]

The hell-raising parties Will and Helen Shuster were noted for
in the city moved to the juniper- and piñon-studded hills in the

country. From what they heard through the Shusters and saw for themselves on the rustic ranch when they attended those affairs, Nina and Mamie learned about homesteading necessities such as cisterns for water catchment and conservation, road maintenance, protection from predators, and, for two small women unused to pioneer living, strong men to handle the heavy work. They also saw the pristine land through the eyes of the artists and felt an added appreciation for the rolling hills and tranquil meadows surrounded by the Jemez and Sangre de Cristo mountain ranges. Nina wrote:

> A glance around showed this a rolling country, with huge mountains for a background. Cedars and piñons tortured by the wind were twisted, bent, knotted and dwarfed. The arroyos had cut through the ground and though they seemed innocent enough were greatly to be feared in the event of a storm, for they were capable of felling trees and rolling boulders as easily as children roll marbles in the spring of each year. . . . So it is with my country . . . beautiful beyond words, but it needs to be watched lest it bruise those not acquainted with its moods."[12]

Here was a place of welcome solitude where Nina could write and have Mamie close by for companionship and support.

As register, Alfred Bergere had access to all the land records in the state, and when he learned of Nina's intentions he found two sections (1,257 acres) still available for homesteading only twelve miles northwest of the city. On March 17, 1930, Nina and Mamie paid fees and commissions to the U.S. Land Office ($34 from Nina, $33.40 from Mamie) and made a homestead application for land which was at that time just north of the "Chili Line," the Denver and Rio Grande Western Railroad's narrow-gauge track running from Santa Fe to Buckman Station on the Río Grande, then north toward Taos. Almost a year later, on February 6, 1931, their application was "allowed" by the Department of the Interior.[13]

They signed an agreement to spend an average of five months a year in residence for four years, and proposed a tentative schedule: from July 10 to November 23, 1931; from April 22, 1932, to Janu-

Mamie Meadors and her Chevrolet, Las Dos, ca. 1932. (Bergere Family Collection, photo no. 23286, New Mexico State Records Center and Archives, Santa Fe, New Mexico.)

ary 16, 1933; from April 1 to November 1, 1933; and from April 1 to November 10, 1934. In addition, they agreed to improve the land by building two houses and a garage, fencing the acreage, installing a surface tank to collect rainwater, preparing an area for cultivation of a bean crop, maintaining the road, developing a natural water catchment basin for wildlife (Lagunita Park), and planting vegetation to control soil erosion.[14]

They wasted no time getting started. In June 1931, soon after the weather moderated, they signed a contract with builders Joaquín Wheeler and Lee Frampton to erect two single-room adobe houses, each with a sleeping porch, on a hill overlooking the Sangre de Cristos on the east and the Jemez range on the west. The foundations for the little houses were to be of rock bound with cement, the rooms were to have two doors and three windows, and the inside of each house was to be plastered with adobe. The two laborers were

Nina Otero-Warren's Las Dos homestead, where she began writing her book, Old Spain in Our Southwest. (Photograph by Charles DeBus, 1992.)

paid one cent per adobe brick and given an advance of $400, but when the final bills were paid three months later the total cost for construction came to $925.86 (Nina paid $492.28, Mamie $433.58). Porches, a *fogón* (a beehive-shaped fireplace) in Nina's room, French doors and locks, the digging of holes for toilets, screen wire for the seats, and additional lumber and labor ran up the cost. When it was finished, they called it Las Dos Ranch.[15]

Las Dos was the name Nina and Mamie had acquired in Santa Fe, given to them by Hispanic friends and business associates who saw them as a devoted twosome, always together in their trips around town and to the outlying county schools. The two women had developed a close friendship based on mutual support and affection, and together they had created an environment in which they

Mamie Meadors's *Las Dos* homestead, site of most family picnics since the 1930s.
(Photograph by Charles DeBus, 1992.)

could live and work independently. Their sustaining and secure relationship became the basis of a productive partnership that lasted for
more than thirty years. With Nina, Mamie felt loved and accepted
even though she had little status or power. And Nina knew she could
rely on Mamie for loyalty and devotion, for companionship without
confrontation. Mamie particularly liked being away from the political
and social realities of the city and felt flattered that colorful Nina had
chosen her as fellow homesteader and helpmate.

Both women were in high spirits when they moved into their
new ranch houses in the spring of 1932. Mamie's old Chevy was
packed to capacity—with kegs of water, kerosene for lamps, a shotgun, shovels, food, liquor, clothing, and bedding for the first five
months they planned to spend at Las Dos. Traveling slowly over rut-

Bedroom with fireplace in Nina's house. (Photograph by author, 1992.)

ted trails that passed for roads, negotiating a total of eleven arroyos along the way, many full of sand or water or both, it took them more than an hour from town to reach the homestead.

Jorge Roybal, the handyman who had agreed to work for them and live on the premises as caretaker most of the year for a monthly wage of $20, followed them on horseback, pulling a wagon full of building materials for a corral, tar for the roofs, screens for the windows, and what tools he needed to repair the one-room frame house moved out from Santa Fe by Wilson Transfer & Storage Company to be used for a storeroom. Two years later, Nina paid $147.41 for the construction of Roybal's own one-room adobe house just down the hill from hers.[16]

While Nina and Mamie had separate houses, the nearness of their living quarters and the isolation both felt because of the distance from Santa Fe and the life they had known there forced them to rely on each other even more closely than before. There were no im-

Dining area with door leading to small bedroom in Mamie's house. (Photograph by Charles DeBus, 1992.)

mediate neighbors to call on in emergencies, only Jorge, and the long trip to town had to be made every week or so to replenish supplies. Nevertheless, the two worked out an arrangement based on equality, reciprocity, and trust, which helped to make their homesteading a joyful experience despite its many challenges. Both women had the inner resources to sustain themselves through long solitary days and nights. Because there was no indoor plumbing, water had to be rationed carefully, particularly if no rain collected in the cistern. Personal hygiene was sporadic at best. Cooking was done on a wood-burning stove indoors, or outside on an open grill, weather permitting. And the weather could be violent, especially in July and August when monsoonlike rain and hailstorms marched across from the mountain ranges to flood the roads and arroyos.

Kitchen with wood-burning stove in Mamie's house. (Photograph by Charles DeBus, 1992.)

For the most part, the days and nights at Las Dos were cool and tranquil, and while many of Nina's friends in town were astonished to see how uncharacteristically reclusive she had become, she remained happy and productive during the months spent in retreat. She took advantage of those quiet days to begin work on her book, and Mamie busied herself about and around the houses, content simply to be with Nina and away from her routine existence in the city. Most of the details of running the place—the baking, preparation of meals, housecleaning, and gardening—were left to Mamie, although Nina did like to chop wood, Eloisa Brown remembered.[17]

During their first four years in residence, from 1932 through 1935, they made substantial improvements. With Jorge's help they maintained the road, fenced in their acreage, added a stable, cultivated a corn and bean crop (with the cooperation of their Tesuque Indi-

The portal of Mamie's house, facing east toward the Sangre de Cristo Mountains. (Photograph by Charles DeBus, 1992.)

an neighbors), and worked with the Civilian Conservation Corps and the U.S. Geological Survey on studies for long-range control of soil erosion.

Growing anything on the semiarid acreage required strong faith—mainly that there would be enough rain for the crops—and backbreaking work. Nina and Mamie spent $300 drilling for water, without success. Their drilling equipment could not break through to the aquifer 750-plus feet below, so they devised a water-catchment basin, connected it to the house gutters, and collected runoff from the infrequent rain storms.

Henry B. Meadors, Mamie's nephew, remembered that Nina made a deal with the Tesuque Indians, whose lands lay just over the ridge from Las Dos, to plant corn and beans for her. In planting the corn, the men would plow and the boys would follow behind, spitting seeds into the furrows. At harvest time they would pull the beans up "stalks and all." To the family's surprise and delight, The Las Dos bolita beans won first prize ($2) at the 1933 Fiesta de Santa Fe.[18]

While all was going as planned on the homestead, tragedy struck in town when John Joseph Kenney, husband of May Bergere, then nine months pregnant, and father of three teenage children, died on November 25, 1934, at the age of forty-four. At the time of his death John Kenney was district attorney for the First Judicial District of New Mexico, a well-respected member of the legal profession, "a grand party-goer," and an avid outdoorsman. He had been stricken with what in the early thirties was called "galloping pneumonia" after returning from a weekend of duck hunting. His daughter-in-law, Joey Kenney, recalled the frantic efforts to save him: "Dr. Robert O. Brown, Rosina's husband, was the doctor on the case. Since the only available oxygen tent at St. Vincent Hospital had a premature baby under it, Dr. Brown had Frank Mendenhall and sixteen-year-old Jack Kenney fashion a homemade oxygen tent, using as a guide a picture of one in a professional journal. Uncle Frank chartered a plane to fly in a supply of the sulfa drug, which had just been discovered but which was not available in Santa Fe at that time.

"Bad weather grounded the plane in Albuquerque until after dark. Since there were no floodlights at the Santa Fe airport, Herbert Mendenhall rallied friends with automobiles and asked them to assemble at the runway and turn on their headlights to help the pilot see to land.

"The response was overwhelming, the plane landed safely, and the drug was rushed to the hospital, but it was too late. Jack, Sr., died surrounded by his family, all kneeling by his bed and saying the rosary. When he was pronounced dead, May fainted and was put to bed. She couldn't even attend the funeral because she was nine months pregnant. She had the baby (Cristina) a week after Jack died."[19]

Jack's sudden death rocked the family. How could a grieving widow possibly cope with three teenagers and an infant when she had no income and no way of earning a living, even if employment could be found in the depression-plagued city? The answer came after a family conference that excluded May, when Nina, Anita, and A. M. Bergere decided to move the Kenney family out of their Palace Avenue home to the Big House, "a move that was at once wonderful and destructive," Joey said. There May would have Teta and Anita to help her with the baby, the older children would have careful supervision, and all would have a supportive family environment, a roof over their heads, and financial security. "Here was the house that grandmother had left lock, stock, and barrel for the widowed, the divorced, the whatever," and so far as Nina and the others were concerned, it was the perfect resolution.

For all their good intentions, the elders of La Casa Grande were accused later of ignoring May's desire to return to her own home where the presence of her husband was strong and where she felt her children would have better memories of him. Nina was overly protective of May and did not encourage her to talk about Jack, fearing that doing so would upset her. Jack Kenney, Sr., had never been a favorite of Nina's, and he had never cared for her either, saying once in exasperation, "What a formidable woman! For God's sake, can you imagine being married to that woman?"[20] May got along with Nina, Joey said, but "regretted that she never had a chance to make it on her own," although she did find a job several years later, first with the National Youth Association and then, when World War II recruiting began, for the draft board. But she lived in the Big House until she died in 1976.

The year following Jack Kenney's death was a better one. On September 6, 1935, President Franklin D. Roosevelt signed the homestead agreement for Las Dos, confirming that the claims of Nina and Mamie had been "established and fully consummated in conformity to law."[21] The land was theirs at last, and Las Dos Ranch became the favorite family getaway. May's sons, Bergere and Jack

Kenney, had vivid memories of picnics on weekends and school holidays and of "greenings" (collecting piñon and juniper branches) in early December before Christmas. The greens were used to decorate the house and were sent to various members of the family living in other cities and states. The late Bergere Kenney recalled that "Nina loved the homestead and shared it very generously with us and others. She always put on her denim skirt for trips to Las Dos, and there was a ritual that went with that country outing at Christmas. Once the greening was finished, Nina would bring out her beverage box, which included hot chocolate for the kids and straight bourbon for the adults. She would pour the whiskey from the flask into a little jigger, and we had to down a shot of straight bourbon, whether we wanted it or not."[22]

The year 1935 also marked the completion of Nina's book, *Old Spain in Our Southwest*, a writing project she began by jotting down memories of her hacienda days at Los Lunas some fifty years earlier. Although she had written a number of articles and book reviews, she was more a political activist than a writer and found the mechanics of organization, structure, and transitions frustrating. Her book is a compilation of memoirs, anecdotes, simplified historical accounts—"A Little History"—and folktales that, taken as a whole, form a charming picture of Hispanic lifestyles in the late nineteenth century.[23]

Curiously, her introductory essay focuses on a "wild and dismal" thunderstorm one night at Las Dos, a storm that made her feel strangely out of place. The wind "hissed like a rattler," thunder and lightning kept her awake for hours watching the quivering flame of one lone candle in her bedroom. At daybreak, with the storm spent, she heard a shepherd lamenting the loss of four little lambs to the wild forces in the night but still welcoming the new day. She saw a half-clad Indian offering his prayer to the rising sun, and she felt a "sense of loss that they were closer to nature" than she who shuddered at the wind and had so little understanding of the elements. "I

Frontispiece and title page from Old Spain in Our Southwest by Nina Otero. (By permission of Richard Herdman for the Estate of Nina Otero-Warren.)

alone," she wrote, "seemed not in complete tune with the instruments of God."[24]

As fearful as Nina was of the unpredictable weather at Las Dos, she treasured her time on the land around her little adobe house, where each day she looked out onto a garden of clouds, scenic ranges, and splendid sunsets—where she had "a feeling of vastness, of solitude, but never of loneliness." She resolved to stay until she had at least the beginnings of a manuscript that she and her literary friends in Santa Fe hoped would help Spanish Americans in New Mexico better understand their rich heritage.[25]

To bring an awareness of the Old World to the New, she began by writing down what she remembered of her mother's stories of the old days, when the first Spanish families in New Mexico, descendants of the conquistadores, lived in haciendas and attended mass in the small chapel where the patron saint of the patrón had a special niche above the altar. Even in church, class divisions were clear: there were chairs for the patrones; the peones knelt and sat on the floor. Servants kept the chapel plastered, the main house clean, the fields tilled, the children tended, the meals prepared, and the guests comfortable at dinner by wielding "huge fans of peacock feathers on long handles." For the benefit of her young nephews, who liked to joke about the early hacendados' slave labor, she wrote that the peones "were not slaves, but working people who preferred submission to the patrón rather than an independent chance alone."[26]

The patrón, she wrote, held court "like a grandee of New Spain. He followed the old customs every day, his home was his court, from his family he received a courtly attention, his servants were his vassals and gave him submission." The servants were "all proud of the masters they served." The peones' "lives were lived close to the soil and to nature. They cherished their traditions, inherited from Spain and adapted to their new life. Theirs was a part of the feudal age, when master and man, although separate in class, were bound together by mutual interests and a close community of human sympathy."[27]

Nina made a conscientious effort to present a balanced perspective of the rural life she knew as a child. But, like several other well-educated Hispanic women involved at the time in the revitalization of their heritage—Concha Ortíz y Pino, Carmen Espinoza, and Fabiola Cabeza de Baca Gilbert—Nina has been criticized for not personally identifying with the class of Spanish Americans she was patronizing in the 1930s. Indeed, many of her friends thought of her as more Anglo than Hispanic. The attitude of Hispanic women such as Nina toward Spanish Americans "not of the elite," Sarah Deutsch points out,

> was virtually indistinguishable from that of their Anglo counterparts. The participation of these women did not make the arts patrons' revival of 'dormant' arts and guidance of living ones indigenous or authentic. Both the Anglo and the Hispanic patrons stood, in large measure, outside the villages and their culture,

and both used the arts to render the villages closer to the romantic vision they wanted Hispanic culture to fulfill.[28]

Actually, Nina was a product of both Hispanic and Anglo cultures, and while she did enjoy upper-class status and moved confi-
dently in the Anglo world, she empathized with those less fortunate
than she and devoted much of her life to helping poor families improve their lot. She was in a unique position to do so because she
had the experience, the intelligence, the education, and particularly
the determination to inform the modern world of the richness and
breadth of Hispanic culture at all levels of society.

The first chapters of her book emphasize the hospitality, dignity,
and Old-World manners of the *patrones* by describing the expectations
and respect they had for each other and the sympathy and concern
they showed a *peón* family grieving over the loss of a loved one. In
chapters titled "An Old Spanish Hacienda," "Asking for the Bride,"
and "The Harvest," she writes in detail about daily living: for the *patrones*, a cup of chocolate in bed in the early morning, followed by a
large breakfast of dried and ground sprouted wheat cereal and hot
milk, fried eggs, pork and hominy, thin batter cakes, fresh or dried
fruit with coffee or more chocolate. "The servants' breakfast consist-
ed of beans, fried meat, chili and coffee with tortillas."[29]

The meal over, the *patrón*, don Antonio, would give the orders of
the day to the foreman and visit the fields and workshops. From
sunup to sundown laborers worked in the fields, "stopping frequently to converse, to doze after the noon meal, to smoke. There was no
need for hurry, since this occupation must continue *mañana*, and then
mañana—tomorrow and tomorrow." The Spanish doñas supervised
the household chores performed by the women servants. Conform-
ing to tradition, the doña of the hacienda "always sat with an air of
great dignity, as if holding Court."[30]

Both *patrones* and *peones* stopped work in the middle of the day to
take a siesta—the workers slept at their posts, the *patronas* "went to
bed as if it were night time," and the men stretched out on lounges

or large chairs. An hour or so later a *merienda* was served—a snack of assorted cakes and chocolate for the *patrones*, who spent the remainder of the day writing letters, calling on friends, walking, and reading. After supper, the men smoked and, for the most part, discussed local politics before retiring for the night.

The reader of *Old Spain* is informed in detail of the food, flowers, animals, folk art, songs, and stories of the early settlers. For weddings, saints' days, and feasts, there was a standard menu: "*caldo blanco*—clear soup; *pollo con arroz*—chicken with rice; *asados*—roast meat; *carne de olla*—boiled meat; *albóndigas con asafrán*—meat balls seasoned with an herb; such vegetables as the garden produced or, in winter, pumpkins, chili and whatever vegetables had been dried. . . . For desert, there was a milk custard called *natillas*, and *arroz con leche*, rice sweetened and cooked in milk. Coffee and chocolate were the beverages."[31]

Spanish-American women treated flowers "like persons" and knew that many, such as the black-eyed Susan and the osha (a wild celery plant), contained healing properties for stomach disorders. The root of the state's indigenous yucca plant was a source for mild soap and shampoo; the cactus, "a brilliant, vital and courageous plant," saved the lives of sheep, goats, and cattle in times of great drought. Water was "the miracle of the country . . . carefully guarded and saved."[32]

Of the ten folktales Nina selected for her book, two stand out: "Count La Cerda's Treasure," the story of a Brazilian gypsy leader's futile search in 1900 for buried gold in the Gran Quivira; and "The Bells of Santa Cruz," the story of young love and sacrifice during the molding of Castilian bells for New Mexico's second oldest Catholic mission. Both tales became popular material for anthologies over the years.

Nina completed the book to her satisfaction in 1935 and had no trouble finding a publisher. Harcourt, Brace and Company in New York published *Old Spain in Our Southwest*, by Nina Otero, illustrated by Aileen Nusbaum (Nina's cousin), in the spring of 1936 in a handsomely illustrated hardcover edition of 206 pages, with attractive endsheets in color, at a list price of $2. Reviews were generally excellent, as were sales (the book went into a third printing within a year of publication), for it was well timed and useful, particularly for young-adult readers in the predominantly Hispanic Southwest.

On April 5, 1936, Anne T. Eaton reviewed it for the *New York Times Book Review* under the heading "The New Books for Boys and Girls" and recommended it for readers twelve years and older. To illustrate the review, the *Times* selected Aileen Nusbaum's wood engraving for the chapter on animals—one of the fourteen "spirited illustrations" that enhanced the book's well-designed format.

Eaton described Nina Otero as "a poet at heart," and her book as a romantic, picturesque account of the New Mexican country she knew well and loved, written with "joy and sympathy."

> It has clearly been a labor of love to bring together in this volume folklore and legend, history and a contemporary life that has its roots so deep in the past. . . . To read it is like visiting the heart of a little known section, where our hosts make it possible for us to see the everyday life of those who live there, and by what they tell us of former times put us in sympathetic touch with today.

Eaton also commended the list of Spanish proper names and the glossary of Spanish words used in the text.[33]

The Santa Fe *New Mexican*'s review praised *Old Spain* as a "delightful picture of the gracious days of the patrones and peones in New Mexico" written by "a member of one of the oldest Spanish families," a knowledgeable author who has "the inherent Spanish gift of story-telling." The reviewer mentioned Nina's dedication of the book to her sisters, Anita, Estella, May, Consuelo, Dolores, Rosina, and Ysabel—"all familiar personalities to Santa Fe."[34]

The *New York Herald Tribune*'s reviewer, Eda Lou Walton, also praised *Old Spain* and its author: "[Nina Otero] loves her country and her people. She understands both. The book is simply written with a kind of child-like charm akin, in a way, to the very manners and modes described."[35]

Other reviewers were more critical, pointing out that the book lacked continuity, that Nina's history of the early days was "naive and sketchy," that there was no definite plan, and that the title was misleading. While Old Spain would never take the place of more conventional historical works on the Southwest, it did offer a

> charming and useful insight into the life of [Spanish-American] people, patient and proud and enduring, so like the land itself. Old Spain . . . takes for granted the wonder, the beauty and the cruelty of mountain and desert, flood and drought, cactus, sage brush and forest, accepting them as natural and inevitable without ever losing the consciousness of their timeless mystery and charm.[36]

In June 1936, more kudos came when Nina was given an honorary degree by her alma mater, Maryville College, for her "outstanding achievement since graduation."[37]

One of Nina's important contributions in writing Old Spain was providing a key source of information for all readers, but mostly for young adults, about life in rural nineteenth-century New Mexico. Such firsthand accounts were, and still are, extremely scarce. Still, she mentioned few of the rough and hard realities of living in that remote, semiarid part of the United States. Instead, she focused on romantic images and the Old-World charm and courtly customs of her forebears, and she made a conscious effort to present Hispanos in the best possible light. Proud of her Spanish heritage and an educator at heart, she saw the book as a teaching tool to educate the multicultural populations in the country and to gain approval, respect, and admiration for her people.

The book more than lived up to her expectations. Requests for permission to reprint selected chapters and passages from Old Spain—in anthologies, textbooks, and study guides for high school and college courses—were sent regularly to Nina throughout the remainder of her life and to her heirs after her death. The *WPA Guide to 1930s in New Mexico* recommended *Old Spain in Our Southwest* for its "general descriptive interest," along with books by Mary Austin, Ruth Laughlin Barker, Harvey Fergusson, and Alice Corbin Henderson.[38]

During the years Nina spent writing *Old Spain*, the depression had deepened, and although she received some money from royalties, she felt it imperative that she find other sources of income. The Lunas, Oteros, and Bergeres were families who had money "up and down—way up or way down," according to Luna Leopold, son of Estella and Aldo Leopold, and it was mostly down during the thirties. Nina's 1935 report to the Internal Revenue Service showed a net income of $5,360.47, which was audited two years later for a $28.98 "deficiency in tax" paid. Nina, though single, had claimed credit as head of a family, listing as dependents

> Elizabeth Doyle, former governess, 78 years old, incapable of self-support, living with taxpayer.
>
> A. M. Bergere, stepfather, 78 years old, incapable of self-support, living with taxpayer.
>
> Isabel Bergere, age 32, mentally incapable of earning her own living, staying in a sanatorium in St. Louis, and principal support contributed by taxpayer.
>
> Anita Bergere, half-sister, age 46, ill and residing with taxpayer. She has no independent means.[39]

Adding to Nina's financial problems was the death of her older brother, Eduardo Otero, who had been managing the N-Bar Ranch, a 640-acre sheep ranch that was the primary source of income for the Bergere family in the Big House. Nina and her brothers actually owned only 640 acres, but they controlled seventy times that number by having access to land for grazing, rights that Eduardo had obtained through the U.S. government's forestry service. Eduardo had been an enterprising businessman and had expanded the Luna sheep industry into Valencia, Socorro, and Catron counties. In the early

A picnic at the N-Bar Ranch, southeast of Albuquerque, ca. 1934. Left to right: Carl Leopold, Anita Bergere, Manuel Otero, Nina Otero-Warren, and Rosina Bergere. (Photograph courtesy of Carl Leopold.)

1900s he was known as the "largest single sheep operator in the United States."[40] His death at the age of fifty-two was a blow not only to his family but to the Republican party as well, which lost his leadership and Valencia County votes when FDR's Democrats came to power.

With Eduardo gone, Nina encouraged her younger brother, Manuel, to take over the sheep business and made a number of trips to the Gila area near the town of Mogollon, west of Silver City, to go over the ranch's financial ledgers with him. Like so many ranching operations in the thirties, the N-Bar was in need of more capital. Manuel and Nina decided to take out a loan to keep things going, money that was repaid "in record time—less than ten years" as a result of Manuel's good management.[41]

Nina had never invited A. M. Bergere, his children, or their progeny to participate in N-Bar Ranch decisions, since she felt the

Separating the ewes from the lambs. Vaqueros at work on the Otero-Luna N-Bar Ranch, n.d.
(Bergere Family Collection, photo no. 21768, New Mexico State Records Center and Archives,
Santa Fe, New Mexico.)

property came under the purview of the Luna-Otero family only.
From the time she was old enough to understand the consequences
of Alfred Bergere's losing his 1898 battle in the Supreme Court over
the Estancia Valley land grant, she distrusted her stepfather's judgment. According to some members of the family, she treated him
like a "second-rate cousin."[42]

By the end of his term as register of the U.S. Land Office in
1933, after twelve consecutive years in office, Alfred had made a
number of enemies. Three years before his retirement at the age of
seventy-seven, he had been reappointed by President Herbert
Hoover, who had not bothered to consult Senator Bronson Cutting.
The senator, a vacillating Republican, had been dissatisfied with A.
M. Bergere's tendency to bend the rules in favor of his friends and attempted to recall the nomination. The publisher of The Record sided
with Cutting, saying that "we do not feel a bit peeved if a register is
appointed who will abide by the law and letter regarding rules laid

Alfred Maurice Bergere (1858-1939). (Photograph by De Castro, courtesy of the Museum of New Mexico, negative no. 105409, Santa Fe, New Mexico.)

down by the department of the interior. Several stunts pulled off by Bergere don't 'set well' with us."[43]

The Record neglected to elaborate on Alfred's "stunts," and he continued in office another three years, much to the approval of most northern New Mexico citizens. The San Juan Review endorsed "Colonel Bergere," saying he had indeed "served efficiently" and had "earned his reappointment with a clean record and sterling character."[44]

Alfred Maurice Bergere died in 1939 at the age of 82, his last six years spent as a consultant for land policies. He had become an expert in Spanish, Mexican, and Pueblo Indian grants, and after his retirement from the land office had opened his own business. For all the rumors about his inadequacies as a businessman—"he sold all the ewes when he was a sheep rancher," Jack Kenney said[45]—"don

Alfredo" held respected positions all his life and was praised for his integrity and his political loyalties. As register, he was liberal and generous with people in need. Even so, the money taken in by his department far exceeded expenditures, by more than $400,000 at the end of his tenure. Judge David Chávez, Jr., onetime chief justice of the New Mexico Supreme Court, had high regard for his friend Alfred, saying he was "one of the finest men I have ever known."[46]

A staunch Republican all his life, Alfred had lived to see, and mourn, the split in his party during the 1930s when progressive-minded Bronson Cutting, a man he considered "more radical than FDR New Dealers," threw his support to the Democrats. And while he was as shocked as all New Mexicans when Cutting's life ended tragically in an airplane accident in 1935, he was relieved to have pro-Hispanic Dennis Chávez succeed Cutting in the Senate. Alfred Bergere also saw the repeal of the Prohibition amendment in 1933, and despite his antipathy toward the Democrats, he was impressed with the improvements in the city made possible with the help of the Works Progress Administration (renamed Work Projects Admin-istration—WPA—in 1939).

Alfred was a devoted family man, and in the autobiography he wrote several years before his death he praised his children for their loyalty to him and their mother: "None of them have ever given me a sorrow or a worry, and among themselves they are the most un-selfish brothers and sisters I have ever known. . . . No father ever loved his children better than I have loved mine." Michael Miller, chief of archival services in Santa Fe, eulogized Alfred in *Southwest Heritage* magazine, saying "the legacy of A. M. Bergere lives on. . . . He was a man of substance and a pioneer of great courage who made Santa Fe and the state of New Mexico a better place to live."[47]

After her stepfather's death, Nina's role as head of the family became official, and one of the first things she did was remove his portrait from the wall in the sun room and replace it with one of her father, Manuel B. Otero. She now was the only breadwinner in the Big House, working once again for the government. Although she was still a strong Republican, she grudgingly admitted that many of Roosevelt's policies and programs to help lift the nation out of the depression were working, and four years before Alfred Bergere died, she took advantage of the New Deal by applying for the position of state supervisor of literacy education, which was sponsored by the WPA Educational Division.

With WPA funding, significant improvements had been made in Santa Fe and employment had been given to many of Nina's friends. The WPA had paid for the 1932 remodeling of the Santa Fe Public Library, supervised by Salome Anthony, who, as acting librarian, had recommended that the building be finished in Territorial-style adobe and that Olive Rush paint the fresco in the entrance hallway.[48] Government funds also helped construct the New Mexico Public Welfare Building and the John Gaw Meem–designed Laboratory of Anthropology. In 1935 the New Mexico School for the Deaf (founded in 1887) was enlarged, and in 1938 Sunmount Sanatorium, no longer needed as a convalescent center for TB patients, was remodeled into a fashionable hotel, the Santa Fe Inn.

The Democrat-sponsored Federal Emergency Relief Administration (FERA) and the WPA also provided jobs for the artists and writers in the community, who, during the thirties, had become an integral part of Santa Fe. Sixty writers from New Mexico were hired to produce the American Guide Series, which offered detailed information for travelers across America. Ina Sizer Cassidy directed the state guide project from 1936 to 1939, when she was replaced by Aileen Nusbaum, author of *Zuni Indian Tales* and illustrator for Nina's *Old Spain in Our Southwest.* Since WPA in Spanish sounded like "*el diablo a pie,*" or "the devil on foot" in English, the editors of the guidebook deleted "WPA" from the title and called it *New Mexico: A Guide to the Colorful State.*[49]

After Mary Austin's death in 1934, her home at 439 Camino del Monte Sol, Casa Querida, became an art center (now the Gerald Peters Gallery) where the creative colony gathered to socialize and discuss ways to preserve the tricultural, "Old World charm and tranquillity of Santa Fe" and to learn of opportunities for government-funded projects.[50] In 1934, Will Shuster's WPA-commissioned frescoes of American Indian rituals appeared on the interior patio walls of the Museum of Fine Art in Santa Fe. The work of Hispanic wood sculptors Patricino Barela and Juan Sánchez also received WPA support, much to the satisfaction of Nina and Witter Bynner, who doggedly continued to promote Spanish colonial arts.[51]

When she first applied for government employment in 1935, Nina sent her "personal history" to the Honorable Lee Rowland, state administrator for FERA. In the letter she fudged a bit on her date of birth, subtracting four years from her total of fifty-four, and said she was "a widow." She listed her accomplishments in the field of education—her twelve years as Santa Fe County school superintendent, her course of study that was adopted for general use in state schools, her two years as general inspector in the Indian Service, her success in promoting and directing public health and child welfare organizations, and her formal education and bilingual skills. She concluded: "I have recently completed a book which is educational in its nature. This book is being published by Harcourt, Brace & Company."[52]

Later, in August 1937, Nina was offered, and accepted, the position of supervisor of literacy education and hired Mamie Meadors as her assistant. Nina approached this newest challenge in her usual methodical, well-organized way by calling a meeting of state educators in Albuquerque and forming an advisory committee to help her uncover the primary causes of illiteracy in New Mexico. Committee members suggested that a survey be made of "typical counties," such as Taos, Socorro, and San Juan. Nina insisted that Santa Fe County also be included because "it attracts the attention of the whole state," and she recommended that volunteer workers proceed with the survey "as soon as possible and before the roads into some of the communities become impassable."[53]

Once the survey questionnaires were sent out and the results came in, Nina wrote a detailed report to the state director for adult education clearly outlining a plan to combat illiteracy in a state where over 13 percent of adults could not read or write in any language at all. Once again, she tried to convince the public that drastic changes had to made. She cited the short school term (usually resulting from a shortage in tax revenue), inadequate school facilities, failure to enforce the school attendance law, poorly trained teachers, and failure to recognize bilingual opportunities as the primary causes of illiteracy in New Mexico.

Nina pointed out that because the greater portion of the state's population was rural, widely dispersed, and poor, having a formal education was of little advantage. A program to eliminate illiteracy "should not be desk made," she insisted, but flexible enough to meet the needs of the communities. "Adults should be taught, first, in the language they know . . . and the instruction should follow their interests. . . . Rural people live from the soil . . . and are not going to enroll in classes for the sake of learning to write their names or read newspapers." The teachers of these people must "understand the language of life, possess qualities of leadership and common sense," and train with experts who know something about agriculture, weaving, tanning, woodworking, auto mechanics, popular arts, music, and physical education, including recreational sports and games.[54]

To promote her ideas, she accepted all offers to speak to groups around the country. At an education conference in Washington, D.C., on June 3, 1937, a teacher from a private eastern school asked her: "At what stage of social development, at what social level, do the people of New Mexico emerge from living in the adobe houses?" Nina's response was cool and brief: "The prominent Cyrus McCormicks, Mr. and Mrs. Simms [Ruth Hanna McCormick and Albert G. Simms], and Mary Cabot Wheelwright all live in adobe houses. I would not pass judgment on their place in the social structure." The woman from Massachusetts, according to the reporter on the scene, "is still absorbing the supervisor's final information that Mary Cabot Wheelwright lives in an adobe house in New Mexico."[55]

Nina was well acquainted with the wealthy families. Mary Cabot

Wheelwright, one of the well-known Cabots of Massachusetts, had moved to the Southwest in 1918 and at the time Nina was with the WPA lived in a beautiful old house, Los Luceros, in Alcalde, north of Santa Fe. She was the principal financial contributor for the Museum of Navajo Ceremonial Art, later renamed the Wheelwright Museum of the American Indian.

Ruth Hanna McCormick Simms (1880–1945), daughter of U.S. Senator Mark Hanna and connected by marriage with the *Chicago Tribune* McCormick family, was the first woman in the country to be elected to the U.S. House of Representatives (1929–31). After her second marriage, to Albert Simms (U.S. congressman from New Mexico) in 1932, she moved to Albuquerque to live in a John Gaw Meem–designed adobe house, Los Poblanos. An active suffragist and Republican party supporter, Ruth Simms later organized the Sandia School and founded the Allied Arts Extension in Albuquerque. The Cyrus McCormicks (the International Harvester Company family) had made their fortune in the early nineteenth century through the invention of the McCormick reaper, a machine that revolutionized the farming industry. For many years they had a large adobe hacienda in Nambe just outside Santa Fe.[56]

On returning to Santa Fe, Nina amused her friends by repeating the "adobe-house" question posed by the sophisticate from Massachusetts and continued on the lecture circuit with increasing self-confidence. In 1939, as Adolf Hitler and his Nazi party were gaining power in Europe, she spoke to members of the Youth Council in Santa Cruz—mostly young girls and their parents—on the importance of leadership and defense. "Soon," she said, "all the women of the nation are going to be organized in a defense program. . . . We have to defend this democracy of ours." She defined a leader as "a person with a magnetic personality. Build personalities that will attract people to you," she urged the young women, and went on to ask them to encourage their parents to join her in combating illiteracy. Perseverance, hard work, and training will open doors to success, she assured them.[57]

Nina's own leadership was noted by Erna Fergusson in her classic book *New Mexico: A Pageant of Three Peoples.*

> Fortunately the work [to combat illiteracy] was directed by Mrs.
> Adelina Otero-Warren, herself a balanced product of two cultures, and she based the courses on actual vocabulary needs and taught teachers to meet their classes with old-fashioned dignity.
> As one result, many older men subscribed for newspapers, and five hundred unschooled youngsters were able to sign up for the draft as literates.[58]

Nina and Mamie focused on such basic skills as writing a letter—how to organize the salutation, text, and closing; how to choose the right words from a vocabulary list (in Spanish and English); and how to address an envelope. The two women had taken on an enormous task in their efforts to overcome the problems of illiteracy in New Mexico, and their efforts were complicated by the uncertainties of funding, given the U.S. military buildup and the hostilities in Europe. But they made progress, and the programs they developed were so practical and helpful that they caught the attention of educational leaders in Washington, D.C.

After five years of hard work, Nina was invited to establish a WPA-sponsored program to help illiterate people in Puerto Rico. Pleased with the prospect of an all-expenses-paid trip to the tropics, she invited Anita to go along with her. May agreed to watch over the Big House, and Mamie stayed home to supervise the courses she had helped develop.

On May 15, 1941, Nina and Anita traveled to Washington, where they joined assistant state recreational supervisor John P. Flores and his wife for a briefing at WPA headquarters. Otero-Warren and Flores were two of the ten educators chosen as special consultants by Albert F. Spina of Puerto Rico to help him establish a community service program, courses that would include "educational and recreational projects, nursery schools, hot lunch projects, art, and music"—all meant to "train citizens of the island to take their places

Nina Otero-Warren, Director of Adult Literacy for the WPA in Puerto Rico, 1941. (Photograph courtesy of John J. Kenney.)

later as administrative officials."[59] A week later the party of four from New Mexico took a steamship from New York to Puerto Rico.

Nina worked on the island for four months. She approached her task there as she had the job at home, surveying the needs of the island's illiterate adult population and then developing programs to meet those needs. She also took time out to enjoy her exotic surroundings. In a letter to the New Mexican a month after her arrival, she wrote: "The country is gorgeous!"

> Vegetation is profuse and the flowers and trees are of vivid color. The flamboyant tree is especially beautiful at this time of the year and you literally drive under a bower of flaming blooms. The ocean is as blue as our New Mexico skies and the royal palms

seem to catch the breeze from the ocean and fan it to the crowded population on the island. Flowers are of all colors and garde-
nias grow wild. We purchase them for 15 cents a dozen—and
the poorest people seem always to be carrying flowers.[60]

For all the island's beauty, the hot sticky climate was "enervat-
ing," living conditions were deplorable, and the poverty crushing. "It
was pathetic to see the sad eyes and undernourished bodies of so
many children of the poor," wrote Nina, yet they all seemed eager
for an education, and she was "working terribly hard." As 56 percent
of the children were without school facilities, she at once submitted
a proposal that, if accepted, would "place 50,000 of these under-
privileged children in school and give employment to 1,000 teachers." Priorities on her agenda included in-service training courses for
adult school teachers and workshops to discuss and solve curriculum
problems. Such workshops, she felt, would give all WPA adult school
teachers an opportunity "to improve themselves professionally so
that they may render a greater service to the people of Puerto
Rico."[61]

Nina found that the teachers of Puerto Rico were like "carpenters without tools and materials" and recommended "well-laid
plans" for bilingual instruction for illiterates, using the language tool
of Spanish before moving on to English. She encouraged a combina-
tion of theoretical and practical approaches to education that considered the social needs of the individual student, "his experience, de-
sires and interests." With the proper teaching methods, the student
would not only escape from the bonds of illiteracy but also "develop
into a self-propelled, intelligent worker with clear views as to what
he is driving at and strong personal motives for accomplishment."[62]

Nina's firm advocacy of bilingual education, her experience and
competence, and her kindness toward the people of Puerto Rico en-
deared her to the island's adult education instructors. As a token of
their affection and gratitude, they sponsored a special program of
speeches, music, dance, and song in honor of "the well known

North American Educator, Mrs. Nina Otero-Warren." El Mundo, the leading newspaper in San Juan, ran an article describing the affair, saying that Nina was "looked upon not as a Director of the project, but as an Orientalist [one who guides and orients students]. . . . and her name will be engraved forever in the minds of all her good friends in Puerto Rico."[63]

One of her student teachers spoke for all who had taken her course, saying that before enrolling "everything looked dark and hopeless," but now "everything has turned white. . . . This miracle was possible because of the enthusiasm and determination of this good American lady. Mrs. Otero-Warren, you must rest assured that the seeds you have sowed in our hearts and minds will yield exuberant fruits of success."[64]

Nina's work was officially commended by the supervisor for educational projects, Pedro Arán, who wrote his superior, Robert Lawrence, saying, "Mrs. Otero-Warren has a dynamic and sympathetic personality capable of making others work hard without using any coercion. . . . She easily grasps problems and situations. . . . She has a very quick mind which enables her to find rapid and adequate solutions for the problems she meets. . . . The training course has been remarkable. It has been one of the most constructive educational enterprises I have observed in my long professional career. . . . Adult Education will be a real success in Puerto Rico in the future as a result of the inspiration and excellent guidance Mrs. Otero-Warren has given us."[65]

A month later, a grateful Pedro Arán wrote to Nina informing her that her educational recommendations had received approval from Washington just in time for the regular school term. "Immediately," he said, "18,250 children will be attending public schools because of this WPA project," the success of which had been far beyond his expectations, "a blessing for the Island."[66]

Nina was extremely pleased that the work had gone well and that she had made a difference in the lives of the Puerto Rican people. After surveying the educational requirements of the Virgin Is-

lands, which were also on her itinerary, and submitting her recommendations for the distribution of $1,037,000 in WPA funds for
schools, teachers, and curricula for all the islands, she bid good-bye
to the puertoriqueños and set sail for New York and home on the S.S.
Borinquen. In an interview before she left she credited the leadership
of the federal WPA education program for the success of her mission
and noted that Puerto Rico was the "only place where the WPA has
supplemented public school work. . . . The program was considered
a defense need." Puerto Rico in 1941 was being used as a U.S. military base and was swarming with soldiers, sailors, airmen, and
marines. She had to train thirty-seven Spanish teachers to help the
250 officers at Borinquen Field learn to speak Spanish.[67]

As to her future, Nina told the reporter, it was "indefinite," but
she planned to remain engaged in government work of some kind.
Hitler and his armies were in the world spotlight, the United States
was mobilizing its military forces, and she had no doubt that she
would be needed on the home front.

CHAPTER SIX

The
Matriarch

Nina had just turned sixty when the Japanese bombed Pearl Harbor on December 7, 1941. After a lapse of only twenty-three years the United States, "with a sense of grim and bitter necessity," was engaged in another world war.[1] While the country had made some preparation—mobilization of troops had begun, the Selective Training and Service Act had been passed the year before, and Congress had grudgingly increased funding for defense—the isolationists, pacifists, and America-firsters had been successful in convincing legislators and the general public that the European conflict was a "phony war."

Like most Americans, Santa Feans had been obsessively antimilitary and hostile to rearming, even though Hitler's forces by 1939 had overrun most of Europe and had begun their blitzkrieg of Great Britain. The United States, with its ill-equipped army mostly made up of volunteers (ranked nineteenth in the world at the time), was at its most vulnerable when Roosevelt finally declared war on Japan and Germany.[2]

The shock of the Japanese attack reverberated throughout Santa

Fe. Nina, Anita, Teta, and May had planned a party that day to celebrate Cristina's seventh birthday but canceled it when they heard the
news. "The Japs ruined my birthday," was Cristina's rueful memory
of that dark day. All that her first-grade friends remembered was their
disappointment and the fun they had missed because of the shocking
bulletins on the radio throughout the day from Manila, Singapore,
Tokyo, London, and Rome.[3]

The large, black headlines in the city's newspaper stunned Santa
Feans. The *New Mexican*, recently acquired by conservative Republican
Frank C. Rand, Jr., had been adamantly opposed to Roosevelt, com-
paring his administration with the system that had led to Hitler's dictatorship. But on that bleak Sunday in 1941, Santa Fe and the rest of
divided America were solidly united. Despite the absence of management (the editor, general manager, and Frank Rand himself were all
duck-hunting in the country), the paper's staff issued an extra supporting the president and denouncing the "gangster-style" tactics of
the Japanese.[4]

The following day six-inch headlines screamed "Manila
Bombed!" and Governor John Miles put his state on full emergency
alert "until our armed forces have time to extract just retribution
from our treacherous, despicable and infamous foe." Still, the governor saw no immediate need to call a special session of the legislature:
"We don't intend to do anything rash," he explained.

While he declared that there would be no detention of Japanese
nationals without cause, Miles ordered peace officers to round up the
few who were living in New Mexico, most of them in Bernalillo, Valencia, and Grant counties. Months later a Japanese internment camp
was constructed just outside Santa Fe, off Buckman Road on the way
to Las Dos. Fearing spies and sabotage and a possible Japanese invasion of California, the United States uprooted, interned, and humili-
ated 146,000 Japanese Americans during the four-year conflict.[5]

Nina's immediate concern was for her nephews and for the Santa Fe boys stationed in the Philippines. Two servicemen from New
Mexico were reported among the dead at Pearl Harbor. In the ex-

tended family, May's sons, Jack and Bergere Kenney, Rosina's Leonard Smith, Connie's Frank Mendenhall, and Estella's Carl, Starker, and Luna Leopold were all eligible for military service.[6]

Only a few months before Pearl Harbor, eighty Santa Fe men in Battery C of the 200th Coast Artillery (Antiaircraft) had been dispatched to Clark Field in the Philippines. Chosen for their fluency in Spanish and their gunnery record for accuracy, the soldiers from Santa Fe had been in the thick of the bombing of their base on December 7, and those who survived had been moved to the Bataan Peninsula. Months later families learned that their sons had been subjected to a forced march—starved, beaten, some bayoneted during the sixty-three–mile death march to the Japanese prison camps located near Cabanatuan.[7]

Although her nephews were not among the men called up for that ill-fated New Mexico regiment, Nina was particularly worried about Jack Kenney, who at her urging and with financial aid from Grandmother Bergere's trust fund had chosen a career in the army. Jack had attended New Mexico Military Institute at Roswell and later the U.S. Military Academy at West Point, graduating in 1940 as a second lieutenant of artillery.

His younger brother, Bergere Alfred Kenney, had graduated from Harvard in 1940 and was in the graduate program in biochemistry at the University of New Mexico when war was declared. Nina felt very close to Jack and Bergere, bright young men who, as teenagers seven years earlier, had moved to the Big House after their father died. For Nina, they were the sons she never had.

Both boys loved and respected her, both had vivid memories of their aunt's generosity and even-handedness during their years in La Casa Grande. She never hesitated to give them a tongue-lashing when they were out of line, Bergere admitted, but "there was no nagging, no recriminations." He laughed when he recalled the time he accidentally drove the family car off an embankment: "She chewed me out, but then she had the car fixed and nothing was ever said again."[8]

Jack gave Nina credit for giving him and his brother direction and opportunity: "I bless her all the time for making it possible for Bergere to go to Harvard and for me to go to West Point, and subsequently to meet and marry our wives. At the height of the depression [1934], Nina pulled strings in the capitol and got me a job with the Santa Fe school system, and later as a page in the state Senate. When she heard that Representative Jack Dempsey wanted to send someone to West Point, Nina and mother told him I would like to go—even though my first ambition was to go to Harvard Law School."[9]

Over the Christmas holidays the year he graduated from West Point, Jack had married Josephine (Joey) Sullivan from Ardsley-on-Hudson, New York. He and Joey were at Fort Ord, California, with the 76th Field Artillery when Pearl Harbor was bombed.

The period between 1941 and 1945 was a time of patriotic fervor and common trial for Santa Feans. When the news of the unprovoked attack by the Japanese first swept through the city, a delegation of boys from the Santa Fe High School senior class, all under eighteen, appealed to Governor Miles to help them join the armed forces right away. He turned them down, of course, but a year later most of them were writing letters home from the European or Pacific theaters of war.[10]

Women were expected to do their patriotic duty and fill men's jobs, and many left Santa Fe for well-paying work in defense industries. Nina promptly applied for and was given the post of director of the Office of Price Administration for Santa Fe County. She just as promptly brought Mamie in as her assistant, and during the war years they fought side by side to help control wartime inflation. Together they canvassed the county to ensure that ceiling prices were maintained on foods, commodities, and residential rents. With the freezing of 90 percent of retail food prices and the rationing of tires, automobiles, gasoline, fuel oil, coffee, sugar, and meat, both women were kept busy making sure merchants complied with the law.

May Kenney worked for the Selective Service in the early 1940s.

Cristina Kenney Herdman remembered how much her mother "hated the job of having to call up boys she had known for years and tell them they had been drafted. She would go by La Fonda and see them on to the bus with tears streaming from her eyes."[11]

For all the sorrow and stress generated by the war, life in the Big House and around the city of Santa Fe continued at a relatively routine pace. Traditional Christmas holiday customs were maintained despite wartime restrictions. During Christmas week of 1941, the leñeros (wood haulers) appeared as usual, playing their violins and guitars as they guided their burros in procession around the plaza lighted by bonfires of pyramided piñon logs. Schoolchildren made their way through the city's twisted streets singing carols in Spanish and English. St. Francis's nativity cribs graced homes, churches, and hotels. Luminarias (also known as farolitos), the traditional festival lanterns made of candles embedded in sand encased in small paper bags, bordered gardens and walks.[12]

Cristina had warm memories of clear, cold Christmas Eves as a child and teenager in Santa Fe during the war years. Bundled up in a heavy coat, scarf, woolen cap, and mittens, she tagged along with her mother, Nina, and Anita as they walked across the plaza and up the hill to García Street to join Rosina and their neighbors for an hour or so of caroling. The comfort of coming in to the Big House from the biting cold outdoors made a lasting impression.

"The fire was roaring, the house was redolent with piñon and juniper, and there on the dining room table was a large punch bowl of spiked eggnog for the grownups and hot chocolate for the kids. It was wonderful!" Out they went again, after warming up with nog and drinks, to attend midnight mass at St. Francis Cathedral. After mass, usually around 2:00 A.M. it was back to La Casa Grande for steaming posole prepared by Anita earlier in the day and the exchange of a few small presents before finally going to bed. Four hours later everyone was up again.[13]

Christmas Day itself was a marathon of activity as relatives and friends came and went from morning till night. Despite shortages, the Christmas dinner table had a turkey (*gallina de la tierra*), traditional baby squash with green chili, corn, tamales, *posole*, and pumpkin pie. After dinner Nina would make her calls and deliver jars of *posole*, the first stop always at the home of Mamie and Salome on Delgado Street. She also stopped by to see the Oteros. "She tried to keep the Oteros in her life," Cristina said, "even though they were not in the 'higher echelons' of Santa Fe at the time."[14]

During and after the holidays in 1941, Santa Feans concentrated on the war, buying defense bonds ($18.75 each) and stamps ($0.10 and up) and doing whatever they could to help at home. For most merchants, however, it was business as usual. Downtown in Sena Plaza, Dorothy Greenwood continued to operate the Villagra Book Shop, one of the Southwest's finest independent bookstores until competition from the large franchises forced it to close in the 1980s. The Woman's Exchange remained open for luncheon and tea and sold Southwestern artifacts. Ina Cassidy, from her home on Canyon Road, stayed busy writing essays for local journals and selling her own marmalades and preserves: "New Mexico Sunshine for your Breakfast Table"—six varieties in attractive glass jars for $2.[15]

During the war, classes in music, creative writing, painting, photography, and the Spanish language were conducted in Mary Austin's former home on Camino del Monte Sol. Through the Arsuna Art School's "At Home" gatherings every first and third Sunday of the month, an attempt was made by the school's staff to fulfill one of Mary Austin's last wishes—to introduce Santa Fe visitors, and subsequently the world, to the work of the city's struggling artists and writers.[16]

The annual Fiesta de Santa Fe continued to be held throughout the war years, and Nina had her party the night before as usual, even though many of her art colony friends had left for the service or had moved away from a town that was beginning to feel the pressure of ever increasing tourism. With rumors flying about the possibility of Japanese planes and submarines invading the West Coast (German submarines had been sinking Allied ships off the shores of the Unit-

ed States, including the Gulf of Mexico), a large number of California "refugees" moved to Santa Fe. Most were wealthy people looking
for a safe haven; others were members of a theosophical cult calling
themselves "I Am." Led by Mrs. Edna Ballard of Los Angeles, the radical believers poured into the city, creating a major housing shortage
and a bonanza for the few real-estate agencies in business at the
time.[17] The influx of tourists, many of whom became permanent
residents, would prompt Nina and Mamie several years later to open
their own real-estate office.

Little did the newcomers to Santa Fe know that they were moving to within thirty-five miles of a laboratory where renowned scientists—Nobel laureates Niels Bohr (1922), Enrico Fermi (1938), and
Ernest Lawrence (1939), and the brilliant physicist Robert Oppenheimer—were developing the world's deadliest bomb. Not until the
New Mexican's banner headlines announced the explosion of the atomic bomb over Japan did Santa Feans learn officially of the secret ex-
periments at Los Alamos. For two years, from the summer of 1943
until August 6, 1945, when Hiroshima was demolished by an explosive force equivalent to twenty thousand tons of TNT, the staff of the
city's paper suppressed all information having to do with happenings
on "The Hill."[18]

From their homestead houses at Las Dos, Nina and Mamie had a
panoramic view of Los Alamos, the tiny community in the Jemez
Mountains where, until the U.S. government took it over for the
Manhattan Project in 1943, the only building of note was a two-story
log ranch house used as a college preparatory school for boys.
Opened in 1917 by Ashley Pond, father of Peggy Pond Church, the
Los Alamos School had fulfilled his dream of creating a place "where
city boys from wealthy families like his own [his was from Detroit]
could regain their heritage of outdoor wisdom at the same time that
they were being prepared for college and the responsibilities which
their position in life demanded."[19]

Through Peggy and her husband, Fermor Spencer Church, who
taught math and science courses at Los Alamos in 1943, Nina and

Mamie had heard of the government's abrupt closing of the school and of the new roads that were replacing the thirty-five miles of dirt trails leading from Frijoles Canyon across the narrow trestle bridge at Otowi to the top of the Pajarito Plateau. The shimmering lights they could see at night across a distance of only seventeen miles from the homestead began to proliferate as more government buildings were quickly constructed. Some days they could see clouds of smoke stretched across the horizon and hear explosions that periodically shattered the tranquillity and stillness of their own hill.[20]

Most Santa Feans had seen military reconnaissance planes circling the West Mesa and had heard rumors that something called a cyclotron had been transported up the steep roads. To relieve tension, Peggy, Nina, and their Santa Fe friends invented stories, speculating that on the high, semiarid plateau at Los Alamos the government was planning a "submarine base in the pond where the ducks swam, and a secret passage would connect it with the Río Grande!" Others guessed that windshield wipers for submarines were being manufactured there, or that the government was using Los Alamos as an internment camp for wayward Republicans or as a home for pregnant WACs. The tight security and strict censorship suggested to Nina and her sisters that more serious projects were under way, that scientists might be working on methods for gas warfare or jet propulsion or death rays—or atomic bombs.[21]

Trucks with large cargoes roared past the Big House on Grant Avenue constantly, and one day May received an overseas letter from Jack, saying: "I had to come all the way to Germany to find out what was going on at Los Alamos." May bragged that her son knew what was happening on the hill. "Next thing you know," Cristina said, "the FBI was at our front door, and we heard later that they were at Jack's station at the same time, wanting to know what Jack knew." Fortunately, May was able to produce Jack's letter for the authorities and persuade them that her son had no subversive intentions. To everyone's relief they let the matter go.[22]

While virtually all the New Mexican staff knew what was happening, news relating to activities at Los Alamos was suppressed:

> The paper even had to give the location of auto accidents on the Los Alamos road as "somewhere north of Santa Fe." . . . The taboo on the mention of Los Alamos was final, complete. . . . A whole social world existed in nowhere in which people were married and babies were born nowhere. People died in a vacuum, autos and trucks crashed in a vacuum. . . . Even the graduates of Los Alamos Ranch School . . . ceased to be graduates of Los Alamos; they bounded direct from Public School No. 7 clear into the classrooms of Harvard and Yale.[23]

Even the experimental shot at the Trinity Site on July 16, 1945, was a well-kept secret, the story buried on page six of the New Mexican and headed "Magazine Lets Go at Alamogordo." The Gallup Independent quoted the officer in charge at Alamogordo as saying, "Yes, there has been an explosion. Nobody hurt. Nothing serious." Yet nearby ranchers "thought they had seen the end of the world."

Margaret Lefranc Schoonover and Alice Marriott, both doing research for María: The Potter of San Ildefonso, had just finished plastering their house in Nambe when a test explosion on the Pajarito Plateau caused the stucco to peel away from the walls and slide to the ground. Astonished and angry, Margaret called the Los Alamos laboratory to ask for compensation for lost time and labor. "I met a brick wall of denial and secrecy," she said. "No one would admit there had been an explosion: 'What blast?' they said. 'There were no tests made. We are not responsible.' "[24]

Nina and Mamie heard through Peggy Pond Church, who had been told by her scientist husband, that Dr. Ernest Lawrence had developed the cyclotron at Berkeley, that Dr. Robert Oppenheimer was known for his research on the structure of the atom, and that "the mysterious project . . . had something to do with atomic research."[25]

"Things—unknown things, were happening" that hot dry summer of 1945, reported Edith Warner, their reclusive friend who lived just down the hill from the laboratories. For two tense years Edith had operated a tea room in her isolated adobe house by the bridge at Otowi, serving the people at Los Alamos simple meals topped off with her magical chocolate cake. Timid, retiring Edith had provided the one temporary escape for the Los Alamos scientists and their wives, most of whom felt that "only their evenings at Edith Warner's kept them human." Once the news of the atomic bomb flashed around the world, Edith Warner felt free to disclose what she knew. In her 1945 Christmas letter to her good friends she wrote that

> Conant and Compton came in through the kitchen door to eat ragout and chocolate cake; that Fermi and Allison, Teller, Parsons, came many times; that Oppenheimer was the man I knew in pre-war years and who made it possible for the Hill people to come down; that Hungarians, Swiss, Germans, Italians, Austrians, French and English have been serious and gay around the candlelit table.[26]

Much as Edith deplored the awesome power of the new weapon, she agreed with Niels Bohr, whom she considered "not only a great scientist but a great man," that only through international control of the bomb and atomic energy could our civilization avoid a fatal catastrophe.[27] Edith died on May 4, 1951, long before Nina and Mamie and the residents in and near Los Alamos fully realized the deadly legacies of the Manhattan Project—fifty years of radioactive and chemical pollution resulting from carelessness and the shortcuts taken in the blitz to develop the bomb.[28]

For all its tragic consequences, the devastating atomic destruction of Hiroshima and Nagasaki ended the largest and costliest war in history. Two months after Japan's Emperor Hirohito surrendered aboard the battleship Missouri in Tokyo Bay on September 2, 1945, the Santa Fe soldiers who had survived the Bataan death march came home to what old-timers declared "the most impressive patriotic ceremony in memory." The turnout for the Armistice Day welcome-home festivities was unprecedented. Thousands packed the plaza.

There were parades and prayers and special awards—even a football game—followed by a cocktail party, supper, and dancing at the Elks Club.

Those boys who returned had vowed to make a pilgrimage to the Santuario de Chimayo to offer prayers of gratitude to the Santo Niño (Holy Child) for the miracle of their salvation. The following spring the famed chapel overflowed with the largest crowd of worshipers ever to attend services there. Twenty-three veterans, three women (two of them wives of the veterans), and Staff Sergeant Rivera's shaggy terrier, Fuzzy, hiked thirty-one miles from Santa Fe across cactus and chamisa-covered hills and mesas to the church in the dusty hamlet of Chimayo.[29]

Except for Leonard Smith, who suffered shrapnel wounds and a hearing loss while in combat, there were no major war casualties in the Bergere family, but there were a number of deaths at home. In 1942, Nina received a startling letter from Santa Barbara, California, signed by Meta Warren, Rawson Warren's wife at the time, announcing Rawson's death on August 9. Nina learned that her ex-husband had retired from the army with the rank of lieutenant colonel and had moved to Santa Barbara, where he died in his Montecito home at the age of sixty-nine. He left no children. His obituary, which appeared in the New York Times, cited his service in the Spanish-American War and in World War I, when he "was in Coblenz with the Army of Occupation after a year in Armenia on a Near East relief detail."[30] After more than thirty years, Nina was officially a widow. Nonetheless, true to her resolve to erase her memories of Warren and the pain of her failed marriage, she kept the letter to herself and volunteered little, if any, information to her family or friends.[31]

Nina had a number of male friends in the years after her separation from Warren, men who enjoyed her company—wealthy Ed Grossman encouraged her to visit New York as his guest from time to time—but the restraints of the Catholic church and her strong religious commitments made it impossible for her to remarry while her estranged husband was still alive. With his death she was free to

John J. Kenney, Jr., at West Point, ca. 1940. (Photograph courtesy of Josephine S. Kenney.)

marry again, but at sixty-two, having managed over the thirty-three years since her separation from Warren to shape a good life for herself, she had apparently lost interest.

She was not the type to brood long over things she could not change, and death was one of them. Her close cousin Miguel Otero died in 1944, and while she missed her kind, generous, and ever supportive friend—the man who had made it possible for her family to move to Santa Fe and a better life at the turn of the century—she was grateful that the eighty-three-year-old former governor, bedridden for three years, had died peacefully. The New Mexican reported that despite Otero's advanced age, the governor before his death "was as mentally alert as in the days when he fought the territorial bad men into submission to law and order."[32]

Josephine "Joey" Sullivan Kenney,
ca. 1939, wife of Jack Kenney.
(Photograph courtesy of Josephine
S. Kenney.)

Nina felt blessed that the war had ended without family fatalities, and when the Kenney boys came home well and whole there was great joy and celebration in the Big House. Jack, the first to arrive, was invited to her room upstairs—a rare privilege since he had never before set foot in that sanctuary—and there she brought out her best liquor and toasted his personal heroism and the Allies' victory. His wife, Joey, joined them later.

While she was dating Jack, Joey had been told about his stern, demanding aunt and had pictured Nina as a tall, severe taskmaster, "at least nine feet tall, dark and Spanish, with long black hair." What she found on her first visit to the Big House was a tiny, energetic woman, her red hair streaked with gray, her brown eyes pleasantly alert, her whole attitude that of a woman who had recently triumphed. Nina had just arrived home from Pecos in a rattletrap truck. "Descending from the driver's side was this creature dressed in a

Bergere A. Kenney, M.D., ca.
1960. (Photograph courtesy of
Dolores K. Kenney.)

bluejean hat, a bluejean jacket, a bluejean skirt, and deep wide clunky shoes. She was carrying a cantaloupe! She jumped out and said, 'Anita, look what I picked up in Pecos!' I turned to Jack and said, 'That's Aunt Nina?' "[33]

Joey soon got over her unwarranted awe of "Tía" (she was told never to call Nina "Mrs. Warren"), and the two became great friends. For Joey, Tía was "always very kind, very forbearing. And when we played poker, she would go to bed early and leave me all her leftover chips."[34]

Nina fully approved of Jack's lovely, vivacious wife, even though there was some resentment when she learned that the Sullivans had had the Bergeres investigated when her nephew and Joey became engaged. Joey was a well-brought-up Catholic girl from a good eastern family. She was a freshman at Mount Holyoke College when she and

*Dolores "Dode" Kornder Kenney,
ca. 1943, wife of Bergere A.
Kenney, M.D. (Photograph courtesy of Dolores K. Kenney.)*

Jack met and decided to marry. Their formal wedding at a nuptial mass in Winnetka, Illinois, attended by the Santa Fe family, met all Nina's criteria for a proper union.

On the other hand, Nina had reservations about Bergere Kenney's marriage in 1945 to beautiful, independent Dolores Kornder, a young woman from Oshkosh, Wisconsin, who had graduated from the University of Wisconsin with a B.S. degree in chemistry and who had been brought up in the Lutheran church. Nina was particularly upset when she heard that "Dode" and Bergere had impulsively decided to avoid possible family friction over religion and have Judge Jones marry them at Chicago's city hall. Dode's parents, the Alfred J. Kornders, sent out announcements once they heard the news, but doubts and disapproval persisted in the Big House until the newlyweds came to Santa Fe eight months later to face the consequences.

Dode remembered meeting Nina and her sisters in the backyard under the apple trees in the early fall of 1945. The women were all dressed in black skirts and white blouses and looked to Dode "like penguins" waiting to meet this newest member of their clan. She soon discovered some of Nina's prejudices. Not only did she openly disapprove of marriages outside the Catholic church, but she also had very conservative convictions when it came to dress codes for women.

Slim and attractive, the modern young Dode Kenney liked to wear bluejeans, much to the dismay of the aunts. Nina's strict upbringing rejected the notion that women who wore pants could still be considered ladies. She never wore jeans herself, rugged as the terrain was in and around Santa Fe, although she did add a split skirt or two to her wardrobe in the fifties. And jodhpurs for horseback riding were perfectly acceptable. "But," said Dode, "we worked it out. I didn't stop wearing jeans—I just didn't wear them around the aunts, and later, after Bergere and I moved to Santa Fe and had a home of our own, I wouldn't go by the Big House when I had them on. We respected her territory, and she ours."[35]

Dode spent two months in Santa Fe in 1946 getting acquainted with Nina and her sisters, easily winning them over with her warmth and honesty, before leaving with Bergere for San Antonio, where he was assigned to the surgeon's office at Fort Sam Houston. Once the young doctor completed two years with the U.S. Army Medical Corps Reserve, he returned to Santa Fe with Dode and their first two children, Katy and David, to establish his medical practice, intending to live there five to seven years at most. Instead they stayed a lifetime.

In general, Nina was fair and generous with her nephews' wives. Both Joey and Dode thought of her as "multifaceted"—warm, vibrant, and affectionate, with a few old-fashioned prejudices, but also a hard-nosed businesswoman who liked to take charge and who insisted on high standards for her nieces and nephews. "She did what was needed," Joey said, "but did it subtly, never with an ax blade."[36]

Jack and Bergere Kenney credited their mother, Tía, Aunt Ana (Anita), and Teta for much of their success in life. In a "Dear Valentine" letter to Anita written in February 1944, while he was still in medical school, Bergere tried to express the affection and appreciation he had for the women who brought him up and for the security their home in Santa Fe had always provided:

> I look upon La Casa Grande as a sort of symbol of permanence and something you can count on—the people, the posole, the 9:15 Mass, and the straight Republican ticket—when actually it is the center of more excitement and change than any place except the White House. Yet there is no event so big, so far-reaching, or so tragic that it causes a real permanent alteration in the way of life.[37]

"What a wonderful job you have done on your mob!" Jack wrote to May on Mother's Day, 1952. "[We] owe all of our little successes and all of our happiness to you, with only the moral and spiritual support of Dad, and to your hard work and many trials. . . . How much we realize and appreciate your pushing us, guiding us, and showing us the better ways to live and to accomplish something."[38]

Thanks to the encouragement and financial support of the family matriarchs, Jack's stellar achievement at West Point made possible his distinguished thirty-year career in the U.S. Army, where he rose to the rank of brigadier general before retiring in 1970 from the Office of the Joint Chiefs of Staff in Washington, D.C., as chief of the Western Hemisphere Division.

His brother Bergere's career was equally impressive. The year Jack entered West Point, 1940, Bergere—at the age of nineteen—earned a bachelor's degree from Harvard. A year later he took an M.S. degree in biochemistry from the University of New Mexico before entering Northwestern University Medical School.[39]

While Bergere appreciated the ambiance of the Big House and

Santa Fe, some of his happiest memories were of picnics with May, Nina, and Mamie at Las Dos. At Nina's urging he and his family spent a great deal of time at the homestead, more than Jack and Joey, since Jack's army career kept them moving around the country after the war. Dode Kenney especially loved the spectacular view of the Sangres during the fall when the aspen trees turned to gold and the mountains began to look like "scrambled eggs and green chili."[40]

For Bergere, the homestead was a wilderness sanctuary where he could escape the stress of his medical practice in town. He knew every hill and arroyo, the habits of most of the wildlife, the generic names of virtually all the indigenous plants struggling for survival in that dry country. "I developed a great love for that land," Bergere admitted in an interview four months before his death in July, 1988: "I think Nina was very much aware of my feeling for Las Dos. Jack was here less often, being off in the military, but he loved it too. And when the time came to settle her affairs, she simply left the land to Jack and me, jointly."[41]

Weekend outings and vacations at Las Dos were not reserved for the Santa Fe families only. Mamie's nephew, Henry B. Meadors, made several trips from Texas to the homestead in the forties and remembered some of the meals prepared by handyman Jorge Roybal: "When Jorge made coffee he would use an entire pound, store it, heat it every morning. The last quart tasted like roofing tar. He would also make camp tortillas using twenty-five pounds of flour, store them, and heat what he wanted for meals, spreading lard on each tortilla and heating as many as the wood-burning stove would hold."[42]

Las Dos in the forties and fifties was a particularly welcome change of pace for Nina's friends as well. She and Mamie generously shared their land and their rustic adobe houses with anyone they felt truly appreciated the bucolic environment. Alice Corbin and Willie Henderson, Peggy Pond Church, Amalia Sánchez, and Ruth Leakey were among the many Santa Feans invited to spend weekends there. Amalia remembered that on every trip barrels of water had to be carried out from town over roads that could be dust-choked or slick with mud or ice, depending on the vagaries of the weather. She recalled her good times at the homestead, sitting on the porch chatting amicably with Nina and watching the red-feathered clouds at sunset over the Jemez Mountains, while Mamie hovered in the background. Amalia thought Mamie "must have been bored with the conversation," she was so quiet. But as different as they were, Nina and Mamie "were always together, you rarely saw one without the other."[43]

When Peggy Pond Church visited Las Dos, she and Nina would walk a mile or so from the houses down one of the main arroyos to a beautiful rock formation Peggy christened the "holy place," where ancient Indian petroglyphs had been carved centuries before on rugged boulders. Much of Peggy's prose and poetry was inspired by the sense of mystical power and peace emanating from that sacred spot and the surrounding land. For her and others it was a contemplative place, and its restorative powers were palpable.

Visits to Las Dos were usually made in mild weather, but even in May and June a frost was possible. On cold nights, weekenders would gather around Nina's small fireplace for drinks, lively conversation, and hearty meals prepared by Mamie on the wood stove in her mud and brick house next door. The cheerful *fogón* with piñon logs standing on end seemed much like a campfire in the wilderness. Outside, dazzling patterns of stars covered clear, dark skies, and the moon, if and when it appeared, lighted the way for those who wanted a late-night stroll despite the piercing cries of coyotes close by.

In the morning guests would wake to see the brilliant sun spotlighting hammered silver candle sconces on white plastered walls and, on the porch, an inlaid tile sculpture of the Virgin of Guadalupe, facing east, blessing the Sangre de Cristos. Alert and busy early-morning birds—flickers, finches, robins, jays, magpies, sometimes a lone hawk—swept over the piñons and junipers, shattering the stillness with their hungry cries; jackrabbits and cottontails boldly checked the back garden for leftovers from the picnic feast the night before.

The solitude of Las Dos made some people uncomfortable, but for most the absence of city noise was welcome, the awe-inspiring stillness of the mountain-framed mesa soothing. As weekends drew to a close, most found it hard to leave the tranquil haven, where at the quietest of moments they could hear the sounds of their own hearts.

Nina herself was more gregarious than introspective, more social than reclusive. "She never intended to live permanently at Las Dos," Bergere Kenney said. "She liked the excitement of the city. She had tremendous charm when she wanted to turn it on. She was very gracious, courtly, and thoroughly enjoyed the parties she gave."[44] Back in town, Nina entertained family and friends in La Casa Grande, that "symbol of permanence," that "center of excitement and change." Her annual birthday parties were splendid events. "Old Santa Fe was represented there," Dode recalled. "John Sloan did marvelous caricatures; one of his best was of a little girl from the big city giving a piano recital. Will Shuster went through his repertoire of old Scottish and English songs, and Witter Bynner read his latest poetry."[45]

"Hal" Bynner was one of the few art-colony writers who stayed in Santa Fe after the war. Lack of work during the Great Depression and the demands of World War II had greatly diminished the colony, so that by 1942 only the literati who had independent incomes or who were ineligible for the draft remained. Bynner, in his sixties at the time, became a regular guest at the Big House for May's weekly bridge games. Nina's game was poker. She liked to gamble and drink with her brother, Manuel, and his friends and handsome Father Pax, a young Catholic priest fresh from the seminary, who, on his arrival in Santa Fe, was quickly taken into the family fold.[46]

Jack Kenney recalled his dismay the first time he came home on leave, a lieutenant colonel in the army, and discovered that his mother and Aunt Nina were socializing with Witter Bynner, a self-acknowledged homosexual. "You know who he is, don't you, Mother?" he asked. "Yes," she replied, "I know who he is. He's one of the

Cristina Kenney, ca. 1954,
daughter of John and May Bergere
Kenney. (Photograph courtesy of
Dolores K. Kenney.)

best bridge players in town. He's a very cultured man, he has very
bright friends, and he's very attentive and very nice to me. Now
what are you talking about?" "But mother," Jack sputtered, "he's a
queer!" When she gave him a withering look and said, "So what?",
Jack knew he was out of line and dropped the subject.[47]

Witter Bynner "was delightful," author Richard Bradford told
John Pen LaFarge in a 1991 interview for El Palacio.

> Hal was very charming, very gentlemanly, rather of the old
> school. . . . He was witty, he was warm, he was friendly, he was
> very well educated, and he told good stories. . . . He helped out
> a lot of people who were on their uppers, without any thought
> of recompense. He exuded a kind of amiability and charm—and
> charm is very hard to define, but you know it when you see it,
> like pornography.[48]

A towering six feet, four inches tall, Witter Bynner and tiny Nina, both in elaborate costumes, usually led the fiesta's "Hysterical Parade" in September each year. The sight of them together, Bergere said, was a "regular annual apparition."[49] There was always great preparation for the parade, Cristina remembered: "As kids we would sit around the dining room table making artificial flowers. One year we made flower garlands to decorate covered wagons borrowed from the old-timers. All the drivers for the romería showed up drunk as lords the day of the parade. Aunt Nina tolerated them, but it was a bit dangerous."[50]

Nina was so popular socially that she could easily have led a life of leisure, but she liked the stimulus of the workplace, the challenge of setting and completing goals and of making money to supplement the income from her mother's trust fund. Using her connections with political friends in high state offices, she had always managed to find jobs that satisfied her. When one ran out she found another. So it was in the postwar forties when the Office of Price Administration was terminated, and with it, her seven-year tenure as director.

But this time, in looking around for gainful employment, she decided, at the age of sixty-five, to establish her own real-estate business. The City Different was attracting more outsiders than ever before, many looking for permanent residences or for rental property during the cool, sunny summer months. In 1947, at an age when most people would have been thinking seriously about retirement, Nina, with Mamie as her business partner, opened Las Dos Realty and Insurance Company at 115 East Palace Avenue in downtown Santa Fe. Mamie was put in charge of insurance matters and took care of most of the bookkeeping. According to Bergere, "Nina liked to sell big houses, such as the McCormick estate, and she had the right connections to make her business a success."[51]

Their small but attractive office in Prince Plaza (next door to Sena Plaza) soon became one of Santa Fe's busiest hubs, another happy gathering place for family and friends who dropped in often to chat and gossip. "Nina had a great wit," Bergere said, "but she never talked negatively about anyone."[52] She and Mamie were always ready for unexpected visitors and had no trouble finding clients. Both had earned considerable respect over the years for their business savvy and hard work. Referrals came easily, and both made comfortable incomes.

Sam Arnold remembered going by Las Dos Realty in the late forties to arrange for the sale of his toy store, La Boutique Fantastique (now the Bull Ring Restaurant). Nina impressed him as a "grande dame of great style and quality, honest, straight, and very wise." Mamie was shorter than Nina and very thin, with "a simian sort of head—lots of prominent teeth—a nice woman."[53] They knew the Santa Fe market well and soon found a buyer for his store. They also found something for Roberta Brosseau, who wanted "an old house in a new part of town."

Nine-to-five days at the office were the norm for both women, with one or two hours off for lunch, usually at home. When they were both out of the office they would ask a friend to watch things for them and keep a list of customers and queries. An April 4, 1948, report showed that photographer Laura Gilpin "stopped in for news of a lost key chain, Mary Chaves came in to make a payment on the house, and Mrs. Edmund Randolph called to make sure that I [Ned, Rosina's teenage son] was really here."[54]

Nina walked to and from Prince Plaza every day. After work she would change into her jean skirt and jacket ("part of her uniform"), and on cold days stand by the fire Anita would have blazing in the sun room. "I don't care whether the Pope was there," Cristina said, "she would back up to the fire and lift her skirt. It really didn't matter who was around. She wasn't at all inhibited."[55]

And there usually was someone around for cocktails and dinner, since this was Nina's time to hold court. Anita would put out bottles of scotch and bourbon, an ice bucket, cashew nuts, and trays of glasses for the cocktail hour. Mamie came by for drinks occasionally,

Bergere family photograph, ca. 1950. Left to right: Rosina Bergere Brown, Nina, Dolores, Teta, Estella, Anita, Cristina, Luna, Rosina Smith Willson, May, and Connie. (Bergere Family Collection, photo no. 21660, New Mexico State Records Center and Archives, Santa Fe, New Mexico.)

but rarely stayed for dinner. Anita, who did not drink alcohol, rang the dinner bell at six no matter how important the conversation in the library and expected everyone to come straightaway.

The dining room in La Casa Grande was the family forum for ideas. Small talk was discouraged. Topics discussed around the dinner table covered virtually every area of interest, but politics, education, and environmental concerns took priority. Rosina's husband, Dr. Robert Brown, called it the "battlefield." When issues of controversy arose, Herbert Mendenhall would usually break the heavily charged silences following Nina's pronouncements by playing devil's advocate and challenging her views, sometimes just for the sake of argument.

For all the heated exchanges, Cristina admitted that hers "was generally a happy family." She and her Aunt Nina had their differ-

ences, but they tried to observe a guarded truce when they were together. "Despite tragedies and disagreements," she said, "we all came
back together when the chips were down."[56]

Nina did have her favorites. She appreciated Rosina's quick
mind and sense of humor—"those two put their heads together for a
couple of the best Hysterical Parades that ever happened in Santa Fe,"
Cristina said. Joey was touched by Nina's sensitive consideration of
May after she lost her husband. And "Nina closely loved Anita, probably because Aunt Ana lived and breathed for Nina. Aunt Ana
planned her own day around Nina's. She always praised her." Joey,
herself an only child, was impressed with the warmth and affection
Nina showed all her sisters.[57]

The men in the family generally treated Nina with respect. She
was a *compadre* they could rely on to give them honest opinions about
major business matters. When she disapproved of the first house
Dode and Bergere considered buying in Santa Fe, they bought another. Of her brothers-in-law, Aldo Leopold was the one Nina thought
"walked on water." He too was an educator and had made a name
for himself as a conservationist. Her admiration for Aldo proved to
be well founded, for decades after his death in 1948 he is still acknowledged as the "father of wildlife management in America." He
taught the students in his popular class, Wildlife Ecology 118, at the
University of Wisconsin in the early forties to see, understand, and
enjoy the land, asking each of them to care for its preservation and
health. Aldo Leopold also influenced Nina and Mamie and urged
them to maintain the integrity and beauty of their Las Dos homestead. Shortly after the publication of his collected writings, *The Sand
County Almanac* (1949), all grazing was prohibited at Las Dos.[58]

Aldo's son, Luna Leopold, a hydrologist and geologist for the
United States Geological Survey after the war, arranged for the USGS
to keep one strand of barbed wire around the entire area to protect it
from excessive grazing while erosion studies were made. Luna
Leopold followed his father, carving out a noteworthy career for
himself and earning in 1991 the Geological Society of America's Dis-

tinguished Career Award and the National Medal of Science Award, the nation's highest scientific honor.[59]

"Aunt Nina was very sensitive to environmental concerns," Cristina said. "We were never allowed to cut down Christmas trees when we went out to Las Dos. The trees were to be left alone to thrive in their natural habitat. Only greenery and mistletoe were brought back to town."[60]

In a family as large as the Bergeres', personalities were bound to clash, and while most acknowledged that Nina was the "umbrella over the family," there were those who felt more warmly toward her than others. Some disliked her intensely. Clearly, she was a strong, controlling woman, impatient with stupidity and carelessness, proud—many would say excessively so—of her rich Spanish heritage. Her sharp tongue, penchant for dirty jokes, quick temper, and ill-concealed favoritism for certain nieces and nephews annoyed her critics, but all admitted that she was a smart, resourceful woman.[61]

Of the friends who cared most for Nina, despite clashes that undoubtedly occurred during thirty years as business associate and companion, Mamie Meadors was the closest. When she died on August 10, 1951, after only four years as co-owner of Las Dos Realty, her loss weighed heavily on her partner. The tuberculosis that had been in remission since Mamie's arrival in New Mexico in 1918 returned in the form of Addison's disease just before her sixty-fourth birthday. She had been critically ill at home for several days before her death, which came while she was in an ambulance racing to St. Vincent Hospital's emergency room.[62]

Funeral services for Mamie were held in the memorial chapel of the First Presbyterian Church in Santa Fe, the Reverend Kenneth M. Koeler officiating and paying tribute to the quiet, hard-working woman who, in her unassuming and efficient way, had contributed so much to the high-profile achievements of others. Of Mamie's immediate family, her brother, J. W. Meadors of Amarillo, Texas, was her only survivor.

In her will, she appointed her cousin, Salome Anthony (she referred to her distant cousin as "my friend"), and Nina as executors of her estate. She left all her property at Las Dos, some 624 acres, to Nina, along with the option to purchase her half of their jointly owned property in Plaza Fatima, a cul-de-sac off Delgado Street. Dode and Bergere were given her old Chevy. Salome inherited Mamie's personal effects and the home they had shared at 429 Delgado.

Shortly after the estate was settled, Salome sold her property at a profit and moved back to Texas, ending her exemplary thirty-year career at the Santa Fe Public Library. As head librarian, she had worked long hours and many years, most of the time with only two assistants, in her desire to provide Santa Feans with the best in public libraries. Before she left she could say with satisfaction that "Santa Fe children for the first time in the public library's history are reading more than their parents." Shortly after Mamie's death, Salome learned that oil had been discovered on property she owned in Oklahoma, another reason for retiring from her meager-salaried job.[63]

Mamie's death closed one of the strongest emotional and intellectual attachments of Nina's life. Without Mamie, Las Dos Realty came to a virtual standstill, and Nina advised her business associates that she would be curtailing her activities—"due to the loss of my partner."[64] Nina was a woman who generally avoided self-revelation and recoiled from intimate discussions of personal matters and outward displays of grief. Over time she came to terms with her loss and resolved to continue living and working as she had always lived and worked. After six months of trying to manage on her own, she decided to hire a part-time assistant and keep her real-estate business open. At seventy, she still had more energy and motivation than most of her colleagues.

In 1952 Nina asked Ruth Leakey to take over for Mamie. Ruth, an army widow, had come from Fort Sill, Oklahoma, to Taos in 1939, spending several summers and one winter there in the house once occupied by Frieda and D. H. Lawrence. At that time Lady

Dorothy Brett lived just behind her in the studio Mabel Dodge Luhan had prepared for the British painter in the twenties when she arrived from England with the Lawrences.

When Ruth Leakey first met Nina in 1947 she was immediately struck by the similarities between Otero-Warren and Brett. "Both were self-sufficient, independent women, but not objectionably so," Ruth observed. "Brett was not as assertive as Nina, and being a polite British lady was never openly confrontational, as Nina could be on occasion." Ruth remembered that "Brett used to load a cot into her station wagon and go fishing. She would fish a while, take a nap, fish some more, then come home in time to cook what she caught and give some to my cat, Adrian. Lady Brett bathed only once a week—at the Taos Inn for fifty cents. She felt there was no need to bathe more than that, water was too scarce."[65]

Ruth Leakey was publishing La Turista magazine—after trying her luck with People and Places in Santa Fe and Taos, a magazine that lasted only nine months in 1951—when Nina asked her to help in the Las Dos office. Nina was desperate for someone to take over the work Mamie had assumed before she died, with the exception of the insurance end of the business. Thanks to Kay Stephens, who owned and operated the Santa Fe Shirts shop next door to the real-estate office, Ruth was recommended to Nina, who hired her at once and launched her new career as a realtor. Like Mamie, Ruth took care of the record keeping and showed prospective buyers available property. Her hours were flexible. She worked part-time for Nina and part-time publishing La Turista, wearing the various hats of writer, editor, artist, and marketing manager.[66] Ruth spent a memorable thirteen years as Nina's valued business associate and friend.

Nina was making "a significant and sometimes very good income from her real-estate ventures," Bergere said, "so she was in a position to do a lot of nice things for people."[67] That income was in addition to revenue from the occasional renting of the Las Dos homestead houses ($65 per month for four months in 1948) and from the family's N-Bar Ranch near Magdalena, which her brother,

Manuel, had been efficiently managing for more than twenty years.

The only surviving male member of the Eloisa Luna–Manuel B. Otero union, Manuel was expected to keep the ranch productive and profitable. A strong, vigorous man, he had firmly taken over the role of patrón after his brother Eduardo's death in 1932. Manuel's vitality and dedication to task were captured by artist Peter Hurd when he dropped by the Otero ranch in 1941. Hurd wrote to his wife, Henriette, describing the sheepman in action:

> About forty people throng the wool shearing camp all working steadily. . . . Everywhere was the Patrón—lashing about the corrals in around the machinery over at the weighing platform yelling, "Mira, mira [Look alive!] . . . to his men. [His name] was don Manuel. . . . He had a fine strong aquiline face with large piercing eyes of a turquoise-matrix, green blue—different from any eyes I have ever seen. He is fair-skinned and large of body— about 55 I'd say. He is one of the old Hidalgo families—descendant of a colonial governor of this land—then New Spain.[68]

In 1953, Manuel had turned seventy and was tiring of his hard life. "He led a tough life," said Luna Leopold. "He lived in a small dirty shack, with no water well—he had to get water from the creek for his coffee—and poor food. He spent most of his time on horseback."[69]

Manuel finally had enough and wanted to sell the ranch and grazing rights. Nina agreed, much to the dismay of her half-brother Luna Bergere and a number of other family members, all of whom thought it was a bad idea. "Nina did not like suggestions from anybody," said Luna Leopold. He and his brother Starker offered to give up their careers (Luna was a geologist and Starker a biologist) and take over the ranch to avoid selling it, but Nina refused, saying, "What do you know about sheep? You never worked with Solomón Luna."[70] Ignoring the dissenters, she sold the property for close to a million dollars but, according to Leopold, had to pay three-fourths of the money to the IRS.

When the family learned that the buyer was a Texan who quickly turned around and sold the land for a large profit, there was a serious rupture. Hostilities came to a head when Nina reportedly told Luna Bergere: "If you have a call on the estate of Eloisa Luna Otero Bergere, take it to court." Fortunately, attorneys for both sides persuaded sisters and brothers, nieces and nephews to compromise and settle matters out of court. Later, in a letter to Estella Leopold, Nina praised Dolores and Carl Leopold for backing her up: "I cannot tell you what a help it has been to us. The minor concessions that we made were so minor that it is unbelievable that a split in the family could arise over such unnecessary insistence on their part."[71]

As in the past, Nina shouldered the responsibility for the difficult decision she made, and her leadership position within the family remained intact. Although hurt feelings and anger festered for a while, most of the disgruntled family members eventually accepted the settlement. Of her sisters, only Consuelo remained bitter to the end of her ninety-five years.

Nina helped ease tensions in the year that followed by using some of the money made from the ranch land sale for a holiday with her sisters in Cuba, Yucatán, and Taxco. The *New Mexican* reported that "those fabulous Bergere sisters," along with "Queen Bee" Nina Otero-Warren, boarded a freighter at Houston and sailed to Cuba. Nina, Anita, May, Rosina, Estella, Dolores, and "one grandchild" virtually took over a ship equipped with staterooms for only twelve passengers. After spending several days at the Veradero Beach Hotel in the "Land of Rhumba," the Bergere "convention" flew in three planes to Mérida on the Yucatán Peninsula, splitting up their party as a precaution against the possibility of a crash wiping out most of the family.

When the women returned to the States they had to hire a truck in El Paso to transport their vacation "loot" to Santa Fe. Nina told Ruth Leakey later that they decided to leave Cuba because of the tinder-box political climate under Fulgencio Batista, whose dictatorship was being threatened by Fidel Castro's forces. Nina and her party flew to Mexico with "Anita saying her beads all the way."[72]

Drawing of Nina made in Cuidad
Mexico, May 9, 1950. (Bergere
Family Collection, photo no.
21708, New Mexico State
Records Center and Archives,
Santa Fe, New Mexico.)

The trip in 1954 was well timed, as the family lost four of its members in the years that followed. The Cuba vacation was one of the last Dolores would take with her sisters before her death two years later at the age of fifty-nine. Both of Nina's half-brothers also died in their fifties, Luna Bergere in October, 1955, and handsome, affable Joe (her favorite brother, "a charmer," according to Ruth Leakey, "much like Nina"), of a sudden heart attack in a motel in Grants, New Mexico, in 1957. Since neither Luna nor Joe left male heirs, the surname Bergere also died, although it was carried on as a first or middle name by nine descendants of Eloisa and Alfred M. Bergere.[73]

The fifties also saw the death of Dolores's husband, Carl Starker Leopold, and Nina's good friends Will Shuster and John Sloan, both dominant figures in the city's early art colony. And a gracious historical period in Los Lunas died when Ted Otero sold the Luna Mansion, that grand symbol of wealth and power held by the Luna and Otero families since 1881. Fortunately, the mansion was preserved and is now the Río Abajo region's most elegant restaurant.

Nina herself enjoyed remarkably good health despite her advancing years and addiction to cigarettes, but she did have some minor problems with embolisms, which young Dr. Bergere Kenney tried to treat. Bergere had undertaken the difficult task of being physician to his mother and all his aunts, but he was often discouraged when the free-spirited—at times obstinate—women ignored his professional advice. One day he finally gave up and told them he was through: "I prescribe medication, but you either refuse to take it or you take only what you want. I'm no longer your doctor." Nina's response was, "All right, Bergere, next time I'm sick I'll just sit by your office door and die." (Bergere's office at 10 Sena Plaza, across from St. Vincent Hospital, was close to Nina's.) With that Bergere laughed and relented, but agreed to keep only Nina as his patient.[74]

Bergere admired his aunts for staying trim and active throughout their lives. Nina, who never weighed more than 100 pounds, walked back and forth from the Big House to Las Dos Realty—eight or ten blocks round trip—every day for eighteen years. She closely followed political events in the state and around the world and remained engaged in the social life of the city as long as she lived. Gifted with a natural ability to charm and entertain, she did so even in her later years, never losing sight of the advantages that could be gained by networking with the politically powerful.

One of her most creative parties was held in 1949 at the old Magoffin House just before it was demolished to make way for a La Fonda hotel parking lot. A fine old Santa Fe landmark, the home was once occupied by Samuel and Susan Magoffin, nineteenth-century pioneers of the Santa Fe Trail. The genial Irish Magoffin brothers, James and Samuel, had made their fortunes as traders while New Mexico still belonged to Mexico. James had served as United States consul to Mexico in the mid-1800s and had helped prepare the way

Nina Otero-Warren, center, surrounded by Will Shuster and friends, preparing to roll dice in the old Magoffin House during a costume-casino party, 1949. Nina was dressed as nineteenth-century gambling hall proprietor Tules Barceló. (Bergere Family Collection, photo no. 24617, New Mexico State Records Center and Archives, Santa Fe, New Mexico.)

in 1846 for the United States occupation of New Mexico by General Stephen Kearney's army.[75]

Under Nina's direction, the Magoffin House was turned into a noisy, smoke-filled casino with a large bar, gaming tables, and posters on the walls inviting guests to try their luck with doña Tules. As in the past, most of the state's important political figures attended, all in costume. Nina arrived gaudily dressed as the notorious nineteenth-century Santa Fe gambling-hall doyenne, La Tules (doña María Gertrudis Barceló), and spent the evening dealing monte.

Back in the early to middle 1800s, doña Tules (an abbreviation of Gertrudis) had come to Santa Fe from Tomé with her husband, Manuel Sisneros, and made a fortune in her plush gambling salon–brothel. A self-assured woman, reputed mistress of the state's

Nina Otero-Warren and Mrs
Gustave (Jane) Baumann during a
joint birthday celebration at a
gay-nineties costume party in
Gonzales Hall on Camino del
Monte Sol, 1953. (Photograph
first appeared in the New Mexican, October 25, 1953.)

last Mexican governor, Manuel Armijo—a woman who drank,
smoked cigarettes, and dealt cards—Tules was nevertheless accepted
by the best of society. Nina, self-confident and secure enough in her
own right to abandon for an evening her conventional lifestyle and
assume the flamboyant airs of Tules, thoroughly enjoyed the role.[76]

One of Nina's most memorable birthday parties took place in a
rented dance hall (Gonzales Hall on Camino del Monte Sol) on October 23, 1953. Since she and her friend Jane Baumann (Mrs. Gustave)
shared the same birthday, both were honored by the elite of Santa Fe,
all of whom arrived in authentic Gay Nineties costumes. The New
Mexican reported that "Santa Fe's First Families—and some of later
vintage—were well represented." The state's governor, Edwin L.
Mechem, and his wife were among the hundred guests, as were the
John Gaw Meems, the Frank Claffeys, the H. S. A. Alexanders, and
the Bergere Kenneys.

Nina, the seventy-two-year-old matriarch, appeared in a Luna family heirloom of heavily embroidered cream silk and lace. Anita wore black, as usual, but carried a Kelly green ostrich boa. May and Rosina were there in vintage gowns, and Cristina chose a black riding habit complete with a tricorn hat that her great-aunt had worn as a teenager in Los Lunas. Toward the end of the splendid evening, Ruth Leakey remembered, one of the tipsy male guests backed his car into a nearby arroyo and had to be hauled out by friends in the wee hours of the morning.[77]

As the 1950s drew to a close, Nina was approaching eighty but showed few signs of slowing down. She took great pleasure in advanced postwar technology—television, jet airplanes, air-conditioning—and the new hot-nut machine in Sears Roebuck, which she operated every day on her way home from work. Always an avid follower of world events, she was particularly impressed with the space programs launched by what was then the Soviet Union and by the United States. Joey and Jack Kenney remembered being invited to join her on the back porch of the Big House on October 4, 1957, to watch for the Soviets' Sputnik I. "Her excitement was contagious," Joey said.[78]

Financially comfortable, Nina gave freely to deserving causes, most of them connected in some way with her sisters, nieces, and nephews. "She bailed out a lot of people," Jack Kenney said. "She kept a considerable amount of cash in her safe deposit box in case someone in the family had problems. She was footing the bills for so many people who were having trouble straightening out their lives, and she never said a word about it."[79]

In 1959, Santa Fe bestowed on Nina the sterling honor of life membership on the Fiesta Board "in recognition of outstanding services given to the perpetuation of Fiesta de Santa Fe." In her hoop-skirted gown of gold and lace, modeled after a court costume worn during the reign of Philip II and enhanced with heirloom jewelry passed along to her from Luna and Otero ancestors, she projected the image of a courtly hidalga, a noblewoman of Old Spain.[80]

First appointed trustees of the Edward Grisso Scholarship Fund of the University of New Mexico. Left to right: W. D. Grisso (Oklahoma City and Santa Fe), Ethel Bond Huffines (Nambe), Nina Otero-Warren, and A. B. Carpenter (Roswell and Phoenix), Albuquerque, 1958. (Bergere Family Collection, photo no. 21724, New Mexico State Records Center and Archives, Santa Fe, New Mexico.)

Three years later, the governor made her an "Admiral in New Mexico's Bi-Partisan Navy" for her outstanding community service and her ground-breaking accomplishments in New Mexico politics. The certificate she received featured two ships and the words, "You have complete and full authority of the Rank to exercise at any and all times aboard our ships, the Defender (D), and the Manhattan (R)." Nina had been made a colonel on Governor Dillon's staff back in 1930. Now she was an admiral.

There were other rewards for her writing. Over the quarter-century since her book was published, she had received queries from publishers around the country for permission to reprint all or portions of Old Spain in Our Southwest for use in textbooks, some in Braille, for children and young adults.

Nina also had the satisfaction of living to see the emergence of the 1960s women's liberation movement, a rebirth of feminist principles she had fought to enforce more than fifty years before. She did not approve of the emerging hippie culture, but she applauded the publication of Betty Friedan's *The Feminine Mystique* in 1963 with its attack on the long-held notion that a woman could be fulfilled only through marriage and motherhood. For even though women were enfranchised, newspapers still advertised male and female jobs in separate columns, airlines routinely fired stewardesses who married, and general discrimination against women prevailed in the workplace, higher education, and politics.

Nina's achievements as an educator were heralded throughout her life and long after her death. On October 26, 1988, the Otero Elementary School in Colorado Springs, Colorado, was "dedicated to Nina Otero (Warren) in recognition of her contributions to the education of Hispanics."[81]

As she approached her eighty-third year, she was still spending time at her Las Dos office (although she would take a short siesta after lunch) and was thinking of writing a book about her uncle Solomón Luna, hoping to put to rest once and for all the rumors that had proliferated over the years concerning the strange circumstances of his death in a sheep-dipping vat. But this was one goal Nina was not to meet.

As she was preparing for mass on Sunday morning, January 3, 1965, she complained to Anita that she felt ill. She asked for a brandy and managed to drink it before collapsing. She was gone before Bergere could get to the Big House, but "she died happy," Jack said. "A quick and painless death after a long and fruitful life—and a good brandy—was all she could have wanted."[82]

Two rosary services were held for Nina, the first, in Memorial Chapel Mortuary, recited in English, the second in Spanish and led by Anita Gonzales Thomas in the Big House, where Nina's body was taken after embalming to lie in state. Crowds of people gathered, including her former devoted pupil, Dominguita Vigíl Ortíz, who "cried and prayed for La Nina." Two days later, after a funeral mass was sung at St. Francis Cathedral with her old friend Father Pax officiating, Nina was laid to rest near her mother in the Rosario Cemetery family plot.

"Mrs. María Adelina Emilia (Nina) Otero-Warren . . . descendant of two pioneer families" was survived by six half-sisters, the obituary in the *New Mexican* reported: Anita, Ysabel, Rosina, May, and Connie—in Santa Fe—and Estella, Mrs. Aldo Leopold, of Madison, Wisconsin. "In keeping with the family history, Nina Otero-Warren left her own mark on the first half of the 20th Century in New Mexico. At a time when most women were confined to the kitchen, she was one of the first to become professionally and politically active."[83]

Author, businesswoman, educator, feminist, homesteader, politician, socialite, and surrogate mother, Nina spent her life well, and mostly on her own terms. A tiny but towering figure in Santa Fe, she transcended the female stereotypes of her time and helped shape the future for other women. She taught and fought for the things she believed in—equality for women, better education for the people of New Mexico, preservation of her native culture, financial independence for herself and those she loved, commitment to family, church, and community. And she did it all with the courage, grace, and pride of her pioneering Spanish ancestors.

Epilogue

rna Fergusson wrote a light-hearted assessment of Santa Fe and its citizens in the fifties, saying "there are no nobodies in Santa Fe. Here everyone is *somebody*." For Fergusson, Santa Fe was the "last outpost of the individual in a standardized and documented world." The City of the Holy Faith was a place where the Indian, the Spanish, and Anglo Americans lived side by side in harmony—"or nearly"—where one could find supportive, tolerant, caring people in a unique setting that its resident artists in the thirties had kept from "going Main Street."[1]

Today, all is changed. Santa Fe has received so much attention worldwide that it is struggling desperately to hang on to its reputation as the City Different, alternately battling developers and media hype bent on turning it into a trendy "Carmel-in-the-Desert." With more than fifty-six thousand permanent or part-time residents (more Anglos than Hispanos now), traffic-choked streets, hotels, restaurants, minimalls, and galleries, Santa Fe is hard pressed to cope with the 1.5 million tourists it has been attracting annually in the nineties.[2]

Mary Austin, Alice Corbin Henderson, and Witter Bynner would be supremely happy to see the work of new and established, national and international artists exhibited in the more than 150 galleries in and around the plaza and up Canyon Road. Although today artists tend to retreat to their studios, seeking isolation for work that since World War II has increasingly focused on individualism and abstract expressionism. Lacking are the close-knit ties, the supportive community infrastructure of the twenties and thirties.[3]

Early art-colonist Willard Clark, still living in 1993 in the two-story "mud hut" he built in the thirties for $2,000, saw the alfalfa field near his property become a posh residential area of multimillion-dollar homes. "Santa Fe had a nice, even growth for a long time," he said, "and then, about fifteen years ago, it just went crazy."[4] Thousands of new homes, apartment buildings, and businesses—downtown and in the suburbs—reflect the boom in real estate during the past decade. And with it has come noise- and air-pollution, congestion, and housing costs so high that people with average incomes must live elsewhere—in Albuquerque or Rio Rancho, Española or Las Vegas—and commute two to three hours a day to jobs in the capital.[5]

The Las Dos land homesteaded by Nina and Mamie in the early thirties is worth millions of dollars on today's market. The rutted roads leading out from town have now been paved, the once treacherous arroyo crossings covered with concrete. Most of the property Nina willed to her nephews Jack and Bergere Kenney has been sold, but the acreage around the original adobe houses still belongs to the heirs of Grandmother Eloisa Luna Otero Bergere. The picnics at the homestead continue and now include the families of those who have built modern adobe homes on the hills nearby.

Bergere and Dode Kenney first opened a portion of Las Dos (about 439 acres) to new settlers in 1980, building all-weather roads, burying telephone and electric cables, and drafting sensible protective covenants to create a conservation community for people drawn to the natural, awe-inspiring beauty of that delicate but pow-

erful land. The roads within the subdivision were named for Bergere's late aunts (Calle Adelina, Vuelta María, Placita Anita) and for
Mamie Meadors (Mamie's Mile). Jack and Joey Kenney sold a portion
of their share in Las Dos to a California family, obviating the division
of the land for multiple residences. Conservation of the richly endowed environment and its most precious commodity, water, is the
primary concern of the new Las Dos homeowners, who have discovered how unforgiving the land can be if exploited through human
carelessness.

After Anita Bergere and May Kenney died in 1976, the Big
House on Grant Avenue was chosen as one of Santa Fe's historic
buildings and was later sold to Harry Bigbee to house his legal firm,
BCO, Inc. Bigbee, with the help of landscape architect Frederick
Liebler, brought the Bergere landmark back to prime condition,
restoring both the interior rooms and the gardens surrounding the
house and winning in 1982 the *New Mexican*'s business landscaping
contest.[6]

The little house in Plaza Fatima that Nina had left to Anita, who
in turn willed it to Cristina Kenney Herdman, remained rental property for years, until Cristina and her husband, Dick, decided to restore it and return to Santa Fe to live there in 1991. When Eloisa
Bergere Brown heard the good news of her cousin's leaving California to move back home, she was ecstatic: "Oh boy, cousins again.
Maybe we can build it back into what it was—the largest extended
family in the world and a town full of cousins waiting on each corner of the plaza for kisses. And Oh, the hugs, and screams of delight
at seeing each other. Almost as though we hadn't just seen each other
last night."[7]

Sadly, Cristina lived less than a year after returning to Santa Fe,
struck down by cancer just a month after settling into her new
home. All the cousins agreed that her early years under the strict
regime of the Nina-dominated Big House had been difficult. She eagerly left the rigid environment and the city once she had the
chance. Yet toward the end of her life she had mellowed, giving Nina

credit for much more than she was willing to admit earlier. Nina had financed her education at Maryville and celebrated her graduation and later her engagement and marriage to Richard Herdman. And Eloisa remembered that as a child, born days after her father died, Cristina had given the depressed women in the Big House comfort and "unconditional love." Anita, "the very religious designated housekeeper, was overwhelmed with love when the Lord blessed the Big House with this beautiful curly-headed baby that, in her mind, resembled the Christ child." Cristina's arrival had turned sorrow to joy in the gloomy house.[8]

Cristina was the last of May and John Kenney's children to die, her sister Dolores the first. Bergere died in 1988, Jack in 1990, both leaving distinguished legacies. Just months before their deaths Bergere and Jack were named Living Treasures by the Santa Fe Network for the Common Good, honored as "wise and wonderful human beings" for the compassion and love they had given others. Bergere had spent all his professional years in Santa Fe, practicing medicine in St. Vincent Hospital and serving as its chief of staff during the late sixties and early seventies. These were difficult years as the hospital transferred its administration from the Catholic Sisters of Charity to a nonsectarian group. "I worked hard to make it all happen as smoothly as possible," he said in an interview six months before his death.[9] On February 21, 1988, the hospital dedicated to Bergere Kenney its cardiac care unit, a department he helped establish in the fifties.

Dr. Bergere Kenney was also a founding board member of the Santa Fe Chamber Music Festival, known today in this country and abroad for its success in bringing to the city every summer some of the world's great musicians. Bergere and Dode opened their home to the artists and permitted them to rehearse in the large, bright living room overlooking Fort Marcy Park.

After retiring from the army as a brigadier general and working in the civilian world for ten years, Jack Kenney returned to his birthplace and bought a house not far from his brother's. Before his death in November 1990, he was active with environmental organizations, serving as chairman of the regional Rio Grande chapter of the Sierra Club and president of the Santa Fe division. For many years he had been a compelling force as a motivator and organizer in bringing environmental concerns to public and governmental attention. Believing in the importance of constant communication between environmental groups—there were more than fifty of them in northern New Mexico at the time—General Kenney proposed ways to help the various organizations keep in touch with each other. He was working with David Knauer in helping to structure NENIX (Northern New Mexico Environmental Exchange) when the same type of cancer that struck down his brother two years before took his life as well.

With the exception of Connie Bergere Mendenhall (1895–1990), all of Nina's half-sisters—Anita, Estella, May, Dolores, and Ysabel—died before the seventies ended. But their children and grandchildren, together with those of Eduardo, Manuel, Luna, and Joe, carry on the family traditions. Today the fourth and fifth generations of Eloisa Luna Otero Bergere's descendants number more than one hundred, but few make their home in Santa Fe.

For those who do, the city and its surrounding land are still far removed from Erna Fergusson's standardized and documented world. The charm and historic richness of Santa Fe, its caring people and healing landscapes, make the difficult challenges to preserve it patently worthwhile.

Chronology

NINA
OTERO-
WARREN

Child and teenager in Los Lunas, New Mexico, 1881–97
Maryville College in Saint Louis, 1892–94
Moved to Santa Fe, 1897
Marriage to Rawson Warren, 1908–1909
State chairman of the legislative committee for the Federation of
   Women's Clubs, ca. 1915
Leader of the suffrage movement in New Mexico, 1915–20
Chairman of the State Board of Health in New Mexico, ca. 1917
Superintendent of public schools in Santa Fe County, 1917–29
Member of the executive board of the American Red Cross, 1918
Chairman of the women's auxiliary board of the New Mexico State
   Council of Defense in the First Judicial District, 1918
Republican party nominee for the U.S. House of Representatives (the
   first woman from New Mexico to be nominated and to run for
   high office), 1922
Chairman of New Mexico's Republican Women's Organization, 1923
Inspector of Indian services in the Department of the Interior (one of
   five, and the first woman), 1922–24

Interpreter and liaison officer with the Pueblo Land Board, 1923

Homesteaded, with Mamie Meadors, 1,257 acres of land called Las Dos outside the city of Santa Fe, 1929–32

Director of literacy education with the Civilian Conservation Corps, 1935

Director of the literacy program of adult education in the state of New Mexico under the Works Project Administration (WPA), 1937

Author of *Old Spain in Our Southwest*, 1936

Director of the Work Conference for Adult Teachers in Río Piedras, Puerto Rico, July 14–26, 1941

Santa Fe County director for the Office of Price Administration (OPA), 1942–45

Owner and manager of Las Dos Realty and Insurance Company, 1947–65

Notes

CHAPTER ONE

1. Lucretia Pittman, S.C., "Solomón Luna: Sheepmaster and Politician of New Mexico" (M.A. thesis, St. Louis University, 1941), 11. Nina's grandfather, Antonio José Luna, built a home in Los Lunas for the priest's convenience.

2. Carl D. W. Hays, "One of Luna Family Was Even Pope in Early 1400s," *Southwesterner* (June 1964), 20; Luna Leopold to author, May 6, 1992; *New Catholic Encyclopedia*, vol. II (New York: McGraw Hill, 1967), 277. Pedro de Luna was born in 1328 in Illueca, Aragón, Spain; he was pontificate of Avignon from September 28, 1394, to July 26, 1417. According to Ludwig Freiherr von Pastor (*The History of the Popes: From the Close of the Middle Ages*, trans. Dom Ernest Graf, OSB, Monk of Buckfast, vol. 1 [St. Louis: B. Herder Book Co., 1952], 189), Benedict XIII and Gregory XII were accused of being "not merely promoters of the Schism, but actually heretics in the fullest sense of the word, because by their conduct they had attacked and overturned the article of faith regarding the One, Holy, Catholic and Apostolic Church."

3. Eloisa Bergere Brown, "A Skeleton in My Closet," *Albuquerque Journal Magazine*, April 10, 1984; James A. Michener, *Iberia: Spanish Travels and Reflections*

213

(New York: Random House, 1968), 106. Álvaro de Luna was a nephew of the "anti-Pope Benedict" and had been "absolute master, for a long generation, of King Juan and of all Castile. He looted the Crown . . . corrupted the Church . . . alienated the nobles by his insolence and arrogance, he infuriated the populace by giving high offices and privileges to Jews and Moors. . . . Many blamed him for all the decay that made the court notorious" (William Thomas Walsh, *Isabella of Spain: The Last Crusader* [New York: Robt. M. McBride, 1930], 2).

4. Carl D. W. Hays, "There Was Even a Luna with Cortés," *Southwesterner* (April 1964), 24.

5. Carl D. W. Hays, "Antonio de Luna Killed by Apaches," *Southwesterner* (May 1964), 2; Alfred M. Bergere, "The San Clemente or Ana de Sandoval y Manzanares Grant," September 1931, A. M. Bergere Family Papers, State Records Center and Archives, Santa Fe, New Mexico; John Collier, *From Every Zenith: A Memoir* (Denver: Sage Books, 1963), 141. The land around what is now Los Lunas was colonized in 1692 and given to don Felix Candelaria two years after his mother, doña Ana de Sandoval y Manzanares de Candelaria, petitioned for the deed in 1716. Doña Ana was the widow of don Blas de la Candelaria and had inherited the lands from her father, don Matío Sandoval y Manzanares. In her petition, doña Ana had asked General Vargas, governor and captain general of the province, to keep the promise he had made when he brought her family from Spain to settle the territory in 1692. At that time he had agreed to give each one of the native citizens tracts of land and fields and stock-raising ranches abandoned in 1680 after the Pueblo Indians rebelled and drove Spain out of New Mexico. She waited several years without hearing from the governor before embarking on her journey to Mexico.

6. Hays, "There Was Even a Luna with Cortés"; Stewart L. Udall, *To the Inland Empire: Coronado and Our Spanish Legacy* (New York: Doubleday, 1967), 203. Juan de Oñate founded the first permanent Spanish settlement in New Mexico. The Bacas, Lunas, and Chaveses are among the fifty-three "Onate families," the "first families of the United States." In the May 1964 issue of the *Southwesterner*, the editor printed a letter from Nina Otero-Warren stating that her grandmother's name was Dolores Chaves y Otero and that "the Chaves spelled their name with an 's' and not

with a 'z'. Those who spelled it with a 'z' are not the original families
that came from Spain." In the June 1964 issue, Dimas M. Chávez challenged Nina's claim, saying that "the spelling of Chaves or Chávez are
both grammatically, historically and ancestrally correct. Both are direct
descendants of Spain. . . . The original Spaniard name was not Chaves
or Chávez, but Llaves, which translated means keys. The Llaves family
of Spain was a blue blood family and of great nobility . . . later dubbed
'keeper of the keys'."

7. *WPA Guide to 1930s in New Mexico*, compiled by the workers of the Writers' Program of the Work Projects Administration in the State of New
Mexico (Tucson: University of Arizona Press, 1989), 248–49. As late as
1880 a band of one hundred Indians attacked Los Lunas, killing seven
people, including two children. Two young girls were taken captive
and several ranches in the vicinity were surrounded and held hostage
until the cavalry rode in and drove the Indians out (Oliver La Farge,
Santa Fe: The Autobiography of a Southwestern Town [Norman: University of
Oklahoma Press, 1959], 99).

8. John Joseph Kenney, "La Reunión de la Familia de Eloisa Luna de Otero
de Bergere: Historia," September 15, 1980:14.

9. John O. Baxter, *Las Carneradas: Sheep Trade in New Mexico: 1700–1860* (Albuquerque: University of New Mexico Press, 1987), 121; Hays, *Southwesterner* (May 1964), 2.

10. Ibid.; Kenney, "La Reunión," 55. "Among the Luna place names on to-
day's maps [June 1964] are Los Lunas, the family seat and county seat
of Valencia County; Puerto de Luna, in Guadalupe County, just south of
Santa Rosa and on the main road between that place and Fort Sumner;
Luna County; Luna, Catron County, named for Solomón Luna and the
headquarters for his sheep operations in that vicinity; Luna Lake in
Apache County, Arizona, where Solomón had another sheep camp; and
Luna Lake Recreation Area, a state project near Alpine, Arizona. . . .
Puerto de Luna in Guadalupe County was one of the stopping places
of Billy the Kid. . . . Miguel Luna and two other boys were playing
marbles at the side of the old Lincoln County jail when the Kid killed
deputies Bob Olinger and J. W. Bell in 1881, and they saw him make
his escape" (Hays, "One of Luna Family Was Even Pope").

11. Pittman, "Solomón Luna," 12.

12. Nina Otero, *Old Spain in Our Southwest* (New York: Harcourt, Brace and Co., 1936), 50.

13. Pittman, "Solomón Luna," 17; Ralph E. Twitchell, ed., *Old Santa Fe: The Story of New Mexico's Ancient Capitol* (Chicago: Rio Grande Press, 1963), 466; Sr. Blandina Segale, *At the End of the Santa Fe Trail* (Milwaukee: Bruce Publishing Co., 1879), 129.

14. Anna Katherine, "Vignette: Consuelo Mendenhall," *Santa Fean* (November 1986), 12.

15. Erna Fergusson, "The Ballad of Manuel B.," in *Murder and Mystery in New Mexico* (Albuquerque: Merle Armitage Eds., 1948), 41; Kenney, "La Reunión," 24.

16. A. M. Bergere, "Early History of the Estancia Valley," AMB Papers, Santa Fe Archives.

17. Manuel Antonio Otero to Manuel B. Otero, transcribed by Nina Otero-Warren, AMB Papers, Santa Fe Archives.

18. Twitchell, *Old Santa Fe*, 466, cited in Kenney, "La Reunión," 6; Andrew K. Gregg, *New Mexico in the Nineteenth Century: A Pictorial History* (Albuquerque: University of New Mexico Press, 1968), 167.

19. Nina Otero, *Old Spain*, 41.

20. *WPA Guide*, 248. "Some of the New Mexico dishes popular today are from this [Los Lunas] section. Two of these are *enchiladas* served with beans (*frijoles*) and *posole*, which is hominy cooked with pork."

21. Fergusson, "Ballad of Manuel B.," 34; Mary Austin, *The Land of Journey's Ending* (Tucson: University of Arizona Press, 1985), 342.

22. Nina Otero, *Old Spain*, 43–44; Austin, *The Land of Journey's Ending*, 342. The ruins of the Manuel Otero home are located not far from Los Lunas, close to the Río Grande, behind the present home of a Mrs. Graham. Most of the onetime adobe structure has melted into mounds of sod with trees and bushes growing around and out of them. The author was shown the site on September 16, 1991, by Edwin Berry, a neighbor who remembered the Oteros.

23. Katherine, "Vignette: Consuelo Mendenhall," 12.

24. Abbreviated history of the Luna Mansion on the back of the Luna Mansion Restaurant menu, 1990. The mansion remained in the Luna-Otero family until it was sold in the fifties. In the twenties, Eduardo Otero's wife, Josefita "Pepa" Manderville Otero, added a solarium, a two-story

porch with four Greek columns, and a decorative wrought-iron fence around the property, and maintained elaborate gardens on the two-acre estate.

25. William MacLeod Raine, "The Baca Land Grant Fight," *Denver Post*, October 25, 1953.

26. AMB Papers, Scrapbook #1, articles from the original 1883 newspapers reporting the incident; *WPA Guide*, 293.

27. *Gringo & Greaser* (August 18, 1883), AMB Papers, Scrapbook #1.

28. *Gringo & Greaser*; Fergusson, "The Ballad of Manuel B.," 38; Miguel A. Otero, *My Life on the Frontier: 1882–1897* (New York: Press of the Pioneers, 1935), 99–103; Bergere, "Early History of the Estancia Valley"; Frank M. King, *Western Livestock*, April 28, 1936; *WPA Guide*, 293. Erna Fergusson claims that two bullets struck Whitney; A. M. Bergere claims eleven. Miguel A. Otero wrote that Whitney was "badly wounded, and, though he partially recovered, he finally died of the wounds." Frank M. King said that Whitney had his "right jaw shot away . . . and had two slugs in his body." *The Optic*, the *Albuquerque Journal*, and other local newspapers ran conflicting stories for weeks after the incident.

29. *Sunday Gazette* (n.d.), n.p., AMB Papers, Scrapbook #1.

30. Fergusson, "The Ballad of Manuel B.," 33–48.

31. Miguel A. Otero, *My Life on the Frontier*, 101–105.

32. Ibid., 108.

33. *Sunday Gazette*, August 18, 1883, AMB Papers, Scrapbook #1. At the time of the Otero-Whitney land dispute, more land-grant claims by the original Hispanic owners were rejected than confirmed. The understaffed surveyor general's office, "a native population which did not understand what was at stake, and politics made for a situation in which fraud and injustice were all too common" (Warren A. Beck, *Historical Atlas of New Mexico* [Albuquerque: University of New Mexico Press, 1969], 21).

34. Beck, *Historical Atlas*, 101-103. Although James Whitney lived almost twenty years after the tragic incident, he suffered emotionally and physically from the experience for the rest of his life.

35. AMB Papers, Scrapbook #1.

36. Nina Otero, *Old Spain*, 37–38.

37. Sarah Deutsch, *No Separate Refuge: Culture, Class, and Gender on an Anglo-Hispanic*

Frontier in the American Southwest, 1880–1940 (New York: Oxford University Press, 1987), 19–40.

38. Katherine, "Vignette," 12; Kenney, "La Reunión," 55. Teta, wrote Eloisa's grandson Jack Kenney in 1980, was "a source of counsel, sharing confidences with all, and supporting the family in all ways."

39. Katherine, "Vignette," 12.

40. A. M. Bergere, "Autobiography," AMB Papers.

41. AMB Papers, 17-A. Alfred Bergere noted in his autobiography that "the Lunas were indirectly related by marriage to the Oteros, Jaramillos, Castillos, Bacas, Sandovals, Chavezes and Gallegoses. . . . The Armijos are intermarried with the Chavez family. The Pereas with the Oteros and the Yrizarri family."

42. AMB Papers; interview with Eloisa Bergere Brown, July 10, 1990; Pittman, "Solomón Luna," 59. Years later family members determined that AMB's parents were Jews when his relatives arrived from England looking for Alfred M. Berger. Alfred Bergere's brother's grandson is John Berger, the author of *Ways of Seeing* and the Booker Prize–winning novel, *G*, the story of a Jewish family brought up in Italy. The Lunas, too, were of Jewish ancestry, according to W. T. Walsh, *Isabella of Spain*, 200: "By the time of Isabel and Fernando, a great many of the ancient houses of the peninsula had Jewish relatives. . . . The de Lunas, the Mendozas, the Guzmans, the Villahermosas, all had Hebrew strains." Sister Lucretia Pittman, in her interviews with Solomón Luna's contemporaries, wrote that not only did Solomón's "appearance lead one to suspect him of Jewish ancestry but many traits of character, his sagacious, unassuming, unobtrusive leadership, the wisdom displayed in the investments he made, his quickness to sympathy and his human understanding, all pointed to the same conclusion." Birth records for A. M. Bergere indicate that he was born *Berger*, without the *e* at the end of his name (Michael Berger to author, September 11, 1991).

43. Bergere, "Autobiography."

44. Ibid.

45. Darlis Miller, "Cross-Cultural Marriages in the Southwest: The New Mexico Experience, 1846–1900," in Joan M. Jensen and Darlis A. Miller, eds., *New Mexico Women: Intercultural Perspectives* (Albuquerque: University of New Mexico Press, 1986), 101–102.

46. Erna Fergusson, *New Mexico: A Pageant of Three Peoples*, (New York: Knopf, 1951), 367.
47. Bergere, "Autobiography."
48. Nina Otero, *Old Spain*, 12.
49. Ibid., 16–17.
50. Darlis Miller, "The Women of Lincoln County," in Jensen and Miller, *New Mexico Women*, 183. Erin Verry, Director, Maryville College Alumnae, to author, April 8, 1991. Not until 1925 did Maryville achieve the status of a senior college. Nina and two other women, Mrs. Lucille Tapin Borden and Miss Florence Magruder Gilmore, were the first Maryville alumnae to receive honorary degrees from the college.
51. Interviews with Consuelo Mendenhall, April 16, 1990, and Eloisa Bergere Brown, July 10, 1990.
52. Sarah Deutch, *No Separate Refuge*, 44.
53. Interview with John J. Kenney, October 12, 1990.
54. Nina Otero, *Old Spain*, 56–57.
55. Nina Otero, *Old Spain*, 48; Pittman, "Solomón Luna," 10.
56. Nina Otero, *Old Spain*, 23.
57. Ibid., 47, 12, 48–49.
58. Nina Otero, *Old Spain*, 16–17; Brian Boru Dunne, "Alfred M. Bergere," *Santa Fe New Mexican*, n.d., cited in John J. Kenney, "La Reunión."
59. Bergere, "Autobiography." In founding Albuquerque in 1706, don Francisco Cuervo y Valdés "honored his patron saint, Francisco Xavier, and the Duke of Alburquerque, viceroy of New Spain, by naming the villa San Francisco de Alburquerque, from which came the common appellation of the 'Duke City'. . . . Eventually the first 'r' was dropped, and it became Albuquerque" (*WPA Guide*, 175).
60. Bergere, "Autobiography."
61. Ibid.
62. Fergusson, *New Mexico*, 320.
63. Bergere, "Autobiography."
64. Miguel A. Otero, *My Life on the Frontier*, 105.
65. Bergere, "The Early History of the Estancia Valley: The First Grant to Bartolome Baca," AMB Papers.
66. Michael Miller, "The Legacy of A. M. Bergere: Pioneer New Mexican," *Southwest Heritage* (n.d.), 8.

67. Fergusson, "The Ballad of Manuel B," 48.

68. Miguel A. Otero, *My Life on the Frontier*, 107.

69. Deutsch, *No Separate Refuge*, 20.

70. Miller, "Legacy of A. M. Bergere," 8.

71. Miller, "Legacy of A. M. Bergere," 8; interviews with John J. Kenney, October 12, 1990, and Eloisa B. Brown, July 10, 1990.

72. Miguel Antonio Otero, *My Nine Years as Governor of the Territory of New Mexico, 1897–1906* (Albuquerque: University of New Mexico Press, 1940), 18; Bergere, "Autobiography."

73. Miguel A. Otero, *My Nine Years as Governor*, 18.

74. Nina Otero, *Old Spain*, 30.

75. Deutsch, *No Separate Refuge*, 42–43.

CHAPTER TWO

1. John Sherman, *Santa Fe: A Pictorial History* (Norfolk: Donning Company, 1983), 76, 115; Erna Fergusson, *Our Southwest* (New York: Knopf, 1940), 273; *WPA Guide to 1930s in New Mexico* (Tucson: University of Arizona Press, 1989), 187; interview with John J. Kenney, October 12, 1990. Anita, Estella, May, and Consuelo, and later Dolores and Rosina, attended grammar school at Loretto Academy. All the girls but Consuelo went on to high school there. Consuelo graduated from Santa Fe High School in 1914.

2. Sherman, *Santa Fe*, 73; Paul Horgan, *Lamy of Santa Fe: His Life and Times* (New York: Farrar, Straus and Giroux, 1975), 122.

3. Miguel A. Otero, *My Life on the Frontier, 1882–1897* (Albuquerque: University of New Mexico Press, 1939), 299; Miguel A. Otero, *My Nine Years as Governor of the Territory of New Mexico, 1897–1906* (Albuquerque: University of New Mexico Press, 1940), 3; Sherman, *Santa Fe*, 76, photograph (neg. #14090, Museum of New Mexico); Lynn I. Perrigo, *Hispanos: Historical Leaders in New Mexico* (Santa Fe: Sunstone Press, 1985), 42–43. Many historical records indicate that Miguel Otero was the first and only officially appointed Hispanic territorial governor, but Donaciano Vigíl served briefly (1847–48) as acting governor after the assassination of Governor Charles Bent in 1847.

4. Miguel A. Otero, *Life on the Frontier*, 277.

5. Miguel A. Otero, *My Nine Years as Governor*, 18; Perrigo, *Hispanos*, 67; Fer-

gusson, *Our Southwest*, 275. Caroline V. Emmett was a young woman from Minnesota whom Otero had married in an Episcopal ceremony on December 19, 1888. "Governor Gilly and his pretty . . . wife entertained lavishly" (*Who Was Who in America* [Chicago: A. M. Marquis Co., 1950], vol. 2, 407–408). Otero later married a Mrs. Maud Pain Frost on October 1, 1913.

6. Interview with John J. and Josephine S. Kenney, April 14, 1990. Nina Otero (*Old Spain in Our Southwest* [New York: Harcourt, Brace and Co., 1936], 72–73) wrote: "The Saints are actually members of the family, interceding for them in event of difficulty and consoling them in times of grief." Like most Spanish-American women of the time, Eloisa believed that multiple patron saints names for girls gave them the advantage of having many friends in heaven to intercede for them in this life and beyond.

7. Interview with Eloisa Bergere Brown, May 27, 1993.

8. Miguel A. Otero, *My Nine Years as Governor*, 283.

9. *Bulletin*, Historic Santa Fe Foundation (n.d.), 4; Sherman, *Santa Fe*, 47.

10. *Bulletin*, 5.

11. Ibid., 5, 8.

12. U.S. Senator Albert J. Beveridge of Indiana was adamantly opposed to statehood for New Mexico, believing that "it was all a diabolical plot on the part of special interests" (Warren A. Beck, *New Mexico: A History of Four Centuries* [Norman: University of Oklahoma Press, 1962], 231–37). See also David J. Weber, *The Spanish Frontier in North America* (New Haven: Yale University Press, 1992), 246.

13. Oliver La Farge, *Santa Fe: The Autobiography of a Southwestern Town* (Norman: University of Oklahoma Press, 1959), 137–39; Andrew K. Gregg, *New Mexico in the 19th Century: A Pictorial History* (Albuquerque: University of New Mexico Press, 1968), 99.

14. *Bulletin*, 7.

15. Anna Katherine, "Vignette: Consuelo Mendenhall," *Santa Fean* (November 1986), 12.

16. Ibid.

17. Sherman, *Santa Fe*, 46; John Pen La Farge, "Música, Mariachis y Maromeros," *El Palacio* 97 (Winter 1991–92), 22.

18. Miguel A. Otero, *My Nine Years as Governor*, 277.

19. Interview with John J. and Josephine S. Kenney, April 14, 1990. "Smoking was another feminine grace"; women would carry "their tobacco, punche, and cornhusk wrappings in tiny silver bottles and boxes" and would roll their own cigarettes and cigarillos (Fergusson, New Mexico, 206).

20. Perrigo, Hispanos, 33.

21. Miguel A. Otero, My Nine Years as Governor, 178–80.

22. Ibid., 323–24.

23. Ibid.

24. Ibid., 257.

25. Ibid., 340, 342; La Farge, Santa Fe: The Autobiography, 255–56, 360; Miguel Otero resumed his mining and sheep-raising ventures after he left the governor's office. He left the Republican party to become a delegate to the Progressive party's national convention in 1912, and later joined the Democratic party. He was treasurer of the territory from 1910 to 1911; president of the New Mexico Board of Penitentiary Commissioners and Parole Board from 1913 to 1917; and U.S. Marshal of the Panama Canal Zone from 1917 to 1921. His son, Miguel A. Otero, Jr., married Katherine Stinson, one of America's "most daring feminine aviators" and the first woman "skywriter," who flew the "first regular airmail route from New York to Washington"; New York Times, November 4, 1936.

26. Interview with Consuelo Bergere Mendenhall, April 16, 1990.

27. Sherman, Santa Fe, 82. On Washington's Birthday in 1900, Nina was one of five bridesmaids for her cousin Carmen Sena, who married Charles Abreu. Seven-year-old May Bergere and Amalia Sena were flower girls.

28. Darien Walker, Director, Stanford Alumni Association, to author, December 16, 1991; Stanford University Alumnae Directory, Class of 1894; (the Rev.) Alice L. Downs, Director, Alumnae Relations, General Theological Seminary, to author, October 29, 1991; Irma Levesque, Development Assistant, Union Theological Seminary, to author, November 7, 1991; Register of Enlistments in the United States Army: 1798–1914 (1899), 334; Francis B. Heitman, Historical Register and Dictionary of the United States Army, from Its Organization September 29, 1789, to March 2, 1903 (Washington: Government Printing Office, 1903), 1004.

29. Carl D. W. Hays, "One of Luna Family Was Even Pope in Early 1400s," *Southwesterner* (June 1964), 20.

30. John J. Kenney, "La Reunión de la Familia de Eloisa Luna de Otero de Bergere: Historia," September 15, 1980:14, quoting Theodore Roosevelt, *The Rough Riders*, 1918 ed., 56–57.

31. *Register of Enlistments in the U.S. Army*, 1798–1914, (1899), L-2 334; Stanford University Yearbook, Class of 1894 Glee Club; Interview with Cristina Kenney Herdman, October 17, 1991.

32. Interview with Ruth Leakey, May 26, 1990.

33. David J. Weber, "Lost Horizons," *SMU Magazine* 42 (Fall 1992), 19, adapted from Weber, *The Spanish Frontier.*

34. Mary Austin, *Earth Horizon: Autobiography* (New York: Literary Guild, 1932), 351.

35. Interview with Ruth Leakey, May 26, 1990; Katherine, "Vignette," 12.

36. Records, St. Francis Cathedral, Marriage Record of Nina Otero and Rawson Warren, June 25, 1908, State Records Center and Archives, Santa Fe, New Mexico.

37. *Santa Fe New Mexican*, June 25, 1908.

38. Katherine, "Vignette."

39. Gregg, *New Mexico in the 19th Century*, 153.

40. Bonnie Domrose Stone and Betty Sowers Alt, *Uncle Sam's Brides: The World of Military Wives* (New York: Walker and Co., 1990), 4, 11. "Times have changed; time has stood still. Although each base, each city of Uncle Sam's, has all the modern conveniences, it is structured along the same lines of demarcation seen in early forts."

41. Stone and Alt, *Uncle Sam's Brides*, 34.

42. Interview with Ruth Leakey, May 26, 1990.

43. Interview with Cristina Kenney Herdman, October 17, 1991.

44. Sarah Deutsch, *No Separate Refuge: Culture, Class, and Gender on an Anglo-Hispanic Frontier in the American Southwest*, 1880–1940 (New York: Oxford University Press, 1987), 46, 59. Deutsch points out that for many nineteenth-century Spanish- Americans, "divorced people and witches existed not simply as eccentric individuals, but as individuals unattached and possibly even hostile to the dense and vital network of family relations that sustained the community."

45. Joan M. Jensen and Darlis A. Miller, eds., *New Mexico Women: Intercultural Perspectives* (Albuquerque: University of New Mexico Press, 1986), 301–31; Territorial Archives of New Mexico, Reel 69, Frame 385, Santa Fe History Library, letter to Henry Stoes, Las Cruces, New Mexico, unsigned, 1908.

46. Jensen and Miller, *New Mexico Women*, 305. Under the new constitution, three-fourths of the voters in each county had to approve amendments to the franchise provisions. Such overwhelming approval was assumed by politicians to be almost impossible to obtain. "If a majority of voters presented a petition to the board of county commissioners requesting disfranchisement of the women, a majority of voters favoring the restoration of the franchise had to present a counter petition before women could vote again."

47. La Farge, *Santa Fe: The Autobiography*, 210–11.

48. Lucretia Pittman, S.C., "Solomón Luna: Sheepmaster and Politician of New Mexico" (M.A. thesis, St. Louis University, 1941), 116.

49. Ibid., 101–103.

50. Kenney, "La Reunión," 10.

51. Interview with John J. Kenney, October, 12, 1990.

52. Jensen and Miller, *New Mexico Women*, 231.

53. Interview with John J. Kenney, October 12, 1990; A. M. Bergere, "Autobiography," AMB Papers, Santa Fe Archives.

54. Bergere, "Autobiography," 18.

55. "A Noble Woman: A Tribute to the Late Mrs. Eloisa Luna de Bergere, by a Santa Fe Woman," *New Mexican*, September 10, 1914.

56. Ruth Loomis Skeen, "The Daughter of a Spanish Don," *Holland* (August 1919).

57. Interview with Ruth Leakey, May 19, 1990.

58. Skeen, "The Daughter of a Spanish Don."

CHAPTER THREE

1. Advertisement sponsored by the Women's Political Union, 13 West 42d St., New York, NY, in *Century* (1913). National Women's Party (NWP) Papers, Texas Women's University (TWU), Reel #1 1913–December 27, 1916.

2. Joan M. Jensen and Darlis A. Miller, eds., *New Mexico Women: Intercultural*

Perspectives (Albuquerque: University of New Mexico Press, 1986), 306.

3. Katherine Patterson to Clara Savage, Misc. Records: Political Issues, "Women's Suffrage in New Mexico, 1917–19," State Records Center and Archives, Santa Fe, New Mexico.

4. Kenneth Florey, "The Artifacts of the Woman Suffrage Movement," *AB Bookman's Weekly* (March 13, 1989), 1132–33.

5. Yolanda Tarango, "La Vida es la Lucha," *Texas Journal* 12 (Spring–Summer 1990), 11.

6. Sarah Deutsch, *No Separate Refuge: Culture, Class, and Gender on an Anglo-Hispanic Frontier in the American Southwest, 1880–1940* (New York: Oxford University Press, 1987), 48.

7. Oliver La Farge, *Santa Fe: The Autobiography of a Southwestern Town* (Norman: University of Oklahoma Press, 1959), 216–17.

8. Nina Otero-Warren to Mable Vernon, March 1, 1920, NWP Papers, Library of Congress, Washington, D.C.

9. Miguel A. Otero, *My Nine Years as Governor of the Territory of New Mexico, 1897–1906* (Albuquerque: University of New Mexico Press, 1940), 75.

10. Jensen and Miller, *New Mexico Women*, 312.

11. John J. Kenney [sr.] Professional Papers, A. M. Bergere Papers, State Records Center and Archives.

12. La Farge, *Santa Fe: The Autobiography*, 196.

13. Ibid., 193.

14. Interviews with Eloisa Bergere Brown, July 10, 1990, and John J. and Josephine S. Kenney and Dolores K. Kenney, April 14, 1990.

15. Jensen and Miller, *New Mexico Women*, 309–10. Estella Bergere had married Aldo Leopold (Oct. 9, 1912), who became a noted conservationist and the author of *A Sand County Almanac: With Essays on Conservation from Round River* (New York: Oxford University Press, 1949).

16. Jensen and Miller, *New Mexico Women*, 314.

17. B. C. Hernández to Nina Otero-Warren, September 1916, NWP papers, TWU, Reel #33, 1913–1916.

18. "The Historic Santa Fe", *Bulletin*, Historic Santa Fe Foundation, (n.d.), 6, AMB Papers, State Records Center and Archives.

19. *The Evening Herald*, Albuquerque, May 19, 1916.

20. Jensen and Miller, *New Mexico Women*, 314.

21. Albuquerque *Morning Journal*, March 2, 1917, Misc. Records: Political

Issues, "Women's Suffrage in NM, 1917–19," State Records Center and Archives.

22. Santa Fe *New Mexican*, March 2, 1917.

23. Alice Paul to Nina Otero-Warren, September 21, 1917, NWP Papers, Library of Congress, Washington, D.C.

24. Nina Otero-Warren to Alice Paul, December 4, 1917, Reel 53, NWP Papers, TWU.

25. Anne Martin to Nina Otero-Warren, December 21, 1917, NWP Papers, Reel 53, TWU.

26. Jensen and Miller, *New Mexico Women*, 311.

27. Florey, "Artifacts," 1132–33.

28. Alice Corbin Henderson, *New Mexico Blue Book* (1919), 96–97, State Records Center and Archives.

29. Ibid., 101.

30. John Sherman, *Santa Fe: A Pictorial History* (Norfolk: Donning Co., 1983), 124.

31. Henderson, *Blue Book*, 97.

32. La Farge, *Santa Fe: The Autobiography*, 237.

33. La Farge, *Santa Fe: The Autobiography*, 95, 207–208, 230; Sherman, *Santa Fe*, 109. Bronson Cutting served in the U.S. Senate from 1927 until 1935, when he was killed in an airplane crash near Macon, Missouri.

34. Michael Miller, "The Legacy of A. M. Bergere: Pioneer New Mexican," *Southwest Heritage* (n.d.), 9, AMB Papers, State Records Center and Archives, Santa Fe, New Mexico; A. M. Bergere, "Autobiography," AMB Papers. A. M. Bergere was selected out of 162 applicants from New Mexico and Arizona for European duty with the Knights of Columbus. He established his huts in Cadillac, Cerons, and Langoran. Buster Keaton was one of the current celebrities he persuaded to entertain the troops. U.S. Infantry bands gave concerts once a week for the men.

35. Jensen and Miller, *New Mexico Women*, 315.

36. Ruth Loomis Skeen, "The Daughter of a Spanish Don," *Holland* (August 1919).

37. Portland *Oregonian*, March 18, 1919; *Christian Science Monitor*, March 14, 1919; Santa Fe *New Mexican*, March 13, 1919; Misc. Records: Political Issues, #40, State Records Center and Archives.

38. Jensen and Miller, *New Mexico Women*, 315; Skeen, "Daughter of a Spanish Don."

39. Jensen and Miller, *New Mexico Women*, 315.

40. *Santa Fe New Mexican*, February 13, 1920.

41. Louise M. Young, *In the Public Interest: The League of Women Voters, 1920–1970* (New York: Greenwood Press, 1989), 37.

42. Alice Paul to Lillian Kerr, February 14, 1920, NWP Papers, TWU.

43. Nina Otero-Warren to Alice Paul, February 17, 1920, NWP Papers, TWU.

44. Jensen and Miller, *New Mexico Women*, 316; Alice Paul to Nina Otero-Warren, February 19, 1920, NWP Papers, TWU. In 1923, Alice Stokes Paul authored the Equal Rights Amendment and crusaded for its passage for the rest of her life. Because of her efforts, the 1964 Civil Rights Act outlawed sex discrimination in the workplace. She died in 1977. In 1992, the Alice Paul Foundation still supported Paulsdale, her birthplace and home, recently named a National Historic Landmark, in Mount Laurel, New Jersey, near Philadelphia (*National Voter* [Mar.–Apr. 1992], 9).

45. Jensen and Miller, *New Mexico Women*, 322.

46. *Santa Fe New Mexican*, July 8, 1921.

47. Ibid.

48. Interview with Eloisa Bergere Brown, March 6, 1992.

49. AMB Papers, Scrapbook #6.

50. AMB Papers, Scrapbook #6; Jensen and Miller, *New Mexico Women*, 322.

51. *New York Times*, September 10, 1922.

52. AMB Papers, Scrapbook #6.

53. Benjamin M. Read, "Mrs. Adelina Otero-Warren," 1922, AMB Papers.

54. Joan M. Jensen, "Women and Politics," *New Mexico Historical Review* 56 (1981), 27.

55. Jensen and Miller, *New Mexico Women*, 323.

56. Marsha Lynn Whicker, *National Voter* (Oct.–Nov. 1990), 13. As the last decade of the twentieth century began, more women than ever before were running for political office. In New Mexico in 1991, over 13 percent of the state legislature was female, and in 1992 one hundred fifty women candidates were campaigning nationwide. In 1992 there were four women in the U. S. Senate and forty-eight in the House of Repre-

sentatives. Supportive fund-raising groups such as WISH ("Women in the Senate and House") for the Republicans and the Democratic party's EMILY's List ("Early Money Is Like Yeast") have made it financially possible for more qualified women to seek high office. See R. W. Apple, Jr., *New York Times*, May 24, 1992; Ellen Goodman, "Women are coming close to breaking political glass ceiling," *Dallas Times Herald*, November 14, 1990.

57. Vivian Gornick, "Who Says We Haven't Made a Revolution?" *New York Times Magazine* (April 15, 1990), 24–53.

58. Interview with John J. Kenney, October 12, 1990.

59. La Farge, *Santa Fe: The Autobiography*, 284.

60. *WPA Guide to 1930s in New Mexico* (Tucson: University of Arizona Press, 1989), 8; Erna Fergusson, *New Mexico: A Pageant of Three Peoples* (New York: Knopf, 1951), 224.

CHAPTER FOUR

1. Interview with Dolores K. Kenney, July 16, 1991. Ysabel Bergere was transferred to an institution in Pueblo, Colorado, after her nurse became ill. In the 1970s Dode and Bergere Kenney brought her back to a nursing home in Santa Fe, where she died at the age of eighty-two.

2. Interview with Consuelo Bergere Mendenhall, April 16, 1990; John Sherman, *Santa Fe: A Pictorial History* (Norfolk: Conning Co., 1983), 68.

3. James Purdy, "The A. M. Bergere House," *Bulletin* 2, The Historic Santa Fe Foundation (Fall–Winter, 1976), 8.

4. Sherman, *Santa Fe*, 81; *New York Times*, September 23, 1990, 16. An ad for Model T Fords appeared in the *New Mexican* on June 7, 1909, boasting of record travel times from Santa Fe to Los Carrillos and Las Vegas.

5. Sarah Nestor interview with Alice Henderson Rossin, *El Palacio* 93 (Winter 1987), 15.

6. John Pen La Farge interview with Anita Gonzales Thomas, "Música, Mariachis y Maromeros," *El Palacio* 97 (Winter 1991–92), 56.

7. Interview with Dolores K. Kenney, July 16, 1991.

8. Anna Katherine, "Vignette: Consuelo Mendenhall," *Santa Fean* (November 1986), 11.

9. Katherine, "Vignette," 11–13; interview with Consuelo Bergere Mendenhall, April 16, 1990.

10. Interview with Eloisa Bergere Brown, July 10, 1990.

11. Nina Otero, *Old Spain in Our Southwest* (Harcourt Brace and Co., 1936), 80; interview with Amalia Sánchez, April 19, 1990.

12. Interview with Eloisa Bergere Brown, July 10, 1990. Isabel of Portugal pursued Álvaro de Luna, "the friend of Jews and *Conversos*, to his doom. . . . By the time of Isabel and Fernando, a great many of the ancient houses of the peninsula had Jewish relatives. *Limpia sangre*, 'clean blood,' was a distinction which many claimed but not all had." *Conversos*, cultural but not practicing Jews, were "powerfully entrenched" in the court. Isabel's confessor was of Jewish descent. Almost all her privy councillors and secretaries "had Jewish ancestors on one side or the other—or both." The king's treasurer, cup-bearer, confidential friends, and advisors were all "of the seed of Abraham." The governor of Aragón was a *converso*, as were most of the judges and lawyers. The inquisitor Torquemada "shattered the power of the great Jewish plutocracy of Aragón" (William T. Walsh, *Isabella of Spain* [New York: Robt. M. McBride, 1930]), 2–6, 200, 206–209, 277, 281).

13. *WPA Guide to 1930s in New Mexico* (Tucson: University of Arizona Press, 1989), 126–29.

14. Oliver La Farge, *Santa Fe: The Autobiography of a Southwestern Town* (Norman: University of Oklahoma Press, 1959), 174.

15. Nina Otero, *Old Spain*, 109.

16. Sarah Deutsch, *No Separate Refuge: Culture, Class, and Gender on an Anglo-Hispanic Frontier in the American Southwest, 1880–1940* (New York: Oxford University Press, 1987), 66, 139.

17. "Education in New Mexico," *New Mexico Blue Book* (1917), 273, State Records Center and Archives, Santa Fe, New Mexico.

18. Adelina Otero, "My People," *Survey Graphic* (May 1931), 149–51.

19. Interview with Anita Gonzales Thomas, May 8, 1992.

20. Adelina Otero, "My People," 149.

21. Interview with Dominguita Vigíl Ortíz, August 13, 1990.

22. Adelina Otero, "My People," 151.

23. *Santa Fe New Mexican* (n.d.), A. M. Bergere Papers, State Records and Archives, Santa Fe, New Mexico.

24. Interview with Henry Meadors, July 7, 1991. Mamie was the only member of her family to pronounce her surname with the last syllable accented.

25. Sherman, *Santa Fe*, 100.

26. Haniel Long, "The Poets' Round-up," in "Alice Corbin: An Appreciation," *New Mexico Quarterly Review* 19 (Spring 1949), 66–72.

27. George Dillon, "A Note on Alice Corbin Henderson and Poetry," in "Alice Corbin: An Appreciation," 42.

28. Interview with Henry B. Meadors, July 7, 1991.

29. Interview with Henry B. Meadors, July 7, 1991. "The idea for a public library in Santa Fe was the dream of a few far-sighted women, who as far back as 1892 under the name of the 'Benevolent Association,' worked for the betterment of the community. . . . The Woman's Board of Trade and Library Association, an organization of nine departments designed for the improvement of the minds of the community . . . established the library in 1896 in a barracks building where the new museum now stands. It was a free public library, one of the first in the territory. A meager four hundred books were available. In 1925 the library had grown till it had 10,000 volumes. . . . In 1936 the library was swelled to 28,000, and the increase is still growing rapidly" (Santa Fe *Tumbleweed*, April 18, 1941).

30. Interviews with Dolores K. Kenney and John J. and Josephine S. Kenney, April 14, 1990.

31. Charles H. Bruce, assistant commissioner, Department of the Interior, General Land Office, Washington, D.C., to A. M. Bergere, March 25, 1921. State Records Center and Archives.

32. La Farge, *Santa Fe: The Autobiography*, 277–81; John Collier, *From Every Zenith: A Memoir* (Denver: Sage Books, 1963), 130–31.

33. Gussie Fauntleroy, *Indian Market* (August 15, 1991), 4–6. Chapman was curator and Hewett director of the Museum of New Mexico.

34. Collier, *From Every Zenith*, 149.

35. Ibid.

36. Benjamin Naranjo to Nina Otero-Warren, September 7, 1923, State Records Center and Archives.

37. La Farge, *Santa Fe*, 281–82; Collier, *From Every Zenith*, 136.

38. Nina Otero-Warren to Charles H. Burke, U. S. commissioner of Indian affairs, September 22, 1923.

39. Nina Otero-Warren to Charles H. Burke, September 22, 1923.

40. J. D. DeHuff, superintendent, U.S. Indian School, Santa Fe, to Nina Otero-Warren, September 22, 1923.

41. Alvin M. Josephy, Jr., *Red Power: The American Indians' Fight for Freedom* (Lincoln: University of Nebraska Press, 1971), 4.

42. *Santa Fe New Mexican* (n.d.), State Records Center and Archives.

43. Fauntleroy, *Indian Market*, 6.

44. Ibid.

45. *Los Angeles Daily News*, June 6, 1924, State Records Center and Archives.

46. Collier, *From Every Zenith*, 147.

47. Charles F. Lummis, *The Land of Poco Tiempo* (New York: Chas. Scribner's Sons, 1893; reprinted, Albuquerque: University of New Mexico Press, 1952), 24.

48. Stewart L. Udall, *To the Inland Empire: Coronado and Our Spanish Legacy* (New York: Doubleday, 1967), 195–97.

49. David J. Weber, *The Spanish Frontier in North America* (New Haven: Yale University Press, 1992), 353–60.

50. Arrell Morgan Gibson, *The Santa Fe and Taos Colonies: Age of the Muses, 1900–1942* (Norman: University of Oklahoma Press, 1983), 30–33.

51. Ibid., 184.

52. Witter Bynner to Anita Bergere, January 8, 1965, State Records Center and Archives.

53. Witter Bynner, "Alice Corbin: An Appreciation," *New Mexico Quarterly Review* 19 (Spring 1949), 38–39.

54. Gibson, *The Santa Fe and Taos Colonies*, 37.

55. "The 1924 Santa Fe Fiesta," *El Palacio* 17 (September 15, 1924), 126–81.

56. "The 1924 Fiesta," 126–81; Gibson, *The Santa Fe and Taos Colonies*, 252.

57. "The 1924 Fiesta," 166.

58. Gibson, *The Santa Fe and Taos Colonies*, 4.

59. Raymond Otis, *Fire in the Night* (New York: Farrar and Rinehart, 1934), 16.

60. George Dillon, "A Note on Alice Corbin Henderson," 42.

61. *El Palacio* 93 (Winter 1987), 4–36 (entire issue devoted to the Henderson family).

62. Gibson, *The Santa Fe and Taos Colonies*, 97.

63. Ibid., 86.

64. Bynner, "Alice Corbin: An Appreciation," 39.

65. Paul Horgan, *The Centuries of Santa Fe* (New York: E. P. Dutton, 1956), 340.

66. Peggy Pond Church, "Admonition;" Haniel Long, "Poems from a Desert Garden," in Alice Corbin Henderson, *The Turquoise Trail* (Boston: Houghton Mifflin, 1928), 90–105.

67. Mary Austin, *The Land of Journey's Ending* (Tucson: University of Arizona Press, 2d printing, 1985), 341–42.

68. Gibson, *The Santa Fe and Taos Colonies*, 212.

CHAPTER FIVE

1. Interview with Eloisa B. Brown, August 15, 1991.

2. *New Mexico Blue Book* (1931–32), State Records Center and Archives, Santa Fe, New Mexico.

3. *Blue Book* (1933–34).

4. Interviews with John J. and Josephine S. Kenney and Dolores K. Kenney, April 14, 1990.

5. Arrell Morgan Gibson, *The Santa Fe and Taos Colonies: Age of the Muses, 1900–1942* (Norman: University of Oklahoma Press, 1983), 216.

6. Nina Otero-Warren to Dr. Herman M. Bumpas, January 30, 1930, State Records Center and Archives.

7. Miguel A. Otero, *My Nine Years as Governor of the Territory of New Mexico: 1897–1906* (Albuquerque: University of New Mexico Press, 1940), 132, 144.

8. *El Palacio* (August 31, 1930), A. M. Bergere Papers, State Records Center and Archives.

9. Joseph Dispenza and Louise Turner, *Will Shuster: A Santa Fe Legend* (Santa Fe: Museum of New Mexico Press, 1989), 64, 66.

10. Ibid., 69.

11. Ibid., 70.

12. Nina Otero, "*El Aire en las Montañas* (The Wind in the Mountains)," first draft of chapter 1 for *Old Spain in Our Southwest* (Harcourt, Brace and Co., 1936), State Records Center and Archives.

13. U.S. Department of the Interior's legal description of Mrs. Adelina Otero-Warren's land: Lots 5, 6, 7, S1/2 NW1/4, SW1/4, Sec. 29; lots 2, 3, 4, 5, SW1/4, W1/2 SE1/4, W1/2 SE1/4, E1/2 SW1/4, Sec. 30,

Township 18 N., Range 9 E., N.M. Meridian, containing 633.09 acres. Mamie E. Meadors applied for lots 5, 6, 7, 8, S1/2 NW1/4, SW1/4, Sec. 19; NW1/4, W1/2 SW1/4, Sec. 30, Township 18 N., Range 9E., N. M. Meridian, containing 624.32 acres. AMB Papers, State Records Center and Archives.

14. AMB Papers.
15. Ibid.
16. Ibid.
17. Interview with Eloisa Bergere Brown, August 15, 1991.
18. Interview with Henry B. Meadors, July 7, 1991.
19. Interview with Josephine (Joey) S. Kenney, August 1, 1991.
20. Ibid.
21. AMB Papers.
22. Interview with Bergere A. Kenney, February, 21, 1988.
23. Interview with Anita Gonzales Thomas, May 8, 1992. Some of the folk-tales in *Old Spain* were selected from those submitted by schoolchildren for a contest Nina sponsored while she was superintendent of public schools. The best of the stories were incorporated into her book.
24. Nina Otero, *Old Spain*, 5.
25. Ibid., 4.
26. Ibid.
27. Ibid.
28. Sarah Deutsch, *No Separate Refuge: Culture, Class, and Gender on an Anglo-Hispanic Frontier in the American Southwest, 1880–1940* (New York: Oxford University Press, 1987), 192.
29. Nina Otero, *Old Spain*, 9–52.
30. Ibid.
31. Ibid., 16.
32. Ibid., 52–55.
33. Anne T. Eaton, "New Books for Boys and Girls," *New York Times Book Review* (April 5, 1936), 10.
34. *Santa Fe New Mexican*, February 26, 1936.
35. Eda Lou Walton, "Books for the Young," *New York Herald Tribune* (n.d.), State Records Center and Archives.
36. "Patient and Proud, Book News of the Day" (n.d.), State Records Center and Archives.

37. Interview with Ellen Verry, Alumnae Office, Maryville College, April, 8, 1991; photo and caption from student newspaper, Maryville College. AMB Papers.

38. *The Southwesterner* 3 (June 1964), 20. Almost thirty years after it first appeared, *Old Spain* went into another edition, published in 1964 by the Rio Grande Press.

39. AMB Papers.

40. John J. Kenney, "La Reunión de la Familia de Eloisa Luna de Otero de Bergere: Historia," September 15, 1980, 18.

41. Interview with Luna Leopold, August 19, 1991.

42. Ibid.

43. "Bergere Appointment," *The Record*, January 17, 1930. AMB Papers.

44. *San Juan Review*, January 20, 1930.

45. Interview with Josephine S. Kenney, August 1, 1991.

46. David Chávez, Jr., "Man of Law—and of the World," *New Mexico Magazine* (February 1974), 31.

47. A. M. Bergere, "Autobiography," AMB Papers; Michael Miller, *Southwest Heritage* (n.d.), n.p., State Records Center and Archives.

48. *WPA Guide to 1930s in New Mexico* (Tucson: University of Arizona Press, 1989), 201.

49. Ruth Laughlin, "Alice Corbin: An Appreciation," *New Mexico Historical Quarterly Review* 19 (Spring 1949), 60; *WPA Guide*, viii.

50. Laughlin, "Alice Corbin," 64.

51. Dispenza and Turner, *Will Shuster*, 93–94; Gibson, *The Santa Fe and Taos Colonies*, 173.

52. Nina Otero-Warren to Hon. Lee Rowland, July 17, 1935, State Records Center and Archives.

53. Nina Otero-Warren to Tom L. Popejoy, October 2, 1936, AMB Papers.

54. "Program for Literacy Classes," memo from Nina Otero-Warren to Tom L. Popejoy (n.d.), AMB Papers.

55. Report on Education Conference, Washington, D.C., June 3, 1937, State Records Center and Archives.

56. John Sherman, *Santa Fe: A Pictorial History* (Norfolk: Conning Co., 1983), 163; Kristie Miller, *Ruth Hanna McCormick: A Life in Politics, 1880–1944* (Albuquerque: University of New Mexico Press, 1992); interview with Katrina McCormick Barnes, May 17, 1992.

57. *New Mexican* (n.d.), AMB Papers.

58. Erna Fergusson, *New Mexico: A Pageant of Three Peoples* (New York: Knopf, 1951), 224.

59. *New Mexican*, May 7, 1941.

60. Ibid., June 1941.

61. Nina Otero-Warren for Albert F. Spina, "The In-Service Training Course," Exhibit A, WPA Educational Projects, Puerto Rico, July 3, 1941. State Records Center and Archives.

62. Otero-Warren, "The In-Service Training Course."

63. *El Mundo*, San Juan, Puerto Rico, July 30, 1941, translated from the Spanish. State Records Center and Archives.

64. *El Mundo*, July 30, 1941.

65. Pedro Arán, coordinator, Department of Education, to Robert Lawrence, director, Community Service Programs Division, WPA, San Juan, P.R., July 26, 1941.

66. Pedro Arán to Nina Otero-Warren, August 20, 1941.

67. Ibid., June 1941.

CHAPTER SIX

1. Santa Fe *New Mexican*, February 17, 1941.

2. *Smithsonian* (September 1991), 91.

3. Interview with Cristina Kenney Herdman, October 17, 1991.

4. Oliver La Farge, *Santa Fe: The Autobiography of a Southwestern Town* (Norman: University of Oklahoma Press, 1959), 353, 359.

5. *New Mexican*, December 8, 1941; Nina Otero-Warren to Santa Fe County Commissioner, April 13, 1948, State Records Center and Archives, Santa Fe, New Mexico; *Smithsonian* (December 1991), 80.

6. Interview with Dolores K. Kenney and Eloisa Bergere Brown, February 10, 1992. Dolores Kenney, sister of Jack and Bergere, married Harry Drypolcher in 1942, and he was also in the service.

7. La Farge, *Santa Fe: The Autobiography*, 367.

8. Interview with Bergere A. Kenney, February 21, 1988.

9. Interview with John J. Kenney, April 14, 1990.

10. *New Mexican*, December 8, 1941.

11. Lesley Poling-Kempes, *The Harvey Girls: Women Who Opened the West* (New York: Paragon House, 1989), 203; interview with Cristina Kenney

Herdman, October, 1991. La Fonda in the forties was a Harvey House hotel that accommodated Los Alamos scientists and, as a contribution to the war effort, sent box lunches to Lamy for the troop trains.

12. Margaret Lohlker, "Yule Logs of Piñon," *Santa Fean Inter-American* (Holiday Number, 1941), 15–16.

13. Interview with Cristina Kenney Herdman, November 29, 1991.

14. Ibid.

15. Lohlker, "Yule Logs."

16. *Santa Fean* (August 1940), 4. The Arsuna Art School opened in June, 1938, and was the second art school to function in Santa Fe. Courses in Hispanic art and music made up the curriculum. See Arrell Morgan Gibson, *The Santa Fe and Taos Colonies: Age of the Muses, 1900–1942* (Norman: University of Oklahoma Press, 1983), 82.

17. La Farge, *Santa Fe: The Autobiography,* 358–59. "The 'I Am' cult . . . claims as its authority a new revelation by Saint Germaine, which complements and to some extent supersedes the Christian revelation."

18. La Farge, *Santa Fe: The Autobiography,* 360.

19. Peggy Pond Church, *The House at Otowi Bridge* (Albuquerque: University of New Mexico Press, 1959), 6.

20. La Farge, *Santa Fe: The Autobiography,* 364.

21. Church, *Otowi Bridge,* 84; La Farge, *Santa Fe: The Autobiography,* 363; Erna Fergusson, *New Mexico: A Pageant of Three Peoples* (New York: Knopf, 1951), 335.

22. Interviews with Cristina Kenney Herdman and Josephine S. Kenney, October 17, 1991.

23. La Farge, *Santa Fe: The Autobiography,* 363.

24. La Farge, *Santa Fe: The Autobiography,* 361; Fergusson, *New Mexico,* 337; interview with Margaret Lefranc Schoonover, January 15, 1992.

25. Church, *Otowi Bridge,* 84.

26. Ibid., 88, 90.

27. Ibid., 90, 96.

28. *Dallas Morning News,* November 3, 1991. With the collapse of the Soviet Union in 1991 and the end of the nuclear cold war, scientists at the Los Alamos laboratories are now focusing on ways to halt nuclear proliferation around the world (*Albuquerque Journal,* February 23, 1992).

29. La Farge, *Santa Fe: The Autobiography,* 369–70; Gibson, *The Santa Fe and Taos*

Colonies, 214–15. In the 1920s Mary Austin had saved the Santuario de Chimayo from abandonment and ruin by raising $5,000 for restoration from friends in the eastern states. She, Frank Applegate, and John Gaw Meem were largely responsible for the preservation of the chapel.

30. Interview with Cristina Kenney Herdman, October 17, 1991; *New York Times*, August 12, 1942.

31. Stanford University alumnae directory (n.d.), 526; Darien Walker, director, Stanford Alumni Association, to author, December 16, 1991. Records show that Warren married a Catharine W. Goodale on June 15, 1912, suggesting that he was married at least three times, unless Catharine Goodale Warren was also "Meta" Warren.

32. La Farge, *Santa Fe: The Autobiography*, 60.

33. Interview with Josephine S. Kenney, April 14, 1990.

34. Ibid.

35. Interview with Dolores K. Kenney, October 17, 1991.

36. Interview with Josephine S. Kenney, August 1, 1991.

37. Bergere A. Kenney to Anita Bergere, February 13, 1944, State Records Center and Archives, Santa Fe, New Mexico.

38. John J. Kenney to May Bergere Kenney, Mother's Day, 1952, State Records Center and Archives.

39. Interview with Dolores K. Kenney, October, 1991.

40. Ibid., February 21, 1992.

41. Interview with Bergere A. Kenney, February 21, 1988.

42. Interview with Henry B. Meadors, July 7, 1991.

43. Interview with Amalia Sánchez, April 17, 1991.

44. Interview with Bergere A. Kenney, February 21, 1988.

45. Interviews with John J. Kenney and Dolores K. Kenney, April 14, 1990.

46. Interview with Josephine S. Kenney, April 14, 1990.

47. Interview with John J. Kenney April 14, 1990.

48. John Pen La Farge, interview with Richard Bradford, "The Cat in the Punch Bowl," *El Palacio* 97 (Winter 1991–92), 18.

49. Interview with Bergere A. Kenney, February 21, 1988.

50. Interview with Cristina Kenney Herdman, October 17, 1991.

51. Interview with Bergere A. Kenney, February 21, 1988.

52. Ibid.

53. Interview with Sam Arnold, February 20, 1992. Arnold is the author of *Eating Up the Santa Fe Trail* (Boulder: University Press of Colorado) and is presently travel correspondent for the *Denver Post*.

54. "Report on Activities at Las Dos Outfit, 2 to 5 p.m., April 4, 1948," AMB Papers, State Records Center and Archives.

55. Interview with Cristina Kenney Herdman, October 1991.

56. Interviews with Eloisa Bergere Brown, February 21, 1992, and Cristina Kenney Herdman, October 1991.

57. Interviews with Cristina Kenney Herdman, October 1991, and Josephine S. Kenney, August 1, 1991.

58. Interviews with Cristina Kenney Herdman, October 1991, and Bergere A. Kenney, February 21, 1988. Archival records indicate that Nina signed a contract in 1951 to permit twenty head of cattle to graze at Las Dos for six months, at $11 per head, the only grazing on the land from the time she acquired it in the early thirties.

59. *Sierra* (March–April 1992), 38.

60. Interview with Cristina Kenney Herdman, October 1991.

61. Interview with Josephine S. Kenney, August 1, 1991.

62. *Santa Fe New Mexican*, August 12, 1951.

63. *New Mexican*, August 12, 1951; June 1944 in "Friends of the Santa Fe Public Library Scrapbook," Santa Fe Public Library; interview with Beth Dreyspring, May 26, 1990. Salome's neighbor Beth Dreyspring's memory of Salome was that she was a quiet woman who made her own soap and grew marijuana in her backyard.

64. Nina Otero-Warren to José Vega, November 6, 1951.

65. Interview with Ruth Leakey, February 3, 1992.

66. Ibid. Ruth Leakey published *La Turista* for thirty years. She celebrated her ninetieth birthday on February 20, 1992, on vacation in Mexico.

67. Interview with Bergere A. Kenney, February 21, 1988.

68. Robert Metzer, ed., *My Land Is the Southwest: Peter Hurd Letters and Journals* (College Station: Texas A & M University Press, 1983), 248.

69. Interview with Luna Leopold, August 19, 1991.

70. Luna Leopold to author, March 6, 1992.

71. Nina Otero-Warren to Mrs. Aldo Leopold, Madison, WI, December 15, 1953. Apparently Manuel wanted to be reimbursed for his work over the years and demanded $10,000 from each of his half-sisters. Some

refused. Interviews with Dolores K. Kenney, April 25, 1991, and with Eloisa Bergere Brown, February 21, 1992.

72. *New Mexican*, April 29, 1954; interview with Ruth Leakey, February 20, 1992.

73. Interview with Ruth Leakey, February 3, 1992; John J. Kenney, "La Reunión de la Familia de Eloisa Luna de Bergere: Historia," September 15, 1980, 52. Descendants with first or middle names: Bergere Alfred Kenney, Eloisa Bergere Brown, Kathleen Bergere Peters, Nancy Bergere Kenney, Dolores Bergere Fredricks, Brooke Bergere Brown, Timothy Bergere Kenney, Erica Bergere Peters, Timothy Bergere Kenney II. Luna Bergere had an adopted son, Thomas B. Catron III.

74. Interview with Dolores K. Kenney and Josephine S. Kenney, October 17, 1991.

75. John Sherman, *Santa Fe: A Pictorial History* (Norfolk: Conning Co., 1983), 171.

76. C. L. Sonnichsen, ed., *The Southwest in Life and Literature* (New York: Debin-Adair Co., 1962), 181; Ferguson writes that General Kearney's men gambled at Tules's place, where Palace Avenue still meets Burro Alley. "Tules Barceló, formerly Governor Armijo's *querida*, had become wholeheartedly *gringa*." Fergusson, *New Mexico*, 254; Lynn I. Perrigo, *Hispanos: Historic Leaders in New Mexico* (Santa Fe: Sunstone Press, 1985), 33–35; Sherman, *Santa Fe: A Pictorial History*, 170–71.

77. *New Mexican* (n.d.), AMB Papers, State Records Center and Archives; interview with Ruth Leakey, May 31, 1990.

78. Interview with Josephine S. Kenney, April 14, 1990.

79. Ibid.

80. AMB Papers, newspaper clipping, State Records Center and Archives, September 2, 1959.

81. John J. Kenney to author, May 9, 1989.

82. Interview with John J. Kenney, April 14, 1990.

83. *New Mexican*, January 4, 1965.

EPILOGUE

1. Erna Fergusson, "Santa Fe of Today," *People and Places in Santa Fe and Taos* (1951–52), 3, State Records Center and Archives, Santa Fe, New Mexico.

2. Robert Mayer, "Santa Fe," *Travel and Leisure* (February, 1992), 87–90.

3. Candelora Versace quoting critic and writer Pamela Tarchinski in the Santa Fe *New Mexican,* "Pasatiempo," April 17, 1992, 6.

4. William Clark, "Great Impressions: The Art of Willard Clark," *El Palacio* 97 (Spring–Summer 1992), 24.

5. Glenn Hunter, "The Commuter Crunch," *Santa Fe Reporter,* April 15–21, 1992, 15.

6. Margaret Johnson, "Native Gardening," *New Mexican,* July 28, 1982.

7. Eloisa Bergere Brown to author, March 2, 1992.

8. Ibid.

9. K. C. Compton, *New Mexican,* February 21, 1988.

Bibliography

Alt, Betty, and Bonnie Stone. *Uncle Sam's Brides: The World of Military Wives.* New York: Walker and Co., 1990.

Armstrong, Ruth W. *New Mexico: From Arrowhead to Atom.* South Brunswick, New York: A. S. Barnes Co., 1969.

Austin, Mary. *The Land of Little Rain.* Albuquerque: University of New Mexico Press, 1974 [first published 1903].

———. *Earth Horizon: Autobiography.* New York: Literary Guild, 1932.

———. *The Land of Journey's Ending.* Tucson: University of Arizona Press, 1985.

Baxter, John O. *Las Carneradas: Sheep Trade in New Mexico, 1700–1860.* Albuquerque: University of New Mexico Press, 1927. Reprint. University of New Mexico Press, 1987.

Beck, Warren A. *New Mexico: A History of Four Centuries.* Norman: University of Oklahoma Press, 1962.

———. *Historical Atlas of New Mexico.* Albuquerque: University of New Mexico Press, 1969.

Boyd, Mrs. Orsemus Bronson. *Cavalry Life in Tent and Field.* Lincoln: University of Nebraska Press, 1982.

Brett, Dorothy. *Lawrence and Brett: A Friendship.* Santa Fe: Sunstone Press, 1974 [first published 1933].

Bullock, Alice. *Living Legends of the Santa Fe Country.* Santa Fe: Sunstone Press, 1972.

Bunting, Bainbridge. *Early Architecture in New Mexico.* Albuquerque: University of New Mexico Press, 1976.

Bynner, Witter. *Journey with Genius: Recollections.* New York: Peter Nevill, 1953.

Cather, Willa. *Death Comes for the Archbishop.* New York: Vintage Books, 1971.

Chávez, Fray Angélico. *My Penitente Land: Reflections on Spanish New Mexico.* Albuquerque: University of New Mexico Press, 1974.

———. *Origins of New Mexican Families in the Spanish Colonial Period.* Santa Fe: Historical Society of New Mexico, 1954.

———. *Chávez: A Distinctive American Clan of New Mexico.* Santa Fe: Wm. Gannon, 1989.

Church, Peggy Pond. *The House at Otowi Bridge: The Story of Edith Warner and Los Alamos.* Albuquerque: University of New Mexico Press, 1959.

Cleveland, Agnes Morley. *No Life for a Lady.* Boston: Houghton Mifflin, 1941.

Coe, Wilbur. *Ranch on the Ruidoso: The Story of a Pioneer Family in New Mexico, 1871–1968.* New York: Alfred A. Knopf, 1968.

Coke, Van Deren. *Taos and Santa Fe: The Artist's Environment, 1882–1942.* Albuquerque: University of New Mexico Press for Amon Carter Museum of Western Art, 1963.

Collier, John. *From Every Zenith: A Memoir.* Denver: Sage Books, 1963.

deBuys, William. *Enchantment and Exploitation: The Life and Hard Times of a New Mexico Mountain Range.* Albuquerque: University of New Mexico Press, 1985.

Deutsch, Sarah. *No Separate Refuge: Culture, Class, and Gender on an Anglo-Hispanic Frontier in the American Southwest, 1880–1940.* New York: Oxford University Press, 1987.

Dispenza, Joseph, and Louise Turner. *Will Shuster: A Santa Fe Legend.* Santa Fe: Museum of New Mexico Press, 1989.

Doyle, Helen MacKnight. *Mary Austin: Woman of Genius.* New York: Gotham House, 1939.

Fergusson, Erna. "The Ballad of Manuel B." In *Murder and Mystery in New Mexico,* Erna Fergusson, ed. Albuquerque: Merle Armitage Eds., 1948.

———. *New Mexico: A Pageant of Three Peoples.* New York: Alfred A. Knopf, 1951.

———. *Our Southwest.* New York: Alfred A. Knopf, 1940.

Fitzpatrick, George, ed. *This Is New Mexico.* Albuquerque: Horn & Wallace, 1948.

Gibson, Arrell Morgan. *The Santa Fe and Taos Colonies: Age of the Muses, 1900–1942.* Norman: University of Oklahoma Press, 1983.

Gregg, Andrew K. *New Mexico in the Nineteenth Century: A Pictorial History.* Albuquerque: University of New Mexico Press, 1968.

Hahn, Emily. *Romantic Rebels: An Informal History of Bohemianism in America.* Boston: Houghton Mifflin, 1967.

Heitman, Francis B. *Historical Register and Dictionary of the United States Army, from Its Organization September 29, 1789, to March 2, 1903.* Washington: Government Printing Office, 1903.

Henderson, Alice Corbin. *New Mexico Blue Book, 1919.*

——. *The Turquoise Trail.* Boston: Houghton Mifflin, 1928.

Hollon, Eugene. *The Great American Desert: Then and Now.* New York: Oxford University Press, 1966.

Horgan, Paul. *The Centuries of Santa Fe.* Santa Fe: Wm. Gannon, 1976 [first published 1956].

——. *Lamy of Santa Fe: His Life and Times* (New York: Farrar, Straus and Giroux, 1975.

Jensen, Joan M., and Darlis A. Miller, eds. *New Mexico Women: Intercultural Perspectives.* Albuquerque: University of New Mexico Press, 1986.

Josephy, Alvin M., Jr. *Red Power: The American Indians' Fight for Freedom.* Lincoln: University of Nebraska Press, 1971.

La Farge, Oliver. *Santa Fe: The Autobiography of a Southwestern Town.* Norman: University of Oklahoma Press, 1959.

Lange, Charles H., and Carroll L. Riley, eds. *The Southwestern Journals of Adolph F. Bandelier: 1880–1882.* Albuquerque: University of New Mexico Press, 1966.

Lea, Henry Charles. *History of the Inquisition.* Vol. 2. New York: S. A. Russell, 1955.

Long, Haniel. *Piñon Country.* New York: Duell, Sloan, and Pearce, 1941.

Luhan, Mabel Dodge. *Lorenzo in Taos.* New York: Alfred A. Knopf, 1932.

Lummis, Charles F. *The Land of Poco Tiempo.* Albuquerque: University of New Mexico Press, 1952.

Manuel, Herschel T. *Spanish-Speaking Children of the Southwest: Their Education and the Public Welfare.* Austin: University of Texas Press, 1965.

Metzer, Robert, ed. *My Land Is the Southwest: Peter Hurd Letters and Journals.* College Station: Texas A & M University Press, 1983.

Michener, James A. Iberia: Spanish Travels and Reflections. New York: Random House, 1968.

Miller, Kristie. Ruth Hanna McCormick: A Life in Politics, 1880–1944. Albuquerque: University of New Mexico Press, 1992.

Morrill, Claire. A Taos Mosaic: Portrait of a New Mexico Village. Albuquerque: University of New Mexico Press, 1973.

New Catholic Encyclopedia. Vol. II. New York: McGraw Hill, 1967.

Otero, Miguel Antonio. My Nine Years as Governor of the Territory of New Mexico: 1897–1906. Albuquerque: University of New Mexico Press, 1940.

————. My Life on the Frontier: 1882–1897. New York: Press of the Pioneers, 1935.

Otero, Nina. Old Spain in Our Southwest. New York: Harcourt, Brace and Co., 1936.

Otis, Raymond. Fire in the Night. New York: Farrar and Rinehart, 1934.

Pastor, Ludwig Freiherr von. The History of the Popes: From the Close of the Middle Ages. Vol 1. St. Louis: B. Herder Book Co., 1952.

Perrigo, Lynn I. Hispanos: Historic Leaders in New Mexico. Santa Fe: Sunstone Press, 1985.

Peyton, Green. America's Heartland: The Southwest. Norman: University of Oklahoma Press, 1948.

Pittman, Lucretia, S.C. "Solomón Luna: Sheepmaster and Politician of New Mexico." Master's thesis, St. Louis University, 1941.

Poling-Kempes, Lesley. The Harvey Girls: Women Who Opened the West. New York: Paragon House, 1989.

Powell, Lawrence Clark. Southwest: Three Definitions. Benson, Arizona: Singing Wind Bookshop, 1990.

Priestley, Herbert Ingram. Tristan de Luna, Conquistador of the Old South: A Study of Spanish Imperial Strategy. Glendale, California: Arthur H. Clark Co., 1936. Reprint. Philadelphia: Porcupine Press, 1980.

Reeve, Agnesa Lufkin. From Hacienda to Bungalow: Northern New Mexico Houses, 1850–1912. Albuquerque: University of New Mexico Press, 1988.

Ruvigny, Marques of. Titled Nobility of Europe. London: Harrison and Sons, 1914.

Schroeter, James, ed. Willa Cather and Her Critics. Ithaca, New York: Cornell University Press, 1967.

Scott, Winfield Townley, ed. The Man with the Calabash Pipe: Some Observations by Oliver La Farge. Boston: Houghton Mifflin, 1966.

Segale, Sr. Blandina. *At the End of the Santa Fe Trail.* Milwaukee: Bruce Publishing Co., 1879.

Sherman, John. *Santa Fe: A Pictorial History.* Norfolk: Donning Co., 1983.

Simmons, Marc. *Ranchers, Ramblers & Renegades: True Tales of Territorial New Mexico.* Santa Fe: Ancient City Press, 1984.

Sonnichsen, C. L., ed. *The Southwest in Life and Literature.* New York: Debin-Adair Co., 1962.

Stedman, Myrtle, and Wilfred Stedman. *Adobe Architecture.* Santa Fe: Sunstone Press, 1973.

Twitchell, Ralph Emerson, ed. *Old Santa Fe: The Story of New Mexico's Ancient Capitol.* Chicago: Rio Grande Press, 1963.

Udall, Stewart L. *To the Inland Empire: Coronado and Our Spanish Legacy.* New York: Doubleday, 1967.

Walsh, William Thomas. *Isabella of Spain: The Last Crusader.* New York: Robt. M. McBride, 1930.

Weber, David J. *New Spain's Far Northern Frontier: Essays on Spain in the American West, 1540–1821.* Albuquerque: University of New Mexico Press, 1979.

————. *The Spanish Frontier in North America.* New Haven: Yale University Press, 1992.

Weigle, Marta, and Kyle Fione. *Santa Fe & Taos: The Writers Era, 1916–1941.* Santa Fe: Ancient City Press, 1982.

WPA Guide to 1930s in New Mexico. Tucson: University of Arizona Press, 1989.

Young, Louise M. *In the Public Interest: The League of Women Voters, 1920–1970.* New York: Greenwood Press, 1989.

Index

Abreu, Charles, 222n. 27
Adams, Abigail, 78
Alamogordo, New Mexico, 175
Albuquerque (Alburquerque), 10
Alexander, H. S. A., 200
Allied Arts Extension, 161
American Indians: in nineteenth-
   century New Mexico, 11–12;
   Navajos, 11, 115; Apache hostility,
   38; school in Santa Fe, 116–19;
   Pueblos, 115, education of, 106,
   120–21; New Mexico Association of
   Indian Affairs, 126; Tesuque, 142–43
American Red Cross, 91
Antelope Springs, 16, 18–19
Anthony, Salome E., 113, 172, 193
Anthony, Susan B., 94
Applegate, Frank, 113
Arán, Pedro, 165
Armijo, Ambrosio, 12
Armijo, Carlos (Charles), 20, 22
Armijo, Manuel, 200

Arnold, Samuel, 4, 189
Arsuna Art School, 172
Atwood, Stella M., 115, 121
Austin, Mary, 3, 62, 113, 123, 129,
   158

Baca Gilbert, Fabiola Cabeza de, 148
Baca, María Nestora Cristina Isabella
   (later Mrs. Antonio José Luna), 11
Baca, Pablo, 20
Bailhache, Arthur, 20
Bakoz, Josef, 113, 135
Ballard, Edna, 173
Barela, Patricino, 159
Bartolomé Baca land grant, 18. See also
   Spanish land grants
Bataan death march, 176–77
Batista, Fulgencio, 196
Baumann, Gustave, 3, 126
Baumann, Jane (Mrs. Gustave), 200
"Bells of Santa Cruz, The," 150
Benedict XIII, 213n. 2

Berger, Francisco Luigi, 27

Berger, John, 218n. 42

Berger, Joseph Charles, 27

Berger, Nina Mandelick (Mrs. Joseph Charles), 27

Bergere, Alfred Maurice (1858–1939): childhood and youth, 27; early business enterprises, 28; courtship and marriage, 25–29; adventures in New Mexico, 34–38; in politics, 40, 84, 102; friendship with Miguel A. Otero, 45, 47–48; supports woman suffrage, 82; in World War I, 91; as register of U.S. land office in New Mexico, 114, 133, 136; death of, 153–57; descendants of, 197

Bergere, Antonio José Luna (1894–1955): childhood, 33; education, 74; World War I, 91; marriage, 102; and Nina Otero–Warren, 195–96; death of, 197

Bergere, Eloisa Luna de Otero de (Mrs. Alfred Maurice) (1864–1914): family matriarch, 31; in Santa Fe, 45; illness and death of, 71–73; descendants of, 197. See also Luna, Eloisa; Otero, Eloisa Luna de

Bergere, Joseph Charles (1905–1957), 49, 62, 102, 133, 197

Bergere, María Alvira Estella (1890–1975), 32, 62, 102. See also Leopold, Estella Bergere (Mrs. Aldo)

Bergere, María Ana (Anita) Isabel Eloisa (1887–1976): childhood of, 32; vocation of, 75, 101; as activist with Congressional Union, 84; as superintendent of schools, Santa Fe county, 131–32; manages the Big House, 153, 189–90; during World War II, 168; and Nina Otero-Warren, 191; at Gonzales Hall party, 201; death of, 209

Bergere, María Bernadette (May) (1893–1976): childhood of, 33; sons of, in World War II, 168–69; with selective service office, 170–71; campaigning with Nina Otero-Warren, 96; marriage of, 102. See also Kenney, May Bergere (Mrs. John Joseph, Sr.)

Bergere, María Edwina Consuelo (Connie) (1895–1990): childhood of, 33. See also Mendenhall, Consuelo Bergere (Mrs. Frank)

Bergere, María Eloisa Berenice Dolores (1897–1956), 49, 62, 102. See also Leopold, Dolores Bergere (Mrs. Carl)

Bergere, María Nestora Cristina Ysabel (1901–1984), 49, 101, 153, 209

Bergere, María Rosina (1898–1972) (Mrs. Leonard Smith; Mrs. Robert Osgood Brown), 49, 62, 102, 144, 191, 201.

Bergere, Suzanne Catron (Mrs. Joseph Charles), 133

Berry, Edwin, 216n. 22

Bigbee, Harry, 207

Big House, The (La Casa Grande): historical landmark, 2; Bergere house, 49; as social center, 52, 133–34; renovation of, 102; at Christmas, 171–72; as family center, 183; sold, 207

Billy the Kid, 54

Bohr, Niels, 173, 176

Bradford, Richard, 187

Brett, Dorothy, 194

Brosseau, Roberta, 189

Brown, Eloisa Bergere, 4, 9, 97, 142,

Brown, Robert O., 144, 190

Burke, Charles H., 117–18

Burns, Lucy, 78

Bursom, Bill, 115

Bursom, Holm, 94

Bynner, Witter (Hal), 3, 113, 122–23, 125–28, 186–88

Cañoncito, New Mexico, 109
Cassidy, Gerald, 130
Cassidy, Ina Sizer (Mrs. Gerald), 172
Castro, Fidel, 196
Cat-and-Mouse Act, 79
Cather, Willa, 123
Catholic Church: in Los Lunas, 8, 29–30; schism within, 9, 213n. 2; and mixed marriages, 62–63, 65; influence on Nina Otero-Warren, 101, 105–6, 177, 182
Catron, Carolyn Updike (Mrs. José Luna Bergere), 102
Catron, Thomas, 49, 55, 82, 84, 91, 133
Catt, Carrie Chapman, 93
Chacón, Mrs. Soledad Chávez, 98
Chapman, Kenneth, 115, 122
Chaves, Mary, 189
Chávez, David (judge), 157
Chávez, Dennis, 157
Chávez, Fray Angelico, 128
Chávez, Ignacio, 10
Chimayo, Santuario de, 177
Church, Fermor Spencer, 173
Church, Peggy Pond, 128–29, 173–75, 184–85
Cinco Pintores, 113
Civilian Conservation Corps (CCC), 143
Claffey, Frank, 200
Clark, Willard, 206
Collier, John, 115–16
Congressional Union (CU), 2, 78, 81
conversos (new Christians), 106, 229n. 12
Coons, Benjamin Franklin, 11
Corbin, Alice, 3. See also Henderson, Alice Corbin
Coronado, Francisco Vásquez de, 7
Cortés, Hernán, 10

"Count La Cerda's Treasure," 150
Crazy Bear Ranch, 135
Cross–cultural marriages, 28
Cutting, Bronson, 90, 132, 155, 157

Davy, Randall, 113
Democratic party, 132
Denver and Rio Grande Western Railroad, 29, 136
Deutsch, Sarah, 80, 148
Dills, J. H., 86
Dodge, Mabel (Luhan), 113, 123
Doyle, Mary Elizabeth (Teta), 24–25, 45, 52, 66, 133, 153, 168
Dreyspring, Beth, 238n. 63

Education: in New Mexico schools, 106–9; improvements by Nina Otero-Warren, 111, 132; adult literacy in Puerto Rico, 164–66
Ellis, Fremont, 113
El Palacio, 122
El Pasatiempo committee, 125
Emmett, Caroline V. (Mrs. Miguel A. Otero), 221n. 5
EMILY'S List ("Early Money Is Like Yeast"), 228n. 56
Esquibel, Jose Santos, 21
Espinoza, Carmen, 148
Estancia Valley, 15, 16, 18, 155
Exchange Hotel (later La Fonda), 46

Fall, Albert, 82, 115
Federal Emergency Relief Administration (FERA), 158
Felton, Rebecca Latimer, 99
Fergusson, Erna, 89–90, 128, 162, 205
Fermi, Enrico, 173
Fletcher, John Gould, 123
Flores, John P., 162
Fort Marcy Military Reservation, 49
Fort Marcy Park, 208

Fort Wingate, 59, 61, 64–65
Frost, Mrs. Maud Pain (Mrs. Miguel A.
 Otero), 221n. 5
Frost, Robert, 128

Garrett, Pat, 54
Gibson, Arell Morgan, 125
Gilpin, Laura, 189
Gonzales Hall, 200
Goodale, Catharine W. (Mrs. Rawson
 Warren), 237n. 31
Grant, Ulysses S., 49
Great Depression, 100, 131
Greenwood, Dorothy, 172
Grossman, Ed, 177

Hagerman, Herbert, 58
Hakluyt, Richard, 121
Hanna, Mark, 161
Hannett, Arthur T., 99
Harding, Warren, 115
Henderson, Alice Corbin (Mrs. William
 Penhallow), 3, 89, 112–13, 123,
 126, 184
Henderson, William Penhallow, 126,
 184
Henríquez, Edward C., 20, 22
Herdman, Cristina Kenney (Mrs.
 Richard), 168, 190–91, 201, 207–8
Herdman, Richard, 207
Hernández, Benigno Cárdenas, 84
Hewitt, Edgar Lee, 115, 124
Hinkle, James, 98
Hitler, Adolf, 161, 167
Hoover, Herbert, 155
Horgan, Paul, 128
Hubbell, Frank, 84
Hughes, Charles Evans, 84
Hughes, Levi, Sr., 113–14
Huning, Franz, 29
Hunter, May Van, 96
Hurd, Peter, 195

"I Am" cult, 173, 236n. 17
Indian market, 115, 120
Isabel (queen of Spain), 9

Jensen, Joan, 87
Johnson, Willard (Spud), 113, 125
Jones, Andrieus Aristiens, 85, 91
Juan II (king of Spain), 9

Kaune's, 46
Kenney, Bergere Alfred: and Nina Otero-
 Warren, 32, 191; birth, 102; at Las
 Dos, 145–46; during World War II,
 169; marriage, 181; memories of the
 Big House and Las Dos, 183–84;
 physician to the family, 198; develops
 Las Dos homestead, 206–7; named
 Santa Fe "Living Treasure," 208
Kenney, Cristina (later Mrs. Richard
 Herdman), 4, 144. *See also* Herdman,
 Cristina Kenney
Kenney, Dolores (Dode) Kornder (Mrs.
 Bergere Alfred), 102, 181–82, 191
Kenney, John Joseph, Sr. 82–83, 102,
 144–45
Kenney, John Joseph (Jack): and Nina
 Otero-Warren, 32; at Las Dos, 145–
 46; marriage, 170; during World War
 II, 169, 174; tribute to May Bergere
 Kenney, 183; criticism of Witter
 Bynner, 186–87; sells Las Dos home-
 stead, 207; named Santa Fe "Living
 Treasure," 208; environmentalist,
 208–9
Kenney, Josephine (Joey) Sullivan (Mrs.
 John Joseph), 144–45, 179–81, 183,
 170
Kenney, María Bernadette (May) Bergere
 (Mrs. John Joseph, Sr.), 82, 144–45,
 174, 201, 209. *See also* Bergere, María
 Bernadette (May)
Kerr, Lillian, 81, 94

Knauer, David, 209
Koeler, Rev. Kenneth M., 192

La Constancia, New Mexico, 8, 15
La Farge, John Pen, 187
La Farge, Oliver, 90, 117, 123
La Fonda, 236n. 11
Land of Poco Tiempo, The (Lummis), 121
Larrazolo, A. O., 92
Las Dos: homestead land, 3, 138–44;
   weekends at, 185–86; grazing on,
   191, 238n. 58; in 1990s, 206–7
Las Dos Realty and Insurance Co.,
   188–89, 203
Laughlin, Ruth, 113, 128
Lawrence, D. H., 123, 193
Lawrence, Ernest, 173, 175
Lawrence, Frieda (Mrs. D. H.), 193
League of Women Voters, 93
Leakey, Ruth, 4, 184, 193–94, 201
Leopold, Aldo, 153, 191
Leopold, Carl Starker, 4, 102, 169,
   196–97
Leopold, Dolores Bergere (Mrs. Carl),
   196–97, 209. See also Bergere, María
   Eloisa Berenice Dolores
Leopold, Estella Bergere (Mrs. Aldo),
   84, 153, 169, 209. See also Bergere,
   María Alvira Estella
Leopold, Luna, 153, 169, 191–92, 195
Leopold, Starker, 169, 195
Lindsay, Vachel, 128
Lindsey, W. E., 88
Long, Haniel, 112, 123
Los Alamos, 173–76
Los Lunas, 2, 7–8, 16, 129
Lucero, Aurora, 84
Luján, Tony, 113
Luján, Manuel, Sr., 132
Lummis, Charles, 121
Luna, Álvaro de, 9, 214n. 3
Luna, Antonio José, 11–12, 18

Luna, Diego de, 10
Luna, Domingo de, 10
Luna, Eloisa (later Mrs. Manuel Basilio
   Otero; Mrs. Alfred Maurice Bergere),
   12–13. See also Otero, Eloisa Luna de;
   Bergere, Eloisa Luna de Otero de
Luna, Isabella Baca de (Mrs. Antonio
   José), 12, 50
Luna, Jesús, 12
Luna, Juan Gómez de, 10
Luna, Luz, 12
Luna Mansion, 17–18, 198, 216n. 24
Luna, Maximiliano, 52, 60
Luna, Melchior de, 10
Luna, Pedro de (Pope Benedict III), 8,
   213n. 2
Luna, places named, 215n. 10
Luna, Solomón: childhood, 12; with
   Alfred M. Bergere, 36–38; in politics,
   41, 50, 66–67; death of, 68–70
Luna, Tranquilino, 12, 18, 41
Luna, Tristan de, 8
Lusk, Georgia, 98

McCormick family, Cyrus H., 160
McFie, John R., 41
McKinley, William, 41, 55
McKittrick, Margaret, 126
Magoffin House, 55, 198–99
Manhattan Project, 173, 176
Manzanares, Ana de Sandoval de, 10,
   214n. 5
María: The Potter of San Ildefonso (Marriott),
   175
Marriott, Alice, 175
Martin, Anne, 86–87
Martínez, María, 125
Maryville College of the Sacred Heart,
   30, 152
Meadors, Henry B., 143–44, 184
Meadors, J. W., 192
Meadors, Mamie: and Nina Otero-

Warren, 3, 112–14, 138–39, 172, 189; homesteading Las Dos, 136–44, 185; with WPA, 159; with OPA, 170; and Las Dos Realty and Insurance Co., 189; death of, 192–93, 229n. 24

Mechem, Edwin L., 200

Meem, John Gaw, 113, 158, 161, 200

Mendenhall, Frank, 144, 169

Mendenhall, Herbert, 104, 190

Mendenhall, María Edwina Consuelo (Mrs. Frank): and Nina Otero-Warren, 4, 196; recounts marriage of her mother and Manuel Basilio Otero, 17–18; memories of her mother and Alfred Maurice Bergere, 62, 64; child and teenager in Big House, 103–4; during World War II, 169; death of, 209

Mera, H. P., 102, 113

Miles, John, 168, 170

Miller, Michael, 157

Monroe, Harriet, 112

Montoya, Néstor, 95

Morrow, John R., 97

Mruck, Walter, 113

Muller, Frederick, 55

Naranjo, Benjamin, 116

Nash, Willard, 113

National American Woman Suffrage Association (NAWSA), 78, 85, 93

National Woman's Party (formerly Congressional Union), 93

N-Bar Ranch, 133, 153, 194–96

Nestor, Sarah, 103

New Mexico: Anglo-American cultural influences, 24, 51; state constitution of 1910, 68

New Mexico: A Pageant of Three People (Fergusson), 162

New Mexico Board of Education, 49, 50

Nineteenth Amendment, 91–92, 94

Nusbaum, Aileen, 150, 158

Office of Price Administration (OPA), 170

Old Spain in Our Southwest (Nina Otero), 3, 12, 32, 146–53, 234n. 38

Oñate, Juan de, 7, 214n. 6

Oppenheimer, Robert, 173, 175, 176

Ortíz y Pino, Concha, 148

Otero, Antonio José, 14

Otero, Caroline Emmett (Mrs. Miguel A., II), 48

Otero, Dolores Chaves (Mrs. Manuel Antonio), 14

Otero, Eduardo, 18, 32, 54, 82, 153–54, 198

Otero Elementary School, 203

Otero, Eloisa Luna de (Mrs. Manuel Basilio), 16, 20, 23, 129. See also Luna, Eloisa; Bergere, Eloisa Luna de Otero de

Otero, Manuel Antonio, 14, 18

Otero, Manuel Basilio: childhood and education, 14–15; marriage to Eloisa Luna, 16; Baca-Estancia land dispute, 18–23, 217n. 28; original homesite, 216n. 22

Otero, Manuel Basilio, Jr.: childhood in Los Lunas, 23, 32; in Santa Fe, 54; in politics, 82, 99; manages N-Bar Ranch, 154, 157, 195

Otero, María Adelina (Nina) Emilia (later Mrs. Rawson Warren): Spanish heritage, 1, 8; in Los Lunas, 18, 22, 38, 42, 43; childhood and education, 30–34; early social life, 54, 56–57; author of Old Spain in Our Southwest, 147–50

Otero, Mariano, 14

Otero, Miguel Antonio, 12

Otero, Miguel Antonio, II: Manuel B. Otero-James Whitney land dispute, 21, 22, 39, 222n. 25; as territorial governor, 41, 46–48; and Alfred M. Bergere, 47; leaves office, 58; and

Thomas Catron, 82, 133; death of, 178

Otero, Pedro, 14

Otero-Warren, María Adelina (Nina) Emilia (Mrs. Rawson Warren): courtship and marriage of, 59–64; and separation from Rawson Warren, 66; in New York, 74; and woman's suffrage movement, 77–78, 81, 83–88, 91–94; as superintendent of Santa Fe county public schools, 87– 88, 106–11, 110; with American Red Cross, 91; as candidate for U.S. House of Representatives, 95–99; and Bergere family, 105, 146, 154–55, 169–70, 191, 204; as inspector of Santa Fe county Indian schools, 114, 117–19; as social leader, 124–25, 134, 186, 189, 199–200; and Mary Austin, 129–32; as educator, 132–33, 159–60, 161–62; as director of adult literacy in Puerto Rico, 162–66; homesteads Las Dos, 134–44; and Mamie Meadors, 138–39, 192–93; begins writing *Old Spain in Our Southwest*, 146; receives awards, 152, 201–2; and World War II, 168–70; with Office of Price Administration (OPA), 170; and Christmas traditions, 172; and death of Rawson Warren, 177–78; and Las Dos Realty and Insurance Co., 188; as environmentalist, 192; travels to Cuba, 196; death of, 203. *See also* Otero, María Adelina (Nina) Emilia

Otowi, 174, 176

Paul, Alice Stokes, 2, 78, 86, 93–94, 227n. 44

Pankhurst, Emmeline, 79

Patterson, Katherine, 79

Penitentes, 105

Peters, Gerald, 158

Poetry magazine, 112

Poets' Roundup, 123

Pond, Ashley, 173

Prince, L. Bradford, 52

Prohibition, 77, 90, 157

Pueblo Indians, 45

Puerto Rico, 2, 162–66

Rand, Frank C., Jr., 168

Randolph, Mrs. Edmund, 189

Raynolds, James Wallace, 56

Republican party, 97–98, 131

Roosevelt, Franklin Delano, 132, 145, 167

Roosevelt, Theodore, 55, 56

Rosario Cemetery, 73

Rossin, Alice Henderson, 103, 112, 123

Rough Riders, 60–61

Rowland, Lee, 159

Roybal, Jorge, 140, 184

Rush, Olive, 158

St. Francis cathedral, 45

St. Vincent hospital, 21, 144, 208

Sánchez, Amalia, 4, 105, 184

Sánchez, Juan, 159

Sandburg, Carl, 128

Sand County Almanac, A (Aldo Leopold), 102

Sandia school, 161

Sanger, Margaret, 77, 79

Sangre de Cristo mountains, 136–37

Santa Fe: in the 1890s, 45–46; central plaza, 53; Indian school, 116; artist colony, 122–30; Sena plaza, 126, 188; School of American Research, 126; Laboratory of Anthropology, 158; Museum of Fine Arts, 159; during World War II, 167–68, 170–73; Japanese internment camp, 168; at Christmas, 171; fiestas, 172; in the 1990s, 205–6; Chamber Music Festival, 208; public library, 230n. 29

Santa Fe railroad, 18
Schoonover, Margaret Lefranc, 175
Seligman, Arthur, 132
Sheep industry, 12
Shuster, Will, 113, 134–35, 159, 186, 197
Simms, Albert G., 160
Simms, Ruth Hanna McCormick, 160–61
Sloan, John, 3, 135, 186, 197
Smith, Leonard, 169, 177
Spanish haciendas, 149–50
Spanish Colonial Arts Society, 130
Spanish land grants: Tiguex, 10; Bartolomé Baca, 15; Estancia, 19; and U.S. courts, 21, 39–40, 217n. 33
Spanish-Pueblo architecture, 51, 102
Spiegelberg, Solomon, 28, 46
Spina, Albert F., 162
Staab, Abraham, 46
Stanton, Elizabeth Cady, 94
Stern, Mabel, 128
Stinson, Katherine, 222n. 25
Sunmount Sanatorium, 102, 112, 158

Thomas, Anita Gonzales, 103, 109–10, 203
Thompson, Ella St. Clair, 84
Tules, doña (María Gertrudis Barceló), 55, 199–200
Turley, Jesse B., 11

Udall, Stewart L., 121
U.S. Geological Survey, 143

Valencia County, 10, 12, 14
Vernon, Mabel, 81, 83–84
Vierra, Carlos, 122
Vigíl, Dominguita Ortíz, 110–11, 203–4

Vigíl, Donaciano, 220n. 3
Vigíl, Toribio, 110
Villagra Book Shop, 172

Walton, William, 85
Warner, Edith, 175–76
Warren, Meta, 177
Warren, Rawson, 59–60, 177, 237n. 31
Weber, David, 122
Wheelwright, Mary Cabot, 160–61
White, Martha, 126
Whitney, James, 18–20
Whitney, Joel P., 19–22
Wilderness Society, 102
Wilson, Woodrow, 85, 88
WISH ("Women in the Senate and House"), 228n. 56
Woman's Journal, 78
Woman's land army, 90
Woman suffrage: early attempts at legislation in New Mexico, 67, 77, 80; periodicals, 80; opposition to, 82, 83; during World War I, 88; victory in New Mexico, 94
Women's auxiliary (later Woman's Committee of the National Council of Defense), 89
Women's Christian Temperance Union (WTCU), 79, 83–84
Women's Clubs, 66–67, 79, 81, 115
Wootton, Richen Lacy (Uncle Dick), 11
Work Projects Administration (WPA), 157, 158
World War I, 88, 90
World War II, 167–69
Wright, E. H., 114

Zozobra, 134

CPSIA information can be obtained
at www.ICGtesting.com
Printed in the USA
BVHW031024160323
660514BV00003B/292